Even More SPECIAL

A Contemporary Collection of Recipes from the
Junior League of Durham and Orange Counties, Inc.
Durham, North Carolina

The purpose of the Junior League of Durham and Orange Counties, Inc. is exclusively educational and charitable and is: to promote voluntarism, to develop the potential of its members for voluntary participation in community affairs, and to demonstrate the effectiveness of trained volunteers.

Book Design by Karen Havighurst
Art Work photographed by Chip Henderson

First printing	March 1986	10,000 copies
Second printing	October 1986	10,000 copies

•

To order additional copies of
EVEN MORE SPECIAL
Use the forms provided in the back of the book or write to:
SPECIAL PUBLICATIONS
900 South Duke Street
Durham, North Carolina 27707
$14.95 per copy plus $1.75 for postage and handling

•

Copyright © 1986

The Junior League of Durham and Orange Counties, Inc.
Durham, North Carolina

•

•

Library of Congress Catalog Card Number 85-82125

ISBN 0-9615845-0-5

Printed in the United States of America

Hart Graphics, Inc.
8000 Shoal Creek Blvd.
Austin, Texas 78758

INTRODUCTION

Cooking is an intensely personal experience; ideally it should be a relaxing and rewarding one as well. For a few, it is the pursuit of excellence; for the majority, it is the challenge of preparing creative, well-balanced meals on a daily basis and finding the energy (and courage!) to entertain friends occasionally.

Trends in food, as in fashion, come and go. Currently our society reflects a dichotomy: we live in a space age, hi-tech, computerized world of ®McDonald's and microwave ovens, yet our cooking style has become more fundamental and basic. The emphasis is on simple, unadorned dishes. This light style is based upon the freshest possible ingredients and has been enhanced by the tremendous diversity of ingredients which is now widely available. Today it is not uncommon to see clay pots sprouting fresh tarragon and basil on tiny terraces in high-rise metropolitan areas!

This trend toward simplicity and freshness is not new; rather, it is a classic approach to cuisine that caring cooks have been practicing for decades.

Even More Special is a collection of recipes assembled by caring cooks, one and all. Some recipes are new; some are not but are so simple and good that they deserve, even in these sophisticated times, not to be forgotten. We have included complete menus as well as serving suggestions for many recipes in order to inspire you. America, in recent years, has certainly become a wine-loving nation, and we have included wine suggestions where appropriate.

The recipes contained in this book are our favorites; most of them are neither elaborate nor taxing. We hope you try and enjoy them all, remembering that cooking is a creative process whose possibilities are limited only by your imagination.

Bon Appétit!

Robin Marin
Recipe Chairman

Cookbook Committee

Chairman
Kathy McPherson

Design and Format

Mary Tatum, chairman   Yolanda Litton, assistant
Anita Brame   Anne Marshall
Mary Haywood   Ellen Rock

Recipes

Robin Marin, chairman   Margaret Rouse, assistant
Marcie Brame   Carroll Haney
Ruth Buchanan   Frances Holman
Brandon Chapman   Trish Lanier
Sims Foulks   Liz Patterson
Louise Glenn   Becky Prestwood
Susan Griffin   Kathryn Walker

Margie Haber

Recipe Collection Coordinator
Jane Thorn

Marketing

Lesli Garrison, chairman   Lee Marks, assistant

Computer Input Typist
Katie Wilson

The cookbook committee owes a special debt to:

• Lloydette Hoof, Perry Van Dyke, and Mary Holderness, presidents of the Junior League of Durham and Orange Counties, who nurtured the cookbook from dream to reality;
• David Barr and Haywood Holderness, whose extraordinary knowledge of wine will be invaluable to the people who use this book;
• Junior League members and friends who tested more than 1,500 recipes to help determine the 416 recipes which appear on these pages;
• Nancy Meadows Taylor, who painted the vibrant watercolor pictures which indeed make this cookbook even more special.

About The Artist

Nancy Meadows Taylor is a native North Carolinian who lives in Raleigh. Her work is constantly seen in juried shows throughout North Carolina and in invitational and solo exhibitions. She is a member of the North Carolina Watercolor Society and the Southern Watercolor Society.

TABLE OF CONTENTS

TRANSITIONS

In 1972, the Junior League of Durham published its first cookbook, **That Something Special.** In the years since that book was published, our Research Triangle area of North Carolina has undergone an amazing transformation. Thousands of people from all over the United States and the world have moved into our area, drawn by opportunities in technological research, medicine, and education, and the attraction of leading a modern lifestyle in a warm and gentle climate. The newcomers have quickened our pace and brought us a rich leavening of cultural influences.

Our new cookbook, **Even More Special**, mirrors the changes in Durham and Chapel Hill in recent years. Our emphasis on fresh ingredients and nutrition-conscious preparation reflects the active, healthy lifestyle of the Research Triangle.

We believe that **Even More Special** captures the unique qualities of life in the Research Triangle—its sophistication, its exciting blend of cosmopolitanism and Southern tradition, and its contemporary style of living.

CRAB MORNAY

No matter how you choose to serve crab, it is always a favorite. How marvelous that this recipe can be used as an appetizer or as an entrée. It is simple to prepare but very elegant.

1 cup butter
2 bunches green onions, chopped
½ bunch parsley, chopped
4 tablespoons flour
2 pints cream

1 pound Swiss cheese, cut into chunks
2 pounds crabmeat
Salt and pepper to taste
4 tablespoons dry sherry
Melba rounds

1.   In a large skillet, melt butter and sauté onions and parsley. Add the flour and mix well.
2.   Stir in cream. Add Swiss cheese and allow to melt. Add crabmeat, salt, and pepper. Heat thoroughly.
3.   Stir in sherry just before serving. Serve in chafing dish.

10-12 servings (main dish) or 60-70 as an appetizer

Hints: Recipe may be halved if a lesser quantity is desired. If using as a main course, serve in patty shells. A simple and economical croustade shell may also be prepared: cut sliced white bread into 2-inch rounds; fit into miniature muffin tins and brush with melted butter. Bake at 350° until lightly browned.

FRESH ZUCCHINI PIZZAS

When zucchini becomes a bumper crop late in summer, and you're out of ideas—why not pizza? Be creative with toppings for this low calorie nibble—include fresh herbs if available.

Fresh zucchini, sliced ½ inch thick (uncooked)
1 can Hunt's Tomato Sauce Special or prepared spaghetti sauce
Grated Monterey Jack cheese

Grated Parmesan cheese
Sliced black olives
Minced green onions
Garlic salt
Freshly ground pepper
Oregano, fresh or dried

1.   Place zucchini slices on a baking sheet. Top each with a dollop of tomato sauce. Sprinkle with cheeses, black olives, green onions, and season to taste with herbs.
2.   Broil until cheese is bubbly.
3.   Serve immediately.

Hint: Substitute chopped mushrooms for black olives.

MEATBALLS POLONAISE

Meatballs:
1½ pounds lean ground
    pork
1 egg
½ cup dry bread crumbs
½ cup milk
½ cup finely chopped
    onion
½ teaspoon salt
½ teaspoon dried
    marjoram
¼ teaspoon pepper
2 tablespoons oil

Sauce:
2 tablespoons flour
1 cup water
1 beef bouillon cube
½ cup sour cream
2 teaspoons lemon juice
Garnish:
¼ cup freshly grated
    Parmesan cheese
Parsley

A very tender meatball with excellent flavor. This recipe would be equally appealing as a main course served over poppy seed noodles.

1. In a large bowl, combine pork, egg, bread crumbs, milk, onion, salt, marjoram, and pepper. Mix lightly until blended.

2. Shape mixture into balls about 1½ inches in diameter.

3. Sauté meatballs in oil until browned on all sides, or bake on broiler rack at 400° for 12 minutes. Set meatballs aside.

4. Measure drippings in sauté pan and add more oil (if necessary) to make 2 tablespoons.

5. Stir flour into drippings until smooth. Gradually stir in water and bouillon cube, bringing to boil to dissolve cube.

6. Remove from heat and add sour cream and lemon juice.

7. Add meatballs and simmer about 15 minutes to heat through.

8. Serve in chafing dish and garnish with Parmesan cheese and parsley.

10-15 servings

Hints: Add thinly sliced mushrooms when serving as an entrée. (This recipe will serve four.)
Make the meatballs ahead of time and keep in the freezer until ready to use.

HONEYED CHICKEN WINGS

A wonderfully versatile dish, this can be served as an appetizer or a main course; it can be oven-baked, or grilled. Also very good cold as a picnic addition.

3 pounds chicken wings or chicken drummettes	2 tablespoons vegetable oil
Salt and pepper to taste	¼ cup tomato catsup
1 cup honey	½ clove garlic, minced
½ cup soy sauce	

1. Cut off and discard wing tips. Cut each wing into two pieces at joint. (Use drummettes if you prefer.) Season with salt and pepper; set aside.
2. Combine remaining ingredients in a saucepan and mix well. Cook for 15 minutes over moderate heat. (It will become frothy and thick.)
3. Place wings in a shallow casserole dish. Pour one-half of the sauce over them and marinate for approximately 1 hour.
4. Bake at 375° for 1 hour, basting with the remaining sauce until chicken is well-done and sauce is caramelized.

6-8 servings

SMÅ KOTTBULLAR

These are great as an appetizer but are equally wonderful as a main course - just make the meatballs larger to suit your need.

¼ cup fine dry bread crumbs	¼ pound lean ground pork
⅓ cup water	1 teaspoon salt
⅓ cup heavy cream	¼ teaspoon pepper
1 tablespoon cooking oil	Dash of cloves
¼ cup finely chopped onion	⅓ cup butter or margarine
¾ pound extra lean ground beef	¼ cup boiling water

1. Soak bread crumbs in mixture of water and cream.
2. Sauté onion in oil until golden brown.
3. Combine onion, crumb mixture, meats, and seasonings. Mix until smooth and shape into balls (about 1-1½ inches in diameter).
4. Fry meatballs in butter until evenly browned, shaking pan continuously.
5. Add boiling water and cover for 5-10 minutes until tender.
6. Serve warm in a chafing dish.

20 servings

Hint: Prepare these ahead of time and microwave at serving time.

AGGIE'S MUSHROOMS AND ARTICHOKES

4 3-ounce cans mushrooms or 1 pound fresh mushrooms	1 6-ounce jar marinated artichoke hearts, undrained
3 scallions, chopped	½ teaspoon dried thyme
1 medium onion, chopped	1 tablespoon minced fresh parsley
1 clove garlic, minced, optional	1 teaspoon Gravy Master or Kitchen Bouquet
1 cup butter (margarine may be substituted if desired)	1 tablespoon flour
	French or Italian bread

This elegant and hearty people-pleaser is a popular addition to any cocktail buffet.

1. Coarsely chop mushrooms.
2. Melt butter in large skillet and stir in mushrooms, onions, and scallions. Add minced garlic, if desired. Sauté for approximately 10 minutes, stirring frequently.
3. Drain artichoke hearts and reserve liquid. Coarsely chop artichoke hearts and add to skillet. Add reserved liquid and thyme, parsley, and Gravy Master. Simmer 20 minutes.
4. Mix flour with a bit of water and add to mushroom mixture. Continue to simmer for approximately 5 minutes.
5. Pour into chafing dish to serve.
6. Serve with warm crunchy French bread or small French rolls. Spoon mixture onto sliced bread.

10-12 servings

Hint: Can be made ahead, refrigerated, and reheated in a microwave.

After Five (Cocktail Buffet)

Patricia's Pâté with Melba Rounds

Curry Vegetable Dip with Crudités

Oyster Cracker Tidbits   Meatballs Polonaise

Caviar Pie with Pumpernickel Bread

Aggie's Mushrooms & Artichokes

Shrimp Spread Supreme with Crackers

SESAME CHICKEN WITH HONEY DIP

A cocktail favorite! Serve bite-size pieces with toothpicks or use chicken wings. Either way these are sure to be enjoyed by everyone.

½ cup mayonnaise
1 teaspoon dry mustard
1 teaspoon minced onion
½ cup dry bread crumbs (very fine)
¼ cup sesame seeds

2 cups cooked chicken, cut into bite-size pieces
Dip:
1 cup mayonnaise
2 tablespoons honey

1. Preheat oven to 425°.
2. Combine ½ cup mayonnaise, mustard, and onion.
3. In a separate bowl, combine bread crumbs and sesame seeds.
4. Coat chicken in mayonnaise mixture, then in crumb mixture.
5. Place pieces on baking sheet and bake for 15 minutes.
6. Combine honey and mayonnaise for dip.
7. Serve chicken hot, accompanied by dip.

6 servings

Hint: Substitute cooked chicken wings for cubed chicken pieces.

CREAMED MUSHROOMS

Serve these lovely mushrooms for any occasion - cocktail buffet, brunch, or as an addition to a main course.

1 pound mushrooms, thinly sliced
2 tablespoons butter
2 tablespoons minced onion
2 tablespoons flour
¼ teaspoon white pepper

1 teaspoon fresh lemon juice
¾ teaspoon celery salt
1½ cups milk
3 tablespoons sherry, optional

1. Melt butter; add onions and sauté over low heat until soft.
2. Add mushrooms, cover, and continue to cook, stirring occasionally, for 8-10 minutes.
3. Stir in flour, pepper, lemon juice, celery salt, and add milk last. Simmer over low heat uncovered until sauce is thick.
4. Add sherry just before serving.
5. Serve in chafing dish with toast tips.

6-8 servings

Hint: If using as a main course, serve over rice or with chicken.

BACON AND CHEESE ROLL-UPS

1 1-pound loaf sliced white bread
½ cup butter or margarine, melted

½ pound Swiss cheese, thinly sliced
1 pound bacon strips, cut in half
Wooden toothpicks

1. Preheat oven to 350°.
2. Trim crusts from bread and cut each slice in half.
3. Brush both sides of bread halves lightly with melted butter.
4. Trim Swiss cheese, if necessary, to fit size of bread slices.
5. Place a slice of cheese on each bread half and roll up. Wrap ½ bacon slice around outside of bread and secure with a toothpick.
6. Place rolls on a cookie sheet and bake for 20 minutes, or until bacon is brown and crispy. Serve immediately.

8-10 servings

A simple hors d'oeuvre that will always disappear quickly.

CHEESE BLINTZES

1 cup butter or margarine
1 8-ounce package cream cheese, softened
1 egg yolk
½ cup sugar

1 loaf sliced fresh white bread
Ground cinnamon
½ pint sour cream, optional

1. Melt 1 cup of butter or margarine. Set aside.
2. Combine cream cheese, egg yolk, and sugar; blend thoroughly.
3. Cut crusts from bread. Roll each slice flat with a rolling pin.
4. Spread cream cheese mixture evenly on each bread slice.
5. Roll up slices like a jelly roll. Dip each roll in melted butter until lightly covered. Cut each roll into thirds. (Can be done ahead to this point and either refrigerated or frozen.)
6. Place the rolls in a shallow oven pan and sprinkle with cinnamon.

A sweet hors d'oeuvre? Why not—these are a wonderful complement to a savory cocktail buffet. Don't overlook them for brunch.

7. Bake for 15-20 minutes at 350°. Serve immediately with sour cream.

100 blintzes

Hints: Although this recipe makes a large quantity, you can freeze the blintzes before baking. They will keep about four weeks in the freezer.

HOT POTATO STRIPS

A spicy, salty hors d'oeuvre that makes tasty use of potato skins. Be prepared— guests will want seconds!

1 large potato per 2 people	**Salt and freshly ground pepper**
Melted butter	**Tabasco sauce to taste**
Garlic salt	

1. Preheat oven to 400°.
2. Bake potatoes whole and unpeeled for one hour or until done.
3. Cool slightly. Cut in half lengthwise. Remove most of the potato pulp and reserve for another use. Cut each half of potato skin into five strips lengthwise.
4. Place on cookie sheet and brush liberally with melted butter. Season heavily with garlic salt, salt, and freshly ground pepper. Sprinkle with Tabasco sauce. (May be made ahead to this point and refrigerated.)
5. Bake at 500° for 10-12 minutes until very hot and crispy. (Check them after 8 minutes to make sure they do not burn!)
6. Serve hot in a basket.

Hint: Use pulp for hash browns, mashed potatoes, or sauté with onion and green peppers for a side dish.

TORTILLA CHIPS

1 package fresh (or frozen) corn or flour tortillas

Vegetable oil for frying

1. In heavy skillet or electric frying pan, heat ½ inch oil until very hot (400°).
2. Stack tortillas and cut stack into six wedges.
3. Fry tortilla wedges, a few at a time, until crisp (one minute for corn tortillas, a little less for flour tortillas). Drain on paper towels. Sprinkle with salt. (May be prepared ahead to this point and stored in airtight container.)
4. Serve warm.

6-8 servings

Hints: To reheat chips, place in preheated 250° oven on cookie sheet for 5 minutes. Leftover chips may be crumbled and used as toppings for soups and salads.

These chips far surpass the commercial variety and are simple to prepare.

CHILE CON QUESO BLANCO

2 8-ounce packages cream cheese, room temperature
1 4-ounce can diced green chilies
1 7½-ounce can hot jalapeño relish

2 medium tomatoes, chopped, or 10-12 cherry tomatoes, halved
Chopped fresh cilantro
Warm tortilla chips

1. In medium saucepan over very low heat, combine cream cheese and green chilies. Stir until cheese is melted.
2. Add jalapeño relish to taste. (One-half can will give a mild con queso.) Stir until ingredients are blended and mixture is hot.
3. Remove from heat and stir in tomatoes.
4. Serve immediately in chafing dish. Garnish with chopped cilantro.

8-10 servings

Hints: Substitute minced fresh parsley if cilantro is unavailable.
Leftovers may be reheated in microwave at medium power setting.

This subtly seasoned con queso is smooth in texture and delicate in color. The use of cream cheese instead of traditional Cheddar guarantees a rich and creamy result.

BLACK BEAN DIP

1 **15-ounce can black beans or black-eyed peas**
1 **tablespoon chopped jalapeño peppers, fresh or canned**
¼ **cup finely chopped onion**
¼ **cup sour cream**
½ **teaspoon salt**
2 **tablespoons picante sauce**
1¼ **cups grated cheese (mild Cheddar or a combination of Cheddar and Monterey Jack)**
Freshly ground pepper

1. Preheat oven to 350°.
2. Drain beans and discard juice.
3. Mash beans with a fork, leaving some chunks. (Do not use blender or processor.)
4. Add remaining ingredients, reserving ¼ cup of cheese, and mix well.
5. Pour into a 1-quart baking dish and sprinkle with remaining cheese. (May be prepared ahead to this point and refrigerated.)
6. Bake for 20-30 minutes or until hot and bubbly.
7. Serve with tortilla chips.

2 cups

Hints: If canned black beans are unavailable, buy dried beans and cook them. A 15-ounce can measures 2 cups of cooked beans. Serve on warmed flour tortillas as a side dish.

MEXICAN SALSA

3   large ripe tomatoes, peeled
1   3¼-ounce can pitted ripe olives
1   4-ounce can mild green chilies, chopped
4   whole green onions, chopped
3   tablespoons olive oil
1½ tablespoons cider or white vinegar
1   teaspoon garlic salt
½   teaspoon freshly ground black pepper
1   cup mild picante or taco sauce
Tortilla chips

1. Coarsely chop peeled tomatoes and ripe olives. Combine in large bowl.
2. Add remaining ingredients and stir to combine. Taste and correct seasonings, if necessary.
3. Serve with tortilla chips.

10-12 servings

Hints: This is a fairly mild sauce. For a spicier version, add 1 minced fresh jalapeño pepper. Leftover salsa may be heated gently and served atop hot pasta.

A wonderfully fresh version of a popular Mexican hors d'oeuvre. It is best made in summer when lush garden tomatoes are at their peak.

MEXICAN LAYERED DIP

3   medium avocados
2   tablespoons lemon juice
½   teaspoon salt
¼   teaspoon pepper
1   pint sour cream
½   cup mayonnaise
1   2-ounce package taco seasoning
2   10½-ounce cans jalapeño bean dip
1   small can salsa, optional
1   cup chopped green onions (including tops)
2   cups chopped tomatoes (approximately 3 medium)
1   6-ounce can pitted ripe olives, drained and chopped
8   ounces Monterey Jack cheese, shredded
Large tortilla chips

1. Mash avocados with lemon juice, salt, and pepper.
2. In a separate bowl, mix together sour cream, mayonnaise, and taco seasoning.
3. On a large serving platter (9x13 inch or 10-inch round), layer ingredients in the following order: jalapeño bean dip, avocado mixture, sour cream mixture, salsa (optional), onions, tomatoes, olives, and Monterey Jack cheese.

For all lovers of Mexican fare, this is a real favorite. Great for after-game parties when a heavy hors d'oeuvre is in order.

4. Cover and chill until ready to use.
5. Serve with large tortilla chips.

12-15 servings

Hints: Refried beans can be substituted for jalapeño bean dip; Cheddar cheese can be substituted for Monterey Jack cheese. Variation: Heat in oven for a few minutes before serving.

GUACAMOLE

A fast and easy version of this versatile Mexican favorite.

1 **large or 2 small ripe avocados, mashed**
1 **small onion, finely chopped**
1 **tablespoon lemon juice, or more to taste**
¼ **teaspoon salt**
¼ **teaspoon chili powder**

Tabasco or Louisiana hot sauce to taste
1 **2-ounce jar diced pimentos, drained, optional**
2 **slices very crisp bacon, crumbled, optional**
⅓ **cup mayonnaise**

1. Mash avocados. Add onion, lemon juice, salt, chili powder, and hot sauce (to taste). If desired, add optional ingredients. Mix well.
2. Spread top with the mayonnaise and chill at least one hour before serving.
3. Stir mayonnaise into mixture before serving. Serve with tortilla chips.

1½ cups

Hints: The mayonnaise spread on top keeps the avocados from turning brown. This recipe can be made entirely in a food processor.

PATRICIA'S PÂTÉ

4 tablespoons butter
1 small onion, chopped
½ pound chicken livers
1 clove garlic, minced
1 tablespoon dry sherry
1 cup chopped pecans
⅛ cup bourbon

⅛ teaspoon salt
⅛ teaspoon
   Worcestershire sauce
⅛ teaspoon allspice
3 hard-cooked eggs,
   chopped

1.   In a skillet, sauté onions and livers in butter for 10 minutes or until done.
2.   Pulse onion, livers, and two of the hard-cooked eggs in food processor with remaining ingredients until the mixture is fairly smooth.
3.   Chill pâté 12 hours. (It will thicken as it chills. If pâté needs to be thinned after chilling, add enough chicken broth to obtain desired consistency.)
4.   Garnish with remaining chopped hard-cooked egg. Serve on thin wheat crackers.

10-15 servings

Chilled and served in a stoneware crock, this do-ahead pâté makes an elegant "tailgate" appetizer. Or serve it with wheat thins as an hors d'oeuvre.

FRUITED CHICKEN SPREAD

2 cups finely chopped
   cooked chicken
1 cup chopped dates
1 cup chopped celery
1 cup pineapple chunks

⅔ cup mayonnaise
½-1 cup slivered almonds,
   toasted
Crackers

1.   Combine chicken, dates, celery, and pineapple. Toss gently with mayonnaise. Refrigerate 1-2 hours.
2.   Top with almonds just before serving.

10 servings

Hints: Also great luncheon fare. Serve on wheat bread with leaf lettuce or in a Bibb lettuce cup for lighter fare.

East meets West in this hearty hors d'oeuvre— serve in a pineapple boat and watch it disappear.

SPINACH SPREAD

This recipe has several variations—try them all or create your own!

1 package frozen chopped spinach (defrosted and drained)
¾ cup mayonnaise
1 cup sour cream
1 8-ounce package cream cheese, softened, optional

½ cup chopped green onions or chives
1 package dried Knorr vegetable soup mix
1 small can chopped water chestnuts, optional
Parsley (garnish)

1. Mix the thoroughly drained spinach with the vegetable soup mix, the water chestnuts, sour cream, mayonnaise, and cream cheese.
2. Cover and refrigerate overnight, if possible, or at least several hours to enhance flavor.
3. Serve with rounds of bread or crackers, as a dip with crudités, even as a salad dressing.

3 cups

Hints: Use 1 cup chopped fresh spinach instead of 1 package frozen chopped spinach. Use ½ cup parsley, ½ teaspoon salt, 1 teaspoon ground black pepper, 1 teaspoon dillweed, and 1 teaspoon oregano instead of 1 package Knorr dried vegetable soup.

CURRY VEGETABLE DIP

This dip is not only good with crudités but also on sandwiches. Serve as an accompaniment to cold roast beef.

1 clove garlic, crushed, or ¼ teaspoon garlic powder
2 cups mayonnaise
3 tablespoons catsup
1 tablespoon Worcestershire sauce

2 teaspoons curry powder
2 teaspoons grated onion
1 teaspoon Tabasco sauce
Pinch of salt

1. Combine ingredients and mix well.
2. Chill until ready to serve.

2 cups

Hint: You may decrease the amount of curry powder to taste.

CREAMY CUCUMBER DIP

1 8-ounce package cream cheese
1 medium cucumber, grated and drained
1 small onion, grated and drained

1 tablespoon mayonnaise
¼ teaspoon white pepper
Salt to taste
Crackers or raw vegetables

1. Combine all ingredients. Chill.
2. Garnish with parsley or chopped green onions and serve with crackers.

8-10 servings

Good with crudités or crackers. In summer, use it as a sandwich filling with sliced garden tomatoes.

FRESH VEGETABLE DIP

⅓ cup sour cream
⅔ cup mayonnaise
2 drops Tabasco sauce
1 teaspoon seasoning salt
¼ teaspoon Accent
½ teaspoon Worcestershire sauce

1 tablespoon dry onion flakes
1 tablespoon dried parsley
1 teaspoon dried dill weed
Crudités

Combine ingredients and chill for several hours before serving.

For a stunning version of the "veggie tray", hollow out a purple cabbage or Chinese Savoy cabbage to hold dip. Use extra cabbage leaves on tray to hold colorful crudités such as yellow squash, cherry tomatoes, zucchini, broccoli, and cauliflower.

HERBED BOURSIN

A less expensive version of a popular herbed cheese. Do use fresh herbs when they are available.

2 8-ounce packages cream cheese, room temperature
8 ounces whipped unsalted butter, room temperature
¼ teaspoon oregano
¼ teaspoon thyme
¼ teaspoon marjoram
¼ teaspoon dill
¼ teaspoon basil
¼ teaspoon pepper
1 clove garlic, minced
Optional: Coarsley ground black pepper or sweet Hungarian paprika or poppy seeds.

1. Cream butter and cream cheese with mixer or food processor until smooth.
2. Add remaining ingredients except black pepper and blend thoroughly.
3. Shape into a ball, log, or pack into ramekins. Chill until firm.
4. For added flavor, roll ball or log in coarsely ground black pepper, sweet Hungarian paprika, or poppy seeds.
5. Remove from refrigerator 10 minutes before serving to soften.
6. Serve with mild crackers.

10-12 servings

Hint: Recipe may be halved.

OYSTER CRACKER TIDBITS

These are great to keep on hand - for cocktails, after school, or midnight snacks. Keep a good supply; they disappear quickly!

6 cups (10 ounces) oyster crackers
1 0.4-ounce envelope original flavor Hidden Valley Ranch dressing (dry)
½ teaspoon dill weed
¼ teaspoon lemon pepper
¼ teaspoon garlic salt
¼ cup cooking oil

1. Mix dry ingredients together. Stir in crackers.
2. Pour oil over cracker mixture and stir from bottom.
3. Seal in airtight container. These will stay fresh for several weeks.

6 cups

MUSHROOM CAVIAR

1 pound fresh mushrooms, finely chopped
¼ cup butter
½ cup dried minced onions
¼ cup lemon juice
4 teaspoons Worcestershire sauce
¼ cup mayonnaise (approximately)
Salt and pepper to taste

1. Sauté mushrooms in butter until soft (approximately 5 minutes). Add minced onions and mix well.
2. Stir in lemon juice and Worcestershire sauce. Remove from heat.
3. Add enough mayonnaise to hold mixture together. Season with salt and pepper.
4. Serve chilled on salted English biscuits or any other mild cracker.

2 cups

Hint: This recipe can easily be halved.

A winner loved by all who tried it!

BLUE CHEESE BALL

2 3-ounce packages cream cheese
1 4-ounce package blue cheese
1 stalk celery, minced
1 tablespoon chives
1 tablespoon minced onion
1 tablespoon minced parsley
1½ tablespoons melted butter, cooled
1 cup chopped pecans, optional

1. Combine all ingredients except pecans.
2. Roll in pecans, if desired.
3. Chill several hours.
4. Serve with crackers.

10-12 servings

Hint: Serve with toasted pita triangles or Granny Smith apple slices.

To be a guest at your own party is a real accomplishment. Since this appetizer can be prepared in advance, you can do just that.

CHEESE BENNES

A Southern treat! A delightful cheese wafer that is wonderful by itself. Also makes a great accompaniment to soups or salads.

1¼ cups all purpose flour, sifted
1 teaspoon salt
½ teaspoon cayenne pepper

½ cup butter, melted
½ cup benne seeds (sesame seeds)
8 ounces extra-sharp Cheddar cheese

1. Combine sifted flour with salt, cayenne pepper, melted butter, and benne seeds.
2. Grate cheese and add to flour mixture. Mix well to form dough.
3. Roll dough out on waxed paper to ¼-inch thickness. Cut, using 1-2 inch cutter, depending on size desired. Place on baking sheet lined with waxed paper. (May be prepared ahead to this point and refrigerated.)
4. Preheat oven to 325°.
5. Bake for 15-25 minutes checking frequently. Bennes should be only slightly browned.
6. Serve warm.

12 dozen

Hint: For spicier bennes, add Tabasco (to taste) to the flour mixture.

WINTERGREEN SPECIAL

An appetizer with zip, or a light summer dessert—try either way served with a fruit such as frosted white grapes.

Saga cheese   **Gingersnaps**

Spread gingersnaps with Saga cheese and serve.

HOT BACON
AND MUSHROOM DIP

¾ pound (16 slices) bacon
1 pound fresh
mushrooms, sliced
1 medium onion, finely
chopped
4 tablespoons flour
½ teaspoon salt

¼ teaspoon pepper
16 ounces cream cheese,
cut into small pieces
4 teaspoons soy sauce
4 teaspoons
Worcestershire sauce
1½ cups sour cream

1. Fry bacon in large skillet until crisp. Drain bacon, and then crumble. Reserve.
2. Discard all but 2 tablespoons bacon drippings from skillet. Add mushrooms and onions; cook until tender, about 6-8 minutes. (Most of mushroom liquid should be evaporated.)
3. Mix in flour, salt, pepper, cream cheese, Worcestershire, and soy sauce. Stir until combined.
4. Remove from heat and add crumbled bacon and sour cream.
5. Serve warm with crackers.

14-16 servings

Hint: This is best served immediately, but can be gently reheated in double boiler or microwaved at low setting.

CAVIAR PIE

6 hard-cooked eggs,
finely chopped
3 tablespoons
mayonnaise
6 scallions, finely
chopped
1 8-ounce package cream
cheese, softened
⅔ cup sour cream

1 3½-ounce jar black
lumpfish caviar
Thin lemon wedges,
optional
Parsley sprigs, optional
Sieved egg yolk, optional
Pumpernickel bread or
crackers

1. Combine eggs and mayonnaise. Spread in the bottom of a well-greased 8-inch springform pan. Sprinkle with scallions.

Although the price of caviar may seem prohibitive, this dressy hors d'oeuvre makes a little go a long way.

2. Combine cream cheese and sour cream in a bowl and beat until smooth (approximately 3 minutes). Drop by tablespoonfuls onto scallions and spread evenly until surface is smooth.

3. Cover with plastic or foil and chill at least 3 hours.

4. Before serving, top with caviar. You can create a lovely effect by arranging the caviar in a flower petal design with sieved egg yolk in the center. Another option is to arrange lemon slices pinwheel fashion in the center.

5. Run a knife around edge of pan to loosen sides, then remove pan.

6. Add parsley sprigs for color. Serve with party pumpernickel bread or crackers.

10-12 servings

Hint: Can easily be doubled. Use a 10-inch springform pan.

SHRIMP SPREAD SUPREME

Pack this seafood appetizer in a crock for serving with crackers, or pipe with a pastry bag into small Belgian endive leaves.

1 **8-ounce package cream cheese**
Juice of one lemon
1 **small onion, grated**
¾ **cup diced celery**
½ **cup mayonnaise**

¼ **cup catsup**
Salt to taste
1 **pound shrimp, cooked, shelled, and coarsely chopped**

1. Combine all ingredients except shrimp with mixer.

2. Stir in shrimp.

3. Chill until ready to serve. Garnish with parsley or watercress. Serve with melba toast or assorted crackers.

10 servings

Hints: Substitute ½ cup sour cream for ½ cup mayonnaise. For a snappier spread, use ¼ cup chili sauce instead of ¼ cup catsup.

ROQUEFORT CHEDDAR CHEESE BALL

6 ounces bacon	¼ pound Roquefort cheese, crumbled
½ pound Cheddar cheese, grated	Pinch ground red pepper
½ pound cream cheese, softened	Pinch garlic salt
1 small grated onion	Dash Worcestershire sauce
	Parsley, for garnish

1. Fry bacon until crisp and drain well. Crumble.
2. Combine all ingredients thoroughly in mixing bowl.
3. Shape into cheese ball. Garnish with parsley and serve with assorted crackers.

A cheese ball with pizazz! Stand-out garnishes—a bed of fanned magnolia leaves for summer, a coating of minced parsley plus a red pimento "bow" for a holiday table.

TARHEEL CROCKS

½ pound sharp New York cheese (black rind)	8 stuffed green olives, chopped
2 hard-cooked eggs, mashed	½ teaspoon salt
¾ cup mayonnaise	¼ teaspoon paprika
1 teaspoon Worcestershire sauce	1 teaspoon minced fresh parsley
	¾ teaspoon onion, grated

1. Allow cheese to soften. Combine all ingredients and blend together by hand. (A food processor will purée the chopped ingredients.)
2. Put in a crock and chill until ready to serve.
3. Serve with crackers, Melba toast, or black bread rounds.

1 large or 2 small cheese crocks

Hint: You may want to grate the cheese before trying to blend with other ingredients.

What is a Tarheel? During the Civil War a North Carolina regiment distinguished itself by holding the line while the Virginia regiments next to it broke and retreated. The Virginia boys were told that some North Carolina tar on their heels might help them stick in the next fight, and when Robert E. Lee heard about the remark, he responded, "God bless the Tarheel boys!" They and their descendants have called themselves Tarheels to this day.

BREADS AND BEVERAGES

CINNAMON APPLE MUFFINS

2 cups sifted all-purpose or unbleached flour
1 tablespoon baking powder
¾ teaspoon salt
⅓ cup brown sugar, firmly packed
1 teaspoon cinnamon
¾ cup milk

1 egg
¼ cup margarine, melted
1 cup coarsely chopped apples
½ cup raisins
½ cup chopped nuts, optional
¼ cup sugar
½ teaspoon cinnamon

1. Preheat oven to 400°. Grease 12 muffin cups or use paper liners.
2. In large bowl, combine flour, baking powder, salt, brown sugar, and 1 teaspoon of cinnamon. Make a well in the center of this mixture.
3. Combine milk, egg, and margarine and pour into well in dry mixture. Stir just until ingredients are combined.
4. Stir in apples, raisins, and nuts.
5. Mound batter high in prepared muffin cups.
6. Mix sugar and remaining cinnamon and sprinkle over the muffins.
7. Bake in preheated oven for 20 minutes or until lightly browned.

12 muffins

APPLESAUCE MUFFINS

½ cup unsalted butter
1 egg
1 cup sugar
½ teaspoon vanilla
2 cups all-purpose or unbleached flour, sifted

½ teaspoon ground cloves
1½ teaspoons cinnamon
1 teaspoon allspice
½ cup chopped pecans, optional
1 cup applesauce
1 teaspoon baking soda

1. Preheat oven to 400°. Grease or paper line 15 muffin cups.
2. Cream together butter, egg, sugar, and vanilla.
3. Sift together flour, cloves, cinnamon, and allspice. Stir in nuts.
4. Combine applesauce and soda.
5. Combine all 3 mixtures and stir well. Spoon into prepared muffin cups, filling ⅔ full.

6. Bake in preheated oven for 15 minutes.

15 muffins

Hints: This batter can be used as a sweet bread baked in loaf pans or as cupcakes spread with cream cheese frosting or sprinkled with confectioners' sugar. Batter may be stored in refrigerator for up to 2 weeks.

MORNING GLORY MUFFINS

4 cups all-purpose or unbleached flour	1 cup raisins
2½ cups sugar	1 cup chopped pecans
4 teaspoons baking soda	1 cup shredded coconut
4 teaspoons cinnamon	1 cup grated carrot
1 teaspoon salt	6 large eggs
4 cups peeled, grated apples	2 cups vegetable oil
	4 teaspoons vanilla

1. Preheat oven to 350°. Grease or paper line 36 muffin cups.
2. Into large bowl, sift flour, sugar, soda, cinnamon, and salt. Stir in apples, raisins, pecans, coconut, and carrot. Mix well.
3. In blender, food processor, or large bowl, combine eggs, oil, and vanilla. Add to flour mixture and stir just until blended.
4. Spoon batter into prepared muffin cups, filling ⅔ full, and bake in preheated oven for 35 minutes or until muffins are springy to the touch.
5. Let cool in pans on wire rack for 5 minutes, then remove from pans to rack to cool completely.

36 muffins

Hint: This recipe yields 100 miniature muffins, so try them for a large crowd.

This recipe from the Morning Glory Cafe in Nantucket was loved by all who tested it.

BREAKFAST MUFFINS

These breakfast treats are a real favorite with the younger set. Try adding chocolate chips for a special after school snack.

1 tablespoon margarine or butter, softened
½ cup sugar
1 egg
⅔ cup Grapenuts cereal
1 8-ounce can crushed pineapple, undrained (1 cup)
1 cup mashed banana
2 cups biscuit mix
1 teaspoon salt
1 teaspoon cinnamon, optional

1. Grease 12-16 muffin cups or line with paper liners. Preheat oven to 425°.
2. Cream margarine with sugar, then add egg. Beat well.
3. Add remaining ingredients and stir just until blended. Mixture will be lumpy.
4. Fill prepared muffin cups ⅔ full and bake in preheated oven for about 20 minutes.

12 large muffins

PROCESSOR ORANGE DATE MUFFINS

A "must" to try. These are absolutely delicious!

1½ cups all-purpose or unbleached flour
1 teaspoon baking powder
1 teaspoon baking soda
1 teaspoon salt
½ cup pecans or walnuts, optional
½ cup dates
¾ cup sugar
1 medium unpeeled orange, cut into eighths and seeded
½ cup butter or margarine
1 large egg
½ cup orange juice

1. Grease 18 muffin cups or line with paper liners. Preheat oven to 400°.
2. Measure flour, baking powder, baking soda, and salt into bowl of food processor. Process until mixed. Add nuts if used. Pulse 1-2 times. Remove and set aside.
3. Process dates and sugar until dates are chopped. Add orange pieces and pulse until they are chopped fine.
4. Add butter, egg, and orange juice. Process to blend well, about 25 seconds. Add dry mixture and pulse until all ingredients are moist.
5. Spoon batter into prepared muffin cups and bake for 15 minutes.

18 muffins

MILDRED'S BLUEBERRY MUFFINS

1 cup unsalted butter
2 cups sugar
4 eggs, beaten
4 teaspoons baking powder
½ teaspoon salt

4 cups all-purpose flour
½ cup milk
1 teaspoon vanilla
2½-3 pints blueberries, fresh or frozen

1. Preheat oven to 400°. Line 30 muffins cups with paper baking cups.
2. Cream butter and sugar.
3. Add beaten eggs and vanilla.
4. Sift together dry ingredients.
5. Alternately add dry ingredients and milk to butter, mixing only enough to make a smooth batter.
6. Fold in blueberries.
7. Fill prepared muffin cups ⅔ full.
8. Bake in preheated oven for 25 minutes.

30 muffins

Hints: Food processor may be used for steps 2-5. Recipe can be halved. Do not thaw frozen blueberries. Fold them into muffin batter straight from the freezer.

Reminiscent of pound cake, these would make a great dessert.

KENTUCKY BLUEBERRY MUFFINS

½ cup unsalted butter
½ cup sugar
1 cup sour cream
2 eggs, beaten
1 teaspoon vanilla
⅓ cup cornmeal
1⅔ cups all-purpose or unbleached flour

1 teaspoon baking powder
¼ teaspoon baking soda
½ teaspoon salt
¾ cup fresh or frozen blueberries
¼ cup chopped nuts
Granulated sugar, optional

1. Preheat oven to 375°. Grease 15 muffin cups or use paper liners.
2. Beat together butter and sugar until light and fluffy.
3. Stir in sour cream, eggs, and vanilla.

Rich but not too sweet, these have just a hint of cornmeal.

4. Combine dry ingredients. Add to creamed mixture.
5. Stir in blueberries and nuts. If frozen berries are used, do not thaw first.
6. Fill prepared muffin cups ⅔ full. Sprinkle with sugar if desired.
7. Bake in preheated oven for 20-25 minutes.
8. Remove from muffin pans to cool.

14-16 muffins

Hint: Best served hot. May be kept hot by wrapping in foil until serving time.

PINEAPPLE BLUEBERRY BREAD OR MUFFINS

½ cup butter or margarine
1 cup sugar
1 teaspoon vanilla
2 eggs
3 cups all-purpose or unbleached flour
½ teaspoon salt
3 teaspoons baking powder

¼ teaspoon baking soda
1 cup pineapple juice or sour cream or combination
1⅓ cups crushed pineapple, well drained
1⅓ cups blueberries, optional

1. Grease a 9x5 inch loaf pan or prepare 18 muffin cups. Preheat oven to 400° for muffins, 350° for loaf.
2. Cream butter with sugar until light and fluffy. Beat in vanilla and eggs. Beat well.
3. Sift together 2½ cups of the flour, salt, baking powder, and baking soda. Add to the butter mixture, alternating with the juice or sour cream. Begin and end with the dry ingredients.
4. Stir remaining flour into pineapple and blueberries, if used. Stir floured fruit into batter. Spoon into prepared pan(s).
5. Bake 20-25 minutes for muffins, 50-60 minutes for loaf. Cool loaf in pan for 10-15 minutes before removing. Serve warm, or cool and wrap to store. Freezes well.

1 loaf or 18 muffins

LEMON HONEY WHEAT MUFFINS

1 cup all-purpose or unbleached flour
½ cup whole wheat flour
2 teaspoons baking powder
½ teaspoon salt

1 egg, beaten
½ cup milk
½ cup honey
¼ cup vegetable oil
Grated zest of 1 lemon

A delicious muffin that's a little bit different.

1. Preheat oven to 375°. Grease 12 muffin cups or line with paper liners.
2. In large bowl, stir together flours, baking powder, and salt. Make a well in the center of dry ingredients.
3. In small bowl, combine remaining ingredients and mix well. Pour all at once into dry ingredients. Stir just until blended. (Batter should still be lumpy.)
4. Fill prepared muffin cups ⅔ full. Bake in preheated oven for 20 minutes. Serve immediately.

12 muffins

Hint: These freeze well and are good when reheated in the microwave.

LEMON CLOUD MUFFINS

½ cup butter or margarine, softened
½ cup sugar
Grated zest of 1 lemon (about 1 tablespoon)
2 tablespoons milk
2 eggs, separated
3 tablespoons fresh lemon juice

1 cup all-purpose or unbleached flour
1 teaspoon baking powder
¼ teaspoon salt
¼ cup finely chopped pecans
1 tablespoon sugar
½ teaspoon nutmeg

These melt in your mouth!

1. Preheat oven to 375°. Grease 12 muffin cups or line with paper liners.
2. Cream butter, sugar, lemon zest, milk, and egg yolks until light and fluffy. Beat in lemon juice.
3. Combine dry ingredients and stir into creamed mixture just until blended.
4. Beat egg whites to soft peaks and fold into batter.
5. Spoon into prepared muffin cups.

6. Combine pecans, sugar, and nutmeg and sprinkle over each muffin.
7. Bake in preheated oven for 15-20 minutes or until lightly browned.

12 muffins

Hint: Vary this by adding 1 teaspoon of almond extract to the batter in step 2 and topping the muffins with ⅓ cup sliced almonds combined with ¼ cup sugar.

DILL MUFFINS

There are many special breads that include dill—this one can be assembled quickly and yields a rich, delicious muffin.

1 cup self-rising flour	½ cup sour cream
½ cup unsalted butter, softened	1 teaspoon dried dill seed

1. Preheat oven to 400°. Grease 18 miniature muffin cups.
2. Blend all ingredients, stirring until well mixed. Fill muffin cups ½ full.
3. Bake 10-15 minutes until lightly browned.

18 tiny muffins

CHEDDAR MUFFINS

An updated version of cornbread, these muffins are made moist by the addition of cheese. Wonderful with soups or chili.

3 ounces sharp Cheddar cheese, cut in cubes	1 teaspoon red pepper flakes, optional
1 large green onion including top, optional	½ teaspoon baking soda
1 cup unbleached or all-purpose flour	½ teaspoon salt
⅓ cup yellow corn meal	1 tablespoon sugar
2 teaspoons baking powder	¾ cup sour cream
	⅓ cup vegetable oil
	2 large eggs

1. Preheat oven to 375°. Grease 10-16 muffin cups.
2. In food processor fitted with steel blade, process cheese and green onion until finely chopped.
3. Add remaining ingredients and process until well mixed.
4. Fill muffin cups ⅔ full.
5. Bake for 15 minutes then remove to wire racks. Serve warm.

10-16 muffins

Hints: Muffins may be frozen for 2 months. For variation, try Monterey Jack or Muenster cheese.

OATMEAL BRAN MUFFINS

½ cup sugar
2 cups whole wheat flour
1½ teaspoons cinnamon
½ teaspoon ground ginger
¼ teaspoon nutmeg
½ teaspoon ground cloves
1 teaspoon salt
2 teaspoons baking soda

1½ cups bran cereal (such as All Bran)
1 cup quick cooking oats
2 cups buttermilk
2 beaten eggs
3 tablespoons oil
⅓ cup dark molasses
⅔ cup chopped dates or raisins, optional

This is it—our best bran muffin! Moist, delicious, and so tasty it's hard to believe it's good for you, too.

1. Preheat oven to 375°. Grease 24 muffin cups or line with paper liners.
2. Combine sugar, flour, spices, and baking soda in a large bowl. Set aside.
3. Measure cereal and oatmeal into a bowl. Pour in buttermilk and mix well. Let stand a few minutes to soften cereal, then add eggs, oil, and molasses.
4. Stir cereal mixture into dry ingredients, mixing until all ingredients are blended. Stir in fruit, if desired.
5. Fill prepared muffin cups ¾ full.
6. Bake in preheated oven for 15-18 minutes.

24 muffins

Hints: Batter can be stored for a few days in the refrigerator. For a sweeter muffin, increase sugar to taste.

OATMEAL BANANA LOAF

1½ cups sifted all-purpose flour
2 teaspoons baking powder
¼ teaspoon baking soda
1¼ teaspoons salt
⅔ cup sugar
¾ cup uncooked rolled oats

¼ cup vegetable oil
2 eggs, beaten
⅓ cup buttermilk (or 1 teaspoon lemon juice and ⅓ cup milk)
1 cup mashed ripe bananas
¾-1 cup chopped nuts, optional

A versatile, not-too-sweet banana bread with the added texture of oatmeal. Try this plain or with the streusel filling and topping.

1. Preheat oven to 350°. Grease one 9x5 inch or two 7½x3½ inch loaf pans.
2. Sift together the flour, baking powder, baking soda, and salt. Add sugar and oats.

3. Combine oil, eggs, buttermilk, and bananas in a large bowl. Add dry ingredients and stir gently to combine. Do not overmix.
4. Pour into prepared pan(s) and bake in preheated oven for about 50 minutes or until toothpick inserted in the center comes out clean.
5. Remove from pan immediately. Cool before slicing.

1 large loaf or 2 small loaves

Hint: Try this variation with a streusel filling: Combine ½ cup sugar, 1 teaspoon cinnamon, 1 tablespoon butter, ½ cup chopped nuts. Pour half of batter into pan. Top with half of streusel mixture, remaining batter, and remaining streusel. Bake as directed.

DATE NUT BREAD

The addition of applesauce gives this wholesome sweet bread a rich moistness. It is a welcome addition to tea or meals and is a much sought-after gift.

¾ cup chopped walnuts
1 cup chopped, pitted dates
1½ teaspoons baking soda
½ teaspoon salt
3 tablespoons shortening
1 cup applesauce, heated
2 eggs
1 teaspoon vanilla
1 cup sugar
1½ cups sifted all-purpose or unbleached flour

1. Combine walnuts, dates, baking soda, and salt. Add shortening and applesauce. Let stand for 20 minutes.
2. Preheat oven to 350°. Grease a 9x5 inch loaf pan.
3. Beat eggs and vanilla with fork. Beat in sugar and flour. Add date mixture and stir until just blended. Pour into prepared pan.
4. Bake 65 minutes or until toothpick inserted in center comes out clean. Cool in pan for 10 minutes. Remove to wire rack. When completely cooled, wrap in foil to store.

1 loaf

Hint: This loaf freezes nicely.

WINE DATE NUT BREAD

6 cups all-purpose or unbleached flour
2 cups brown sugar, firmly packed
2 tablespoons baking powder
4 teaspoons pumpkin pie spice
1 teaspoon salt
1 16-ounce package chopped dates

2 cups chopped pecans or walnuts
4 eggs, beaten
2⅔ cups Chablis or other dry white wine
1 cup butter or margarine, melted
1 cup sifted confectioners' sugar
2½ tablespoons Chablis
1 teaspoon pumpkin pie spice

1. Preheat oven to 350°. Grease two 9x5 inch loaf pans.
2. In large bowl combine flour, brown sugar, baking powder, 4 teaspoons spice, and salt. Stir well. Add dates and nuts and stir to coat.
3. In smaller bowl combine eggs, 2⅔ cups Chablis, and butter. Add to dry ingredients, stirring just until blended.
4. Pour batter into prepared pans and bake in preheated oven for 1 hour 25 minutes or until toothpick comes out clean when inserted in center.
5. Cool for 10 minutes in pans while combining confectioners' sugar, remaining spice, and remaining Chablis. Drizzle over warm loaves. Remove from pans to cool when mixture has soaked in.

2 loaves

Wonderful and lovely gift bread. Great for morning coffee or special brunch.

CHRISTMAS CRANBERRY BREAD

2 cups flour
1½ teaspoons baking powder
1 cup sugar
½ teaspoon salt
½ teaspoon soda
Juice and grated zest of 1 orange

2 tablespoons melted shortening
Boiling water
1 egg, beaten
1 cup halved cranberries
¾ cup chopped nuts

1. Grease a 9x5 inch loaf pan. Preheat oven to 325°.
2. Sift dry ingredients into a large bowl.

Wonderful for Christmas morning breakfast, this bread is also a welcome gift for friends.

3. In 2-cup measure place the juice of the orange, the grated zest, and the melted shortening. Add enough boiling water to make ¾ cup. Add the egg to this mixture.
4. Mix nuts and cranberries with dry ingredients to coat well. Add liquids and stir just until well blended.
5. Pour mixture into prepared pan and bake for 1 hour. Cool in pan for 10 minutes, then remove to rack to cool completely. Wrap and store for 24 hours before serving.

1 loaf

BLACKBERRY BREAD

One of the best sweet breads! Good served as cake topped with vanilla ice cream, too.

3	cups all-purpose or unbleached flour	1	cup chopped pecans
2	cups sugar	2	cups blackberries-frozen, canned, or fresh
1	teaspoon cinnamon	4	eggs, well beaten
1	teaspoon baking soda	1¼	cups vegetable oil
1	teaspoon salt		

1. Grease two 7½x3½ inch loaf pans. Preheat oven to 350°.
2. Mix together flour, sugar, cinnamon, soda, and salt. Stir in pecans and blackberries to coat well.
3. Mix eggs with oil and combine with dry mixture.
4. Pour into prepared pans. Bake in preheated oven for about 1 hour.
5. Cool in pans for 10 minutes then remove from pans to cool completely.

2 loaves

Hint: *Strawberries can be substituted for the blackberries.*

APRICOT NUT BREAD

Tangy and flavorful, this bread is perfect for breakfast, afternoon tea, or gifts. It freezes beautifully.

1½	cups apricot nectar	1	tablespoon butter, melted
¾	cup white raisins		
¾	cup diced dried apricots	2	cups all-purpose flour
		2	teaspoons baking soda
1	tablespoon fresh lemon juice	½	teaspoon salt
		⅓	cup milk
¾	cup sugar	½	cup chopped pecans
1	egg		

1. Preheat oven to 350°. Grease a 9x5 inch loaf pan.

2. Combine nectar, raisins, apricots, and lemon juice in a saucepan. Cook over medium-low heat for 5 minutes. Cool.
3. Beat sugar, egg, and butter together.
4. Combine flour, soda, and salt. Stir in nuts.
5. Combine sugar mixture, flour mixture, and apricot mixture. Mix well.
6. Stir in milk.
7. Pour into prepared pan and bake in preheated oven for 1 hour.

1 loaf

CHOCOLATE PUMPKIN BREAD

½ cup butter, melted	1 teaspoon baking soda
1 cup canned pumpkin	1 teaspoon cinnamon
2 eggs	½ teaspoon nutmeg
½ cup water	¼ teaspoon ground cloves
1½ cups sugar	¼ teaspoon salt
1¾ cups all-purpose or unbleached flour	½ cup chopped dates
	½ cup chopped nuts
¼ teaspoon baking powder	½ cup chocolate chips, optional

The richest, most tasty pumpkin bread you'll ever try - with or without chocolate chips!

1. Grease a 9x5 inch loaf pan and set aside. Preheat oven to 350°.
2. Beat together butter, pumpkin, eggs, and water. Set aside.
3. Sift together the sugar, flour, baking powder, baking soda, spices, and salt. Stir in dates, nuts, and chocolate chips to coat well.
4. Combine dry ingredients with pumpkin mixture until well blended.
5. Pour batter into prepared pan and place in preheated oven. Bake for 1¼-1½ hours. Check for doneness after 1¼ hours by inserting a toothpick into center. Bread should be very moist.
6. Cool in pan.

1 loaf

Hints: This bread freezes well. It is great warm or cold, with cream cheese or butter.

WHOLE WHEAT FRUIT BREAD

2½ cups whole wheat
   pastry flour
1   teaspoon baking soda
½   teaspoon salt
1   teaspoon cinnamon
½   teaspoon nutmeg
2   large eggs
¼   cup vegetable oil
1   cup dark brown sugar,
   firmly packed

½   cup milk
1   teaspoon vanilla
2-2½ cups diced peaches,
   pears, or other fruit.
   Use fresh, canned and
   drained, or dried
   (soaked in warm water
   for 15 minutes and
   drained)

1.   Grease a 9x5 inch loaf pan or two 3x7 inch loaf pans. Preheat oven to 375°.
2.   In large bowl, stir together the flour, soda, salt, spices, and fruit.
3.   In small bowl, beat the eggs. Mix in oil, sugar, milk, and vanilla. Add to dry mixture stirring only until well mixed.
4.   Pour into prepared pan(s) and bake in preheated oven 50-60 minutes for the large loaf or about 40 minutes for the smaller loaves. Bread is done when a toothpick inserted in the center comes out clean.
5.   Cool in pan for 15 minutes, then turn out onto a rack to cool completely. Wrap tightly to store.

1 large loaf or 2 small loaves

Hints: Spices may be varied according to the fruit used. Allspice makes a nice addition with apples or apricots. This bread freezes well.

HAM AND CHEESE BREAD

1 cup milk
½ cup water
4½-5 cups sifted unbleached or bread flour
¼ cup sugar
1 tablespoon salt
2 tablespoons or packages active dry yeast

1½ teaspoons dry mustard
Pinch cayenne pepper
½ pound sharp Cheddar cheese, cut in chunks
2 cups ground smoked ham

Try this in the food processor for a quick hearty loaf.

1. Combine milk and water and heat until very warm.
2. In bowl of food processor fitted with steel blade, combine 2 cups of the flour, sugar, salt, yeast, mustard, and cayenne. Process 2-3 turns to mix. Add chunks of cheese and process until coarsely chopped (12-15 turns). Add liquids and process to mix. Add 1-1½ cups of flour and process.
3. Turn dough mixture onto floured board and knead in as much remaining flour as is needed to form a soft but manageable dough. Knead until smooth and elastic.
4. Place dough into large greased bowl, cover, and let rise until doubled in bulk.
5. Punch down, divide in half, and roll each half into a 9x15 inch rectangle. Sprinkle each with 1 cup of the ground ham and roll, jelly roll fashion, to form a 9-inch cylinder. Place in greased 9x5 inch loaf pan. Cover and let rise until doubled.
6. Preheat oven to 375°.
7. Bake loaves 30-35 minutes. Cool in pans covered loosely with towel for 10 minutes. Remove from pans and serve immediately or cool on wire racks. Store in refrigerator or freeze for later use.

2 loaves

Hints: To make bread without food processor, mix ingredients as in step 2 above but stir vigorously with a wooden spoon or use electric mixer. Add cheese coarsely grated.
This makes a wonderful cheese bread without the ham.

CRACKED WHEAT FRENCH BREAD

A wonderfully rustic bread with the crunchy texture of cracked wheat, crispy on the outside with a moist center. This recipe is a bonus for the novice or rushed bread baker in that it does not require kneading.

1¾ cups warm water (110°-115°)
1 tablespoon or 1 package active dry yeast
1 tablespoon sugar
⅔ cup cracked wheat (bulgur)
4½ cups bread flour
2 teaspoons sugar
2 teaspoons salt
½ cup instant milk powder

1. Pour water into a small bowl. Sprinkle in yeast and 1 tablespoon of sugar. Add cracked wheat. Stir and set aside.
2. Sift flour into a large bowl. Sprinkle with 2 teaspoons of sugar, salt, and milk powder.
3. Make a well in the center of the dry ingredients and pour in the yeast mixture. Stir until all ingredients are well-blended. Use hands if necessary but do not knead.
4. Cover and let rise until doubled, 1-2 hours.
5. Punch down and divide in half. Spray French bread pans or cookie sheet with non-stick spray or grease with shortening.
6. Stretch each half of dough into oblong shape to fit length of bread pan. Make slits in top of loaves if desired.
7. Cover to let rise until doubled. Preheat oven to 425° with a pan of hot water in bottom of oven.
8. Bake loaves on upper rack for 15 minutes; reduce oven temperature to 375° and bake an additional 15 minutes.
9. Remove loaves from pan directly onto oven rack for about 5 more minutes or until bottoms of loaves are crusty. Serve immediately or cool, wrap tightly, and freeze.

2 baguette loaves

Hint: To reheat: Place completely thawed loaves directly on rack in moderate (350°) oven until hot and crisp, about 10 minutes.

PROCESSOR FRENCH BREAD

1 tablespoon active dry
   yeast (1 package -
   regular or rapid rise)
1 cup warm water (110°-
   115°)

1 teaspoon sugar
2⅓ cups unbleached or
   bread flour
⅔ cup cake flour
½ teaspoon salt

1. Dissolve yeast in warm water to which sugar has been added.
2. Place flours and salt in bowl of food processor fitted with steel blade and pulse to blend 5 to 7 on/off motions.
3. With processor running, slowly pour liquid through feed tube. Process until mixture forms a ball that cleans sides of bowl. Add more flour or water if necessary to obtain a moderately stiff dough.
4. Process an additional 30 seconds.
5. Let dough rest in processor 2 to 3 minutes.
6. Process again 30-45 seconds.
7. Place dough in greased or oiled bowl, turning to coat ball of dough.
8. Cover dough and let rise in warm place until doubled in bulk (about 1 hour).
9. Prepare French bread pan or baking pan by lightly greasing then sprinkling with corn meal.
10. Form dough into 1 long or 2 short loaves and place in prepared pan. Cover and let rise until doubled in size.
11. Set a shallow pan of water in lower part of oven and preheat to 425° at least 10 minutes before baking to create steam for a crisp crust.
12. Place bread in oven and reduce oven temperature to 400°.
13. Bake for 20-25 minutes. Remove bread from pan and place on oven rack for about 2 minutes to brown bottoms. Watch carefully.
14. Serve immediately or cool on rack to freeze.

1 long or 2 short loaves

Hint: To reheat frozen loaves, defrost and wrap in foil. Heat thoroughly at 325° (about 20 minutes).

This recipe combines contemporary and traditional methods for French bread. The dough is made in a food processor so kneading is not required. A pan of water is used in the oven for baking to ensure an authentic French crust.

CRISPY WHITE BRAIDS

A lovely bread that is an asset to any meal. Try shaping this bread into large, round, peasant loaves for a picnic or tailgate party.

4-4½ cups unbleached or bread flour
2 tablespoons or 2 packages active dry yeast
½ cup vegetable oil
1½ teaspoons salt
2 cups warm water (110°-115°)
3 tablespoons sugar
1 beaten egg white
Sesame or poppy seeds, optional

1. In large bowl of electric mixer, combine 2 cups of the flour and the yeast. Add oil, salt, water, and sugar. Beat with mixer on low speed for ½ minute. Scrape sides of bowl as necessary. Beat on high speed for 3 minutes. Add enough additional flour to make a moderately stiff dough.
2. Turn dough onto floured surface and knead for 8-10 minutes, or until smooth and elastic. Place dough in greased bowl, turning to coat all sides. Cover and let rise until doubled in bulk, about 90 minutes.
3. Punch dough down and divide in half. Divide each half into 3 equal pieces. Cover and let rest for 10 minutes.
4. Grease a large cookie sheet.
5. Roll each piece of dough into a 16-inch rope. Line up 3 ropes on greased sheet. Braid, pinching ends together and tucking under. Repeat with remaining ropes. Cover lightly and let rise until doubled (30-40 minutes). Brush with beaten egg white and sprinkle with seeds if desired.
6. Bake in preheated 375° oven for about 30 minutes.

2 loaves

WHEAT OAT RAISIN BREAD

Well worth the preparation time. A hearty bread with a wonderful texture.

2 tablespoons or packages active dry yeast
½ cup warm water
2¾ cups boiling water
1 cup oatmeal
2 teaspoons salt
2 tablespoons shortening at room temperature
1 cup raisins
1 cup bran
¾ cup molasses
1 cup cracked wheat or whole wheat flour
6 cups all-purpose, unbleached, or bread flour

1. Grease two 9x5 inch loaf pans. Set aside.

2. Pour boiling water over oatmeal, salt, shortening, raisins, bran, cracked wheat if used, and molasses in large bowl. Stir well and allow to cool to lukewarm (below 120°), stirring often.

3. Dissolve yeast in warm water and stir. Set aside to proof.

4. Stir yeast into oatmeal mixture. Mix well. Stir in whole wheat flour if used and 2-3 cups of white flour. Beat well. Stir in enough remaining flour to make a dough that is not sticky. Turn onto lightly floured surface and knead for 8 minutes. Shape dough into a ball and place in greased bowl. Cover with damp towel and let rise until doubled in bulk (about 1 hour). Punch down.

5. Divide dough into 2 parts and shape each into a cylinder. Place each in a prepared pan. Cover and let rise until nearly doubled (about 45 minutes).

6. Preheat oven to 350°. Bake loaves for 40 minutes to 1 hour. Remove from oven and cover with clean cloth.

2 loaves

SESAME BREAD

1 **cup milk**	1 **cup warm water (110°-115°)**
2 **teaspoons salt**	
½ **cup sugar**	7-8 **cups unbleached or bread flour**
4 **tablespoons unsalted butter**	2 **beaten eggs**
2 **tablespoons or 2 packages active dry yeast**	1 **egg white**
	Sesame seeds

1. In small saucepan, scald milk. Add sugar, salt, and butter. Stir well. Set aside to cool.

2. Pour warm water into large mixing bowl. Add yeast and stir until dissolved.

3. To yeast mixture add cooled milk and 3½ cups flour. Beat until smooth with electric mixer if possible.

4. Add beaten eggs. Beat well. Gradually add enough remaining flour to make a soft dough that can be handled easily.

5. Turn dough onto floured surface and knead for 10 minutes, or until smooth and elastic. Place in large greased bowl. Cover and let rise in warm place until doubled in bulk (about 1½ hours).

6. Punch down dough and divide into thirds. Divide each third into 3 pieces and roll each piece into a rope about 15 inches long. Pinch tops of 3 ropes together and braid. Pinch ends together and tuck under.

This prizewinning bread recipe yields a bountiful three loaves. An elegant dinner bread with a fine texture and crumb, it is great for baking ahead, freezing, and reheating when ready to serve.

7. Place each braid in a greased 9x5 inch bread pan, or place on greased baking sheet. Cover and let rise until doubled in bulk.

8. Beat remaining egg white with 1 tablespoon of water. Brush on loaves. Sprinkle generously with sesame seeds. Bake in preheated 425° oven for 10 minutes. Reduce oven temperature to 375° and continue baking until golden, 10-15 minutes.

9. Remove from oven. If soft crust is desired, rub tops of bread with soft butter. Remove from pans to wire racks to cool completely before storing airtight or freezing.

3 loaves

FINE BREAD

What more special way to greet your guests than with the glorious aroma of freshly baked bread.

2 **heaping tablespoons active dry yeast (3 packages)**	¾ **cup dry milk**
	¾ **cup corn meal**
	5 **cups hot water (115°-120°)**
½ **cup warm water**	
2 **tablespoons + 2 teaspoons salt**	10 **cups whole wheat flour**
	2 **cups unbleached or bread flour**
1 **cup molasses**	
1 **cup oil**	

1. Grease four 9x5 inch loaf pans.

2. Dissolve yeast in ½ cup warm water.

3. Combine the salt, molasses, oil, dry milk, corn meal, and hot water. Add yeast mixture. Stir in flours.

4. Turn dough onto floured surface and knead for 8-10 minutes or until smooth and elastic. Cover, place away from drafts in warm place, and let rise until doubled.

5. Punch dough down. Divide into four pieces. Form each into a loaf and place in prepared pans. Cover to let rise until doubled.

6. Preheat oven to 350°.

7. Bake loaves in preheated oven for 35-45 minutes. Remove and cover pans with clean cloth for 5 minutes to soften crust, if desired. Turn out on wire racks to cool.

4 loaves

Hint: For a lighter bread, reduce whole wheat flour to 8 cups and increase bread flour to 4 cups.

HERB BREAD

1	cup rolled oats	½	teaspoon dried parsley
2	cups boiling water	1	teaspoon dried basil
2	tablespoons or packages active dry yeast	½	teaspoon anise seed, optional
⅓	cup warm water (110°-115°)	2	teaspooons dried summer savory
2½	teaspoons salt	¼	teaspoon dried thyme
2	tablespoons butter or margarine, softened		Pinch dried marjoram
½	cup molasses		Pinch dried sage
		6	cups bread flour

1.   Pour boiling water over oats in large bowl. Stir and allow to cool to lukewarm.
2.   Soften yeast in ⅓ cup warm water.
3.   Add salt, butter, molasses, and herbs to oats and stir well. Add yeast mixture.
4.   Stir in 4 cups of the flour and beat well. Add an additional 1 cup of flour and continue mixing until dough is moderately stiff, adding more flour as necessary.
5.   Turn dough onto floured surface and knead 8-10 minutes, or until smooth and elastic.
6.   Place in greased bowl, turning to coat evenly with oil. Cover and let rise until doubled in bulk.
7.   Punch down and form into loaves for two 9x5 inch pans or braid.* Place in greased pans. Cover and let rise until almost doubled.
8.   Bake in preheated 350° oven for 25-30 minutes.
9.   Remove pans from oven and rub tops of loaves with butter or margarine. Remove loaves from pans and cool on wire racks.

2 loaves or 1 large braid

Hints: Whole wheat flour may be substituted for some of the bread flour.
*See Sesame Bread for braiding instructions.

Any leftovers make wonderful sandwiches the next day—our favorite is egg salad. Try fresh herbs in this bread whenever they are available.

POPPY SEED RYE

This no-knead rye is moist and hearty—the addition of poppy seeds is unexpected but yields a wonderful texture. This bread is worth making for sandwiches alone!

2 cups rye flour	⅓ cup poppy seeds
3-3½ cups bread flour	1 cup warm milk (110°-115°)
2 tablespoons sugar	
2 teaspoons salt	1 cup warm water (110°-115°)
2 tablespoons or packages active dry yeast or rapid rise yeast	
	2 tablespoons margarine, softened
	2 tablespoons molasses

1. Grease and set aside two 9x5 inch loaf pans.
2. Combine the rye flour, 1 cup bread flour, and remaining dry ingredients in large bowl.
3. Combine milk, water, margarine, and molasses; add to dry ingredients and beat well.
4. Stir in enough of the remaining flour to make a stiff dough. Kneading is not necessary, so dough will be a little sticky.
5. Place dough in greased bowl, turning to coat with oil. Cover and let rise until doubled in bulk.
6. Punch down dough and divide in half. Form each half into a cylinder to fit prepared bread pans. Turn each loaf to coat with shortening. Cover and let rise until doubled in bulk.
7. Preheat oven to 375° and bake loaves for about 30-40 minutes. Remove from oven and rub tops of loaves with butter or margarine. Cool slightly and remove to racks to cool completely.

2 loaves

DILL BREAD OR ROLLS

An exquisite savory bread loved by all who tasted it! The dough is very easy to work with, so if you've never tried to braid a loaf, don't hesitate to practice with this one.

1 tablespoon or 1 package active dry yeast	1 green onion with top, finely chopped, or 1 teaspoon onion flakes
¼ cup warm water (110°-115°)	2 tablespoons sugar
½ teaspoon sugar	1 tablespoon dried dill seed
1 cup sour cream, room temperature	
1 beaten egg, room temperature	1 tablespoon dried dill weed
	1 teaspoon salt
1 tablespoon butter or margarine, softened	2¾-3 cups bread flour
	1 beaten egg yolk
	2 tablespoons water

1. In large bowl sprinkle yeast over warm water. Stir in ½ teaspoon of sugar. Let stand until foamy.
2. Stir in sour cream, egg, butter, onion, 2 tablespoons sugar, dill seed, dill weed, salt, and 1 cup of the flour. Beat with a spoon until well blended (or use mixer).
3. Stir in as much of the remaining flour as possible with a spoon, then turn dough onto a floured surface. Knead in enough additional flour to make a moderately stiff dough. Continue kneading until dough is smooth and elastic, about 8 minutes.
4. Place in greased bowl, turn dough to coat with oil. Cover and let rise until doubled, about 1¼-1½ hours.
5. Punch dough down. For braid: Divide dough into 3 pieces. Roll each piece into an 18-inch rope and braid 3 pieces together. Place on ungreased baking sheet. Cover, and let rise until doubled. For rolls: Turn dough onto lightly floured surface and roll to 1½-inch thickness. Cut with biscuit cutter. Place on greased baking sheets. Cover and let rise until doubled, 30-60 minutes.
6. Combine egg yolk with 2 tablespoons water. Brush on rolls or loaf. Bake in preheated 350° oven: 25 minutes for loaf, 15-20 minutes for rolls.

1 loaf or 24-30 rolls

BUTTERMILK ROLLS

2 tablespoons or 2 packages active dry yeast	¼ cup melted margarine or butter
¾ cup warm water (110°-115°)	4 tablespoons sugar
1¼ cups buttermilk, warmed slightly	2 teaspoons baking powder
4½-5 cups bread flour	2 teaspoons salt
	Butter or margarine, melted

1. In a large mixing bowl, dissolve yeast in warm water. Let proof about 5 minutes.
2. Add buttermilk, 2½ cups flour, ¼ cup butter, sugar, baking powder, and salt.
3. Blend well, then beat for approximately 2 minutes using an electric mixer or wooden spoon.
4. Stir in just enough additional flour to make a soft dough.
5. Knead well on lightly floured surface (about 5 minutes).
6. Place in a greased bowl; turn dough to cover with oil. Cover and let rise until doubled.
7. Punch down dough and let rest while melting butter.

Light as a feather, these buttery rolls also make tasty sandwich buns for special occasions.

8. Form dough into small balls of desired size. Dip each ball into melted butter. Place each ball into a muffin pan or into square baking pan depending upon whether you desire "pull apart" or individual rolls.
9. Cover and let rise until doubled.
10. Bake in preheated 375° oven for 15-20 minutes, depending upon size.
11. Cover with cloth immediately after removing from oven for a very soft roll.

24-36 rolls

Hint: Dough may also be made into a loaf. Bake loaf at 375° for 30-35 minutes.

WHOLE WHEAT BISCUITS

Delicious!

1 **tablespoon or package active dry yeast**	½ **teaspoon baking soda**
3 **tablespoons warm water (110°-115°)**	½ **teaspoon salt**
2½ **cups whole wheat flour**	¼ **cup margarine, softened**
½ **cup unbleached, bread, or all-purpose flour**	1 **tablespoon honey**
2 **teaspoons baking powder**	1 **cup buttermilk, slightly warmed**
	Melted margarine

1. Lightly grease a baking sheet. Preheat oven to 400°.
2. Dissolve yeast in warm water. Set aside.
3. Combine dry ingredients. Cut in margarine until mixture resembles coarse meal. Add yeast mixture, honey, and buttermilk, mixing well.
4. Roll dough to ½-inch thickness on floured surface. Cut with 2-inch round biscuit cutter and place biscuits on prepared baking sheet. Brush with melted margarine.
5. Bake for 12-15 minutes.

12 biscuits

MURPH'S MOM'S CHEESE BREAD

1   5-ounce jar Old
    English cheese spread
½   cup butter or
    margarine, softened

1   loaf unsliced white
    bread

1.   Stir cheese spread and butter together until they are well-blended.
2.   Remove crust from 3 sides of bread loaf leaving bottom crust on. Cut lengthwise down middle of loaf not quite through to bottom crust, then cut loaf cross-wise making slices about 1-1½ inches thick. Again, do not cut through.
3.   Spread cheese mixture on all cut surfaces and "ice" the loaf.
4.   Place on lightly greased cookie sheet and bake in preheated 400° oven until cheese is crusty and bread is hot (5-10 minutes). Watch carefully as cheese can slide off bread and burn if over-cooked.

1 loaf

Nothing could be simpler than this hearty bread. Serve it as an accompaniment to main course salads in summer or with steaming bowls of chili on snowy winter nights.

PROCESSOR PIZZA DOUGH

1   cup warm water (110°-
    115°)
1   tablespoon or 1
    package active dry
    yeast
1   teaspoon sugar
2   tablespoons oil
¾   teaspoon salt

3½-4 cups white flour (all-
    purpose, unbleached,
    or bread) or 1½ cups
    whole wheat flour and
    2-2½ cups white flour
Desired sauce and
    toppings

1.   In small bowl combine water, yeast, and sugar. Stir and let stand until bubbly. Add oil.
2.   In bowl of food processor fitted with steel blade, combine 3½ cups of flour and salt. Process a few turns to mix.
3.   With processor running, pour in liquid mixture. Process until dough forms a ball. Add more flour if necessary to make a dry dough that forms a ball. (Can be made ahead to this point and frozen.)

Use 6 9-inch pie pans for individual "make your own" pizzas. Try this when feeding a crowd of teenagers.

4. Transfer dough to a greased bowl. Cover to let rise until doubled.

5. While dough rises, prepare two 12-inch round or two 10½x15½ inch rectangular pans by coating with shortening or spraying with vegetable coating.

6. Prepare desired toppings.

7. Preheat oven to 425°.

8. Punch dough down and divide in half. Press each half into a prepared pan. Top with desired toppings.

9. Place pizzas in lower half of preheated oven and bake for 10-20 minutes (depending upon thickness) until crust is brown and crisp.

2 pizza crusts

HOT CROSS BUNS

The best hot cross buns we've tasted! Omit the crosses and serve anytime.

1 **tablespoon or 1 package active dry yeast**
¼ **cup warm water (110°-115°)**
1 **cup warm milk (110°-115°)**
2 **tablespoons butter, melted**
⅓ **cup sugar**
¾ **teaspoon salt**
¾ **teaspoon cinnamon**
½ **teaspoon nutmeg**
2 **beaten eggs**

¾ **cup currants**
½ **cup chopped, candied peel - grapefruit, orange, lemon, or mixture**
4 **cups unbleached or bread flour**
1 **egg yolk**
Frosting:
1 **cup confectioners' sugar, sifted**
1-2 **teaspoons cream or milk**
1 **teaspoon lemon juice**

1. In large bowl dissolve yeast in warm water. Stir in milk, butter, sugar, salt, cinnamon, and nutmeg. Stir in eggs, currants, and peel. Slowly add flour to make a soft dough.

2. Turn dough onto a floured surface and knead for 8-10 minutes, or until smooth and elastic. Place in a lightly greased bowl and let rise in a warm place, covered, until doubled in bulk.

3. Punch down dough and divide into 24-36 balls depending on the size buns desired. Place balls on well-greased cookie sheets. Combine egg yolk with 1 tablespoon water. Brush tops of rolls with egg wash. Cover lightly and let rise until doubled.

4. Bake in preheated 400° oven for 12-15 minutes. Cool for at least 5 minutes before frosting.

5. Combine frosting ingredients and use to form a cross on each bun.

24-36 buns

ORANGE COCONUT SWEET ROLLS

Dough:
1 tablespoon or 1 package active dry yeast
¼ cup warm water (110°-115°)
¼ cup sugar
1 teaspoon salt
2 eggs, slightly beaten
½ cup sour cream
6 tablespoons butter, melted
2¾-3 cups all-purpose flour
4 tablespoons butter, melted

Filling:
¾ cup sugar
¾ cup shredded coconut, lightly toasted
2 tablespoons grated orange zest

Glaze:
¾ cup sugar
½ cup sour cream
2 tablespoons orange juice
¼ cup butter

Topping:
¼ cup toasted coconut

These won a blue ribbon. Try them and you will understand why!

1. In a large bowl, soften yeast in warm water. When foamy, add sugar, salt, eggs, sour cream, and 6 tablespoons butter. Mix well. Gradually beat in flour to form a stiff dough. Cover and let rise in warm place until doubled.
2. Combine filling ingredients and set aside.
3. Punch dough down and knead on floured surface about 2 minutes. Divide dough in half.
4. Roll each half of dough into a 12-inch circle and brush each circle with 2 tablespoons of the melted butter. Sprinkle each circle with half of the filling mixture. Cut into 12 wedges and roll each wedge up "croissant style" beginning at wide edge.
5. Place rolls, seam side down, in 3 rows in a greased 9x13 inch baking dish. Cover and let rise until doubled in bulk, 20-30 minutes.
6. Bake in preheated 350° oven for 18-20 minutes. Remove from oven and leave in pan.
7. Combine glaze ingredients in saucepan. Bring to a boil and boil for 3 minutes. Pour over rolls in pan. Sprinkle with ¼ cup toasted coconut.

24 rolls

CROISSANT DAINTIES

Pretty and delicious pastry. Great for a coffee, brunch, or tea.

2 cups all-purpose or unbleached flour
¼ teaspoon salt
1 cup butter, room temperature
1 egg yolk, slightly beaten
¾ cup sour cream
½ teaspoon vanilla
¾ cup sugar
1 teaspoon cinnamon
¾ cup chopped pecans

1. In large bowl, combine flour and salt. Cut in butter with pastry blender until mixture resembles small peas.
2. In small bowl combine egg yolk, sour cream, and vanilla. Add to flour mixture blending with a fork until well mixed. Divide dough into thirds. Wrap and chill several hours or overnight.
3. Mix sugar, cinnamon, and nuts in a small bowl.
4. Preheat oven to 375°.
5. Roll ⅓ of the dough into a 12-inch circle on lightly floured surface. Sprinkle with ⅓ of the nut mixture. Cut into 16 wedges. Roll each wedge firmly starting at outer edge. Place on ungreased baking sheet with the point side down. Curve into crescent shape. Repeat with remaining dough and nut mixture.
6. Place in preheated oven and bake for about 18 minutes or until lightly brown. Remove to wire racks to cool.

48 pastries

Neighborhood Coffee

Morning Glory Muffins

Kentucky Blueberry Muffins

Wine Date Nut Bread　　　Chocolate Pumpkin Bread

Ham & Cheese Bread

Croissant Dainties　　　　　Plum Coffee Cake

Russian Tea

Hot Coffee

CREAM CHEESE ALMOND COFFEE CAKE

Dough:
1 cup sour cream
⅓ cup sugar
1 teaspoon salt
½ cup butter or margarine, melted
2 tablespoons or 2 packages active dry yeast
½ cup warm water (110°-115°)
2 eggs, beaten
4 cups unbleached or bread flour

Filling:
2 8-ounce packages cream cheese, room temperature
⅔ cup sugar
1 egg, beaten
⅛ teaspoon salt
2 teaspoons vanilla
Topping:
1 cup sliced almonds
Glaze:
2 cups confectioners' sugar
4 tablespoons milk or cream
2 teaspoons vanilla

These rich sweet "braids" melt in your mouth, and they are so easy! Be sure to start ahead, though, as the dough should be refrigerated overnight.

1. Heat sour cream gently over low heat. Stir in sugar, salt, and butter. Cool.
2. In large bowl, sprinkle yeast over warm water. Stir and let stand until bubbly. Add sour cream mixture, eggs, and flour and mix well. Cover and refrigerate overnight.
3. Prepare filling: With mixer, beat cream cheese. Add remaining filling ingredients and mix well. (If prepared ahead, refrigerate filling. Bring to room temperature before assembling braids.)
4. Divide chilled dough into 4 equal parts. On a well-floured surface, roll each section into a 12x8 inch rectangle. Spread with ¼ of filling. Roll up jelly roll fashion beginning with long side. Pinch edges and tuck under.
5. Place rolls, seam side down, on well greased baking sheet. Slit tops of rolls at 2-inch intervals about ⅔ of the way through. Cover and let rise 1 hour. Sprinkle with the almonds.
6. Bake in preheated 375° oven for about 15 minutes. Cool on pan placed on rack.
7. Combine glaze ingredients and drizzle over cooled "braids".

4 loaves

Hints: May vary the flavor of the filling by substituting 1 teaspoon almond extract and 1 teaspoon vanilla for 2 teaspoons vanilla.

MAKE AHEAD COFFEE CAKE

A simple and delicious coffee cake that is assembled in the evening, baked and served hot in the morning.

¾ cup butter or margarine, softened
1 cup sugar
2 eggs
1 8-ounce carton sour cream
2 cups all-purpose or unbleached flour

1 teaspoon baking powder
1 teaspoon baking soda
½ teaspoon salt
½ teaspoon nutmeg
¾ cup brown sugar, firmly packed
½ cup chopped walnuts
1 teaspoon cinnamon

1. Grease and flour a 9x13x2 inch pan.
2. In large bowl of electric mixer combine butter and sugar. Beat with mixer until light and fluffy. Add eggs and sour cream. Mix well.
3. In small bowl combine flour, baking powder, baking soda, salt, and nutmeg. Add to butter mixture and mix well. Pour into prepared pan.
4. Combine remaining ingredients and mix well. Sprinkle evenly over batter. Cover and chill in refrigerator overnight.
5. The next morning preheat oven to 350°. Place coffee cake in oven uncovered and bake 35-40 minutes - until a toothpick comes out clean.

12-15 servings

PLUM COFFEE CAKE

¼ cup fine crisp cookie crumbs (gingersnaps or vanilla wafers)
6 tablespoons unsalted butter, softened
¾ cup sugar
1 egg
1 tablespoon grated lemon zest
1 teaspoon vanilla
2 cups all-purpose or unbleached flour
2 teaspoons baking powder

½ cup milk
3 cups peeled, sliced plums (about 1½ pounds)
Topping:
⅓ cup flour
½ cup chopped walnuts (or other nuts if preferred)
1 teaspoon cinnamon
½ cup sugar
2 tablespoons unsalted butter, softened

1. Grease an 8-inch springform pan. Dust with the cookie crumbs and set aside. Preheat oven to 375°.
2. Cream butter and sugar in large mixing bowl. Beat in egg, zest, and vanilla.
3. Sift together dry ingredients. Add these to the creamed mixture alternately with the milk. Fold in the sliced plums. Spread batter in prepared pan.
4. For topping, mix all ingredients blending butter with fork or fingertips. Sprinkle evenly over cake.
5. Bake in preheated oven for 60-70 minutes or until a toothpick inserted in center comes out clean. Cool for 10 minutes before removing outer ring from springform pan. Serve warm.

6-8 servings

Moist and crunchy but not too sweet, this is a perfect brunch cake. Try varying the fruit by using pears or peaches alone or combined with the plums.

HOT APPLE WINE

Great party punch! Good for informal use too.

3 cups apple cider
¼ cup sugar
1 3-inch stick of cinnamon
6 whole cloves

Sliced peel of ¼ lemon
1 fifth dry white wine
2 tablespoons fresh lemon juice

1. In a 2-quart saucepan combine cider, sugar, cinnamon stick, cloves, and lemon peel, and bring to a boil. Stir until sugar is dissolved, then simmer, uncovered, for 15 minutes.
2. Strain cider mixture to remove spices and peel; add wine and lemon juice. Heat through but do not boil. Serve warm in punch cups or mugs garnished with lemon slices.

6-8 cups

NORTHWOODS APPLE SOUR

Serve this special cocktail as a prelude to a fall supper or tailgate luncheon before a football game.

½ cup whiskey
2 cups apple juice or apple cider
4-6 tablespoons fresh lime or lemon juice

2 tablespoons maple syrup
⅛ teaspoon cinnamon
⅛ teaspoon ground cloves
Club soda

1. Mix all ingredients except club soda in blender and pour into ice-filled glasses. Top glasses with club soda.

2-4 servings

HOMEMADE AMARETTO

Make a large batch of this early in December. In glass decanters or carafes tied with holiday ribbon, it makes wonderful Christmas gifts.

4 cups boiling water
2 pounds brown sugar
4 ounces almond extract

1 fifth peach brandy
½ gallon vodka

1. Add brown sugar to boiling water. Remove from heat and stir until sugar is dissolved. Cool slightly.
2. Stir in remaining ingredients. Mix well. Stores indefinitely in glass bottles.

1 gallon

HOLIDAY WASSAIL

1½ cups sugar
1 quart water
12 whole cloves
4 sticks cinnamon
4 whole allspice
2-4 tablespoons chopped, crystalized ginger

3 cups orange juice
1 cup lemon juice, fresh preferred
2 quarts apple cider
Bourbon or dark rum, if desired

Wonderful hot punch with the subtle flavor of ginger. Great for all ages.

1. In 5-quart pot simmer water and sugar for 10 minutes. Remove from heat. Add cloves, cinnamon, and allspice. Cover and let stand for 1 hour.
2. Strain mixture. Add ginger, orange juice, lemon juice, and apple cider. Let stand at room temperature, covered, for 24 hours.
3. Before serving, strain, heat, and stir. As an option stir in desired amount of bourbon or dark rum.

About 16 cups

HOT BUTTERED RUM

1 pound butter, softened
1 pound light brown sugar
1 pound confectioners' sugar
2 teaspoons cinnamon

2 teaspoons nutmeg
1 quart vanilla ice cream, softened
Light rum
Whipped cream, optional
Cinnamon sticks, optional

Wonderful on a cold winter night.

1. Combine butter, sugars, and spices. Beat until fluffy. Add ice cream and blend well. Place in a 2-quart container and freeze.
2. To serve: Place 3 heaping tablespoons of mixture plus 1 jigger of rum in a large mug. Fill with boiling water. Stir well. Top with whipped cream and cinnamon stick stirrers.

15-18 cups

RUSSIAN TEA

1 stick of cinnamon	4 cups boiling water
1 tablespoon whole cloves	4 oranges, sliced, or 1 6-ounce can orange juice concentrate
1 cup sugar	2-3 cups pineapple juice
4 cups water	Juice of 2 lemons
3 teaspoons tea leaves	

1. Tie cloves and cinnamon together in a small cheesecloth bag. In a large saucepan, combine the bag of spices, sugar, and 4 cups water. Boil for 5 minutes.
2. In a separate container, add the tea to 4 cups boiling water. Steep for 5 minutes.
3. Strain tea into spice mixture along with juices and sliced oranges, if used. Heat to boiling to serve, but do not boil.
4. Store in refrigerator for up to 2 weeks to heat and serve as desired.

10-12 servings

TUXEDO DRINK

This rich concoction will please chocolate and coffee lovers alike. Try it in place of dessert for a special ending to a dinner party.

3 cups vanilla ice cream	2 tablespoons cognac
2 teaspoons instant coffee powder	½ cup milk
2 tablespoons chocolate syrup	Grated semi-sweet chocolate, optional garnish

1. Place ice cream in blender or food processor container fitted with steel blade.
2. Add remaining ingredients.
3. Blend until milkshake consistency. Pour into glasses and garnish with shaved chocolate. Serve immediately.

2 servings

Hint: Fudge ripple ice cream is equally good.

LIQUID GODDESS

1 quart Breyers or other high quality peach ice cream	½-¾ cup Amaretto 2-4 tablespoons white rum

Place all ingredients in container of blender. Blend just until ingredients are mixed. Pour into stemmed glasses and serve.

4 servings

So quick and easy. Try this for dessert with a chocolate snap or ginger cookie.

COFFEE PUNCH

1 gallon strong coffee	½ gallon rich vanilla ice cream
2 cups sugar	
1 tablespoon vanilla	1 pint heavy cream, whipped

1.   Mix hot coffee with sugar. Stir to dissolve. Cool and add vanilla. Chill until very cold.
2.   Chill large punch bowl.
3.   Soften ice cream and mix with the coffee mixture in chilled punch bowl. Garnish with whipped cream.

About 30 servings

Hints: This punch freezes well before adding cream.
Vary by decreasing whipping cream to ½ pint and using ½ gallon each of vanilla ice cream and chocolate ice cream or 1 gallon of fudge ripple. Very rich!

A very dressy punch — try it during the holidays.

SOUPS AND SANDWICHES

Soup is one of cuisine's kindest courses. In our country's early days, it was not unusual to have a pot of warming nourishment cooking on the open hearth where the family gathered. It was a meal within itself; however, today our culture identifies soup with lunch or as a first course for an evening meal.

The versatility and variability of soups are limitless. Hot soups, served in hearty portions and accompanied by bread and a simple salad, can comprise a meal. Cold soups are appropriate as first courses or snacks and are often a welcome palate refresher on a summer afternoon.

The following pages are filled with interesting and delectable soups for all seasons. In the fall, try the Borscht or Spicy Vegetable Soup and when winter arrives, prepare the Cream of Cauliflower or Texas 12-Bean Soup. Serve the Spring Soup when the flowers and trees are budding and the Chilled Melon or Gazpacho when the hot days of summer are upon us.

Since many soup recipes call for chicken stock, we have included a basic recipe which follows. In a pinch, canned stock may be substituted; instant granulated broth is also available in a variety of flavors. Be judicious in the use of salt with these substitutes as they may already contain enough to season the soup.

HOMEMADE CHICKEN STOCK

2 **pounds bony chicken pieces (any combination of necks, backs, or wings)**	1 **large onion, peeled and stuck with 3 cloves**
2 **carrots, coarsely chopped**	1 **bay leaf**
3 **celery stalks with leaves, coarsely chopped**	2 **sprigs fresh parsley**
	6 **whole black peppercorns**
	2 **teaspoons salt**
	6 **cups cold water**

1. In a 5-quart stockpot combine chicken pieces and all remaining ingredients.
2. Bring to a boil.
3. After 5 minutes, remove the scum that forms on the surface with a large spoon.
4. Reduce heat and simmer, covered, for 1-2 hours.

5. Remove chicken pieces and strain stock through a sieve lined with 2 layers of cheesecloth. Discard vegetables.
6. Chill stock and when it is cold, remove layer of fat that has formed on the surface. Stock may be refrigerated for 2 days or frozen for later use.

5 cups

Hint: Stock freezes beautifully. Make a double batch and freeze in small quantities.

HERBED TOMATO SOUP

½ cup unsalted butter
2 tablespoons olive oil
1 large sweet onion, thinly sliced
1 teaspoon fresh dill weed, or ½ teaspoon dried
1 teaspoon fresh thyme, or ½ teaspoon dried
1 teaspoon fresh basil, or ½ teaspoon dried
6 large tomatoes, peeled and chopped, or 1 28-ounce can and 1 16-ounce can tomatoes, drained and chopped

3 tablespoons tomato paste
3¾ cups chicken stock
¼ cup all-purpose flour
Salt
Freshly ground black pepper
½-1 teaspoon sugar
Freshly grated Parmesan cheese
Croutons, optional garnish

This lovely soup captures the essence of tomatoes even when they are out of season and the canned variety is substituted. It is a natural addition to a wide variety of menus and couldn't be simpler to prepare.

1. In 5-quart saucepan, melt butter with oil over medium heat.
2. Add onion, dill, thyme, and basil. Cook, stirring occasionally, until tender and very lightly browned.
3. Add tomatoes and tomato paste to onion mixture. Simmer, uncovered, 10 minutes.
4. Combine ½ cup chicken stock with flour in small bowl and whisk until smooth. Add to tomato mixture. Blend in remaining stock and simmer 30 minutes.
5. Transfer soup (in batches) to food processor fitted with steel blade and purée.
6. Return to saucepan and season to taste with salt, pepper, and sugar.
7. Serve hot. Sprinkle Parmesan cheese and croutons on top.

6-8 servings

Hint: This soup freezes very well.

CRAB BISQUE

Be prepared to be embarrassed when guests demand this recipe. They will not believe how simple such an elegant soup can be!

1 **pound fresh crab clawmeat**
1 **10½-ounce can cream of mushroom soup**
1 **10½-ounce can cream of asparagus soup**
3 **cups half and half**
4 **tablespoons dry sherry**
Paprika
Fresh parsley

1. Pick through crabmeat and remove any shells.
2. In top of a double boiler, combine all ingredients except sherry.
3. Cook, stirring often, until bisque boils and thickens.
4. Just before serving, stir in sherry. Garnish with paprika and a sprig of fresh parsley.

6 main course servings

SALMON BISQUE

The northwest region of the country is well known for its fresh salmon, and this recipe captures salmon at its best! Complete this full flavored gourmet bisque with a sprig of parsley and a bottle of wine for a delightful prelude to an evening meal.

6 **tablespoons butter**
1 **tablespoon chopped onion**
5 **tablespoons flour**
2 **bay leaves**
1¾ **cups chicken broth**
½ **cup dry white wine**
1 **tablespoon tomato paste**
8 **ounces fresh salmon, poached, or 1 7¾-ounce can pink salmon (undrained)**
1 **cup half and half**

1. Melt butter in saucepan and sauté onion until tender. Blend in flour. Cook until bubbly, stirring constantly.
2. Add bay leaves. Gradually stir in broth; cook, stirring constantly, until smooth and thick.
3. Stir wine into sauce. Cook at low heat for 10 minutes, stirring occasionally. Discard bay leaves. Drain salmon and reserve liquid. Stir tomato paste and salmon liquid into sauce.
4. Mash salmon (making sure all bones and skin have been discarded) and stir it into sauce.
5. Place small amount of soup in blender or food processor and blend until smooth. Repeat with remaining soup.
6. Return to saucepan. Add half and half and heat thoroughly.

4 servings

DEED'S CRAB SOUP

1 small beef soup bone
3 slices bacon, cooked until crisp, crumbled
2 tablespoons bacon fat
3-4 stalks celery, including tops, coarsely chopped
1 small onion, finely chopped
2 small carrots, sliced
1 small head green cabbage, chopped
4-5 tomatoes, coarsely chopped
½ pound fresh green beans, cut into 1-inch lengths
½ pound fresh lima beans
2 ears fresh corn, cooked
1 teaspoon dried thyme or 2 teaspoons fresh thyme
½ teaspoon dried red pepper flakes
6 quarts water
Salt and freshly ground pepper
2 pounds crab clawmeat

1. With a sharp knife, remove corn from cobs.
2. In a large stockpot, combine all ingredients except crabmeat.
3. Simmer, uncovered, for one hour.
4. Add crabmeat and simmer slowly for an additional 2-3 hours, adding more water if necessary.
5. Remove soup bone and serve.

12 servings

This family recipe is a summer tradition during vacations at the shore. Serve it as the sun is setting accompanied by a crusty bread and a green salad.

MUSHROOM AND ONION SOUP

8 ounces fresh mushrooms, rinsed and patted dry
2 tablespoons unsalted butter
1 medium onion, finely diced
2 tablespoons flour
½ teaspoon salt, or to taste
Pinch of black pepper
1 10¾-ounce can condensed chicken broth
1¼ cups milk
Minced parsley or chives, garnish

1. Coarsely grate mushrooms using shredding disc of food processor.
2. In a medium saucepan, melt the butter; add onion and cook gently until golden brown and tender. Stir often.

An easy-to-prepare soup with a hearty flavor.

3. Increase heat to high, add mushrooms, and cook rapidly, stirring often until wilted. (Have heat high enough so that mushrooms do not give off their liquid.)
4. Stir in flour, salt, and pepper.
5. Remove from heat and gradually stir in broth and milk, keeping smooth. Cook over medium heat, stirring constantly, until thickened.
6. Serve with minced parsley or chives as garnish.

2-3 servings

CHESAPEAKE OYSTER AND SPINACH SOUP

Oysters are a popular holiday food, and this soup is a great beginning to a festive meal. The combination of spinach and oysters is unique and pleasing.

¾ **quart oysters**	**Pinch garlic powder**
1 **pound frozen chopped spinach**	**Pinch nutmeg**
3 **tablespoons butter**	1 **tablespoon Worcestershire sauce**
⅓ **cup finely chopped onion**	**Salt**
1 **stalk celery, finely chopped**	**Pepper**
3 **tablespoons flour**	1 **pint milk**
	1 **pint light cream**

1. Cook oysters in 1½ cups water until they are firm; drain liquid and reserve.
2. Cook spinach and drain well. Place oysters and spinach in food processor to purée.
3. Melt butter in saucepan and sauté onions and celery until tender. Move onions and celery to one side of pan and add flour to butter to make a paste. Add oyster liquid to roux, using a whisk to make mixture smooth. Simmer 15-20 minutes, stirring occasionally.
4. Add oyster and spinach purée and seasonings to simmering liquid - mix well.
5. Stir in milk and cream and continue to cook over low heat for 5-10 minutes, but do not boil.

6 servings

LEEK AND STILTON CREAMED SOUP

2 tablespoons butter	1½ cups heavy cream
1 tablespoon finely chopped shallots	Salt
	Pepper
2 cups coarsely chopped leeks	Nutmeg
	Lemon juice
¾ cup diced potato	3 ounces Stilton cheese, crumbled
2 cups chicken stock, heated	

1. Melt butter in 2-quart saucepan. Add shallots and leeks. Cover and cook over medium heat until translucent.
2. Add potatoes and hot chicken stock. Cover and cook until potatoes are done, about 20 minutes. Place in blender or food processor and purée.
3. In 1-quart saucepan, bring cream to a gentle boil over medium heat. Reduce heat to very low and cook, stirring frequently, until reduced and slightly thickened, about 45 minutes.
4. Add cream to leek-potato mixture and bring to boil. Add salt, pepper, nutmeg, and lemon juice to taste.
5. Pour into individual bowls and top each with crumbled Stilton cheese.

4 servings

Hint: This soup is also delicious made with light cream.

Leeks have always been widely used in European cooking and are now more available in our own markets. The combination of leeks and Stilton cheese adds a rich flavor to this creamed soup.

Soup's On

Hot Potato Strips

Honeyed Chicken Wings   Barley Soup

Chesapeake Oyster & Spinach Soup

Cheddar Chowder   Spicy Vegetable Soup

Cracked Wheat French Bread

Murph's Mom's Cheese Bread

Herb Bread

Classic Pound Cake   Carrot Cake

Chocolate Cinnamon Cake

CHEDDAR CHOWDER

This wonderfully soothing soup can be assembled quickly, so try it for a Sunday night supper or during the hectic Christmas holidays. Teamed with hot bread and a green salad, a satisfying meal can be created with little effort.

½ cup chopped onion
1 clove garlic, minced
2 stalks celery, sliced
3 carrots, peeled and sliced
1 large potato, peeled and cubed
3½ cups chicken broth
1 17-ounce can sweet corn, drained
¼ cup butter

¼ cup flour
2 cups milk
1 tablespoon Dijon mustard
¼ teaspoon freshly ground black pepper
¼ teaspoon paprika
2 tablespoons chopped pimento
2 cups (8 ounces) grated mild Cheddar cheese

1. Combine chicken stock, onion, garlic, celery, carrots, and potatoes in 3-quart saucepan. Bring to a boil. Cover, reduce heat, and simmer until vegetables are tender, approximately 20 minutes.
2. While vegetables are cooking, melt butter in separate saucepan. Add flour, whisking until smooth. Cook 1 minute, stirring.
3. Gradually add milk to roux; cook over medium heat, stirring until thick and bubbly.
4. Add mustard, pepper, paprika, pimento, and cheese to white sauce. Stir until cheese melts.
5. Gradually add cheese sauce and corn to vegetable mixture. Heat, stirring, until hot.

6-8 servings

Hint: Substitute 1 cup grated Monterey Jack and 1 cup mild Cheddar or 2 cups sharp Cheddar cheese.

BORSCHT

1½ cups thinly sliced
   potato
1 cup thinly sliced beets
4 cups water or chicken
   stock
2 tablespoons butter or
   margarine
1½ cups chopped onion
1 stalk celery, chopped
2 carrots, sliced
3 cups chopped cabbage

2 teaspoons salt
Black pepper
¼-½ teaspoon dried dill
   weed
1 tablespoon plus 1
   teaspoon red wine
   vinegar
1 tablespoon plus 1
   teaspoon honey
1 cup tomato purée

1. Cook potatoes and beets in chicken stock until tender - 15-20 minutes. Drain, reserving stock.
2. In a 4-quart saucepan, cook onions in butter until soft and translucent. Add celery, carrots, and cabbage. Add the stock from beets and potatoes and cook covered until vegetables are tender.
3. Add beets and potatoes and all other ingredients. Cover and simmer slowly at least 30 minutes.
4. Taste and correct seasonings.

4-6 servings

Hints: When seasoning with vinegar and honey, remember that borscht is best when slightly more tangy than sweet. Serve with a dollop of sour cream sprinkled with dill weed. Freezes well.

Fresh beets are wonderful in season. However, canned ones are just as rich in flavor and color, and can be used when fresh are not available. A borscht is a heartily flavored soup, and even if beets are not everyone's favorite, this soup will be a pleaser to most.

SPRING SOUP

2 tablespoons butter
2 leeks, chopped (about 1
   cup)
1 small onion, chopped
1½ quarts hot water
2 potatoes, peeled,
   quartered, and thinly
   sliced
2 medium carrots, peeled
   and thinly sliced

2 teaspoons salt
¼ cup uncooked white
   rice
8 stalks fresh or frozen
   asparagus, cut in ½-
   inch pieces
½ pound fresh spinach,
   washed and chopped
1 cup light cream

1. Melt butter in 3-quart saucepan. Add leeks and onions. Cook over low heat, covered, about 5 minutes.

A very delicate soup that can be prepared a day ahead. Asparagus is one of spring's greatest gifts, so try this when the season is right.

2. Add hot water, potatoes, carrots, and salt. Bring to a boil, reduce heat, and simmer covered 15 minutes.
3. Add rice and asparagus; simmer covered for 25 minutes.
4. Add spinach and simmer 10 minutes longer. Stir in cream. Bring just to boiling.

8 servings

Hint: Tastes best made day before and reheated at serving time.

CREAM OF CAULIFLOWER SOUP

Here is a delicious, dramatically flavored, and easily assembled soup. It includes a "bouquet garni", which is either dried or fresh herbs tied in cheesecloth. Add the bouquet to the mixture to impart its flavor and then remove before serving. All testers agreed this soup was unbeatable!

2 tablespoons oil	Bouquet garni of whole
1 small onion, chopped	pepper, bay leaf,
1 small carrot, grated	parsley
3 stalks celery, chopped	¼ cup butter or
1 head cauliflower, cut	margarine
into florets	¾ cup flour
2 tablespoons minced	1½ cups milk
fresh parsley	1½ cups half and half
8 cups chicken bouillon	1 tablespoon salt, or to
	taste
	1 cup sour cream

1. Heat oil in 8-10 quart pot. Add onion and sauté until golden. Add carrot and celery and cook two minutes, stirring frequently.
2. Add cauliflower and 1 tablespoon parsley. Cover, reduce heat to low, and cook 15 minutes, stirring occasionally to prevent sticking.
3. Add chicken broth and bouquet garni and bring to a boil over medium heat. Reduce heat and simmer 15 minutes.
4. Melt butter in a 2-quart saucepan. Stir in flour; slowly add milk, stirring constantly to blend. Boil until thick and smooth. Remove from heat and stir in half and half. Stir into cauliflower mixture. Season to taste with salt and simmer about 15 minutes.
5. Just before serving, remove bouquet garni and add sour cream.

8 servings

FRENCH ONION SOUP

½ cup butter or margarine	1 cup water
4 large onions, thinly sliced and separated into rings	¼ cup dry white wine
	¾ teaspoon salt
	⅛-¼ teaspoon pepper
1 tablespoon all-purpose flour	1 6-ounce package Mozzarella cheese slices, cut in half
2 cups chicken broth	Croutons
1 10¾-ounce can beef broth	

1.   Melt the butter in a 5-quart pot. Add onion and cook over medium heat until tender. Blend in flour, stirring until smooth.
2.   Stir the chicken broth, beef broth, water, and wine into onion mixture. Bring to a boil, reduce heat, and simmer 15 minutes. Add salt and pepper to taste.
3.   Preheat oven to 350°.
4.   Ladle soup into individual baking dishes. Top each with six to eight croutons and a cheese slice.
5.   Bake for 10 minutes or until cheese melts.

6 servings

Hints: Use food processor for slicing onions.
For croutons: Cut a good-quality bread into ½-inch cubes and spread on baking sheet. Toast in 400° oven until crisp and brown.

Nothing can compare to the rich aroma of onions simmering in a meat broth. This onion soup can also be expanded into a hearty one-dish meal with the addition of a sandwich.

HAMBURGER MINESTRONE SOUP

Souptime is for anytime, but try this one on a cold winter night. Using ground beef instead of cubed beef makes it pleasing to children as well as adults. Add bread, a salad, and voilà - the meal is complete.

1 pound ground beef	1 bay leaf
1 cup chopped onion	½ teaspoon dried thyme
1 cup cubed potatoes	¼ teaspoon dried basil
1 cup diced carrots	5 teaspoons salt
½ cup diced celery	¼ teaspoon pepper
1 cup shredded cabbage	1½ quarts water
1 28-ounce can tomatoes	Freshly grated Parmesan
¼ cup uncooked rice	cheese

1. In large Dutch oven, brown beef and onions over medium heat. Add potatoes and simmer for several minutes.
2. Add remaining ingredients except cheese. Bring to a boil. Reduce heat and simmer, covered, for 1 hour.
3. Serve sprinkled with cheese.

6-8 servings

TEXAS 12-BEAN SOUP

This recipe makes a unique gift idea. Give friends a cannister of the 12 beans, premeasured, and a copy of the recipe. 1½ pounds of the first four types of beans and 1 pound of the others will yield 7 packages for gifts. A neat idea and inexpensive too!

All beans are dried:	1 ham hock or ½ pound
½ cup navy beans	salt pork or 1 cup
½ cup small white beans	cubed ham
½ cup great northern	2 16-ounce cans stewed
beans	tomatoes
½ cup baby limas	2 medium onions,
⅓ cup black-eyed peas	chopped
⅓ cup pink beans	6 stalks celery, chopped
⅓ cup pinto beans	Salt and pepper
⅓ cup small red beans	1 12-ounce can beer
⅓ cup lentils	½ pound thinly sliced
⅓ cup green split peas	smoked sausage
⅓ cup yellow split peas	1-2 pounds raw chicken,
⅓ cup black beans	boned and cubed

1. Wash and drain beans, discarding stones. Place beans in 8-10 quart pot. Add 3 quarts water and ham (or salt pork or hock). Bring to a boil, reduce heat, cover, and simmer approximately 3 hours.

2. Add tomatoes, onion, celery, salt, pepper, and beer. Simmer uncovered 1½ hours.

3. When soup gets to creamy stage, add sausage and chicken pieces. Continue to cook 20-30 minutes more, or until chicken is done.

8-10 servings

Hints: Other beans may be substituted - whatever the combination, use ½ cup any white bean and ⅓ of the others. This is reminiscent of a stew - very hearty and delicious. Delicious winter meal served with cornbread and a green salad or sliced tomatoes and onions.

BARLEY SOUP

¾ cup medium pearl barley	½ cup minced celery
11 cups chicken broth	3 tablespoons butter
1½ cups minced onion	Salt and pepper
1 cup minced carrot	Garnish:
1 cup thinly sliced mushrooms (reserve a few slices for garnish)	Minced parsley
	¼ cup sour cream
	Reserved mushroom slices

1. In a saucepan, combine barley and 3 cups chicken broth. Bring to a boil, reduce heat, and simmer until liquid is absorbed, approximately one hour.

2. In a 4½-quart saucepan, melt butter and sauté onion, carrot, mushroom slices, and celery for 5 minutes until softened.

3. Add 8 cups chicken broth and simmer, uncovered, 30 minutes. Add cooked barley and simmer 5 minutes. Add salt and pepper to taste.

4. Serve in heated bowls. Garnish with dollop of sour cream, sliced mushrooms, and parsley.

6-8 servings

This is a simple but unusual soup. It is very pretty when garnished with mushrooms, parsley, and a dollop of sour cream. Try it as a first course when winter has arrived.

CREAM OF ONION SOUP

Your taste buds are in for a treat with this rich, well-seasoned soup. The bay leaf adds a savory flavor. Ingredients are few, but flavor is plentiful.

¼ cup butter
2 medium sweet onions, chopped (Vidalias are best)
½ cup flour
1 14-ounce can chicken broth or homemade stock

1 14-ounce can evaporated milk
1½ cups water
½ teaspoon dried thyme
1-2 bay leaves
½ teaspoon salt

1. Melt butter in saucepan and sauté onions until tender.
2. Mix flour with broth and add to onion mixture.
3. Add milk, water, thyme, bay leaf, and salt. Cook slowly and stir almost constantly for 20 minutes until soup thickens.

6 servings

Hint: Serve garnished with large, toasted croutons.

LENTIL SOUP

Hearty main dish for cold weather.

2 cups dry lentils
6 cups water
8 slices bacon, diced
½ cup diced salt pork, or ham hock, optional
1 large onion, chopped
1 clove garlic, minced
2 medium carrots, diced
2 celery ribs, diced
1 medium potato, diced

3 tablespoons minced fresh parsley
Smoked sausage, sliced, optional
2 tablespoons flour
Salt and pepper to taste
Accent, optional
4-5 cups water or milk or combination

1. Wash lentils. Bring 6 cups water to boil, add lentils, and cook gently until tender, about 30 minutes. Do not drain.
2. In skillet, sauté bacon and salt pork (if used) until crisp and light brown. Add onion and garlic to bacon for last few minutes. Remove bacon, onion, and garlic from pan and drain, reserving 3 tablespoons fat in skillet.
3. Add the remaining vegetables, seasonings, sausage, and flour. Sauté briefly and set aside.
4. Add vegetable-bacon mixture to lentils plus the 4-5 cups water. Cover loosely and simmer 30 minutes or until tender. Skim fat off top and serve.

8 servings

SPICY VEGETABLE SOUP

1	16-ounce can tomatoes	2	16-ounce cans V-8 juice
1	quart water	1	10-ounce package
2	pounds boneless beef		frozen green beans
	chuck roast, cut in 1-	2	cups sliced carrots
	inch cubes	1	12-ounce can corn,
1	beef shin bone,		drained
	optional	1½	cups thinly sliced
1	teaspoon salt		onion
1	teaspoon pepper	1-2	teaspoons mixed dried
1	cup sliced celery		herbs
	(include some tops)	1	teaspoon
1	tablespoon minced		Worcestershire sauce
	fresh parsley	2	beef bouillon cubes
1	bay leaf		

1.   Drain tomatoes, reserving liquid. Add water to tomato liquid and place in 6-quart saucepan along with meat, shin bone, salt, pepper, celery, parsley, and bay leaf. Cover and simmer one hour.

2.   Add V-8 juice, tomatoes, frozen beans, carrots, corn, onion, herbs, Worcestershire sauce, bouillon cubes, and another cup of water if soup seems too thick. Simmer, uncovered, 1-1½ hours.

3.   Remove bone, bay leaf, and celery tops. Cool and refrigerate soup.

4.   After chilling, remove any fat congealed on top. Reheat slowly before serving.

8 servings

Hints: May substitute or add other vegetables.
Use any combination of herbs such as basil, thyme, oregano, marjoram, cumin.

This will surely become one of your favorite vegetable soups. The various ingredients simmer together to form an unforgettable flavor. Make it and keep it on hand during the holidays to satisfy those hungry relatives.

VICHYSSOISE

Served hot or cold, this vichyssoise is one of the best. Remember that the best leeks to buy are never more than 1½ -2 inches in diameter. The slender leeks cook quickly and should be trimmed lengthwise, leaving no more than 2 inches of green above the base.

6 leeks	1 teaspoon salt
3 onions	1 teaspoon white pepper
½ cup butter	1 cup heavy cream
2 quarts chicken stock	1 cup sour cream
1 pound potatoes, peeled and sliced	Chopped chives, garnish

1.   Finely chop leeks and onions. Melt butter in 4-quart Dutch oven and sauté leeks and onions until soft; do not brown.
2.   Add stock, potatoes, salt, and pepper. Cook until potatoes are soft.
3.   In small batches, purée mixture in food processor or blender. Return to soup pot.
4.   Add heavy cream and sour cream. Blend and serve hot or cold garnished with freshly chopped chives.

8 servings

CUCUMBER SOUP

Summer activities often leave little time and energy for preparing food. This soup can be made in twenty minutes, leaving plenty of time to enjoy a leisurely stroll at sunset. This cool liquid version of those tasty cucumber finger sandwiches is always a hit!

1 cup chicken broth	3 tablespoons fresh lemon juice
¼ cup finely chopped onion	1 cup plain yogurt
1 teaspoon salt	1 cup sour cream
½ teaspoon dried dill weed	3 cucumbers, peeled, seeded, and chopped
Dash garlic powder	Lemon slices
1 teaspoon freshly grated lemon zest	Cucumber slices

1.   Combine chicken broth, onion, salt, dill weed, garlic powder, lemon zest, and lemon juice in blender or food processor fitted with steel blade. Blend until smooth.
2.   Combine yogurt and sour cream. Add to blender (or processor) mixing a few seconds just to blend.
3.   Add chopped cucumber. Quickly turn blender on and off to combine. Cucumbers should be finely grated but not liquefied.
4.   Chill for 1 hour.
5.   Serve garnished with lemon and cucumber slices.

4-6 servings

Hints: Delicious first course for a chicken, shrimp, or crab salad meal.
Looks pretty served in clear glass bowls.

AVOCADO WHOOPER

1 ripe avocado, peeled, pitted, and cut into chunks
3 medium tomatoes, peeled and chopped
½ cup sour cream
1 tablespoon chopped green pepper
1 tablespoon chopped onion
1 tablespoon chopped celery
1 tablespoon lemon juice
Tabasco to taste
Salt to taste
1¼ cups chicken broth
Sour cream and parsley, garnishes
4-6 ounces vodka, optional

1. Blend all ingredients except broth, garnishes, and vodka in food processor or blender until smooth.
2. Stir in chicken broth and correct seasonings.
3. Serve cold in bowls with garnish and present with a jigger of vodka.

6 servings

Hint: A few fresh herbs, processed first, might be a nice addition and would add a bit of color. Try fresh basil, chives, or dill.

A "zippy" first course for a summer supper. Try this in lieu of gazpacho.

CHILLED MELON SOUP

1 ripe cantaloupe
¾ cup heavy cream
¾ cup apricot nectar
¼ cup white wine
¼ teaspoon grated lemon zest
1 teaspoon fresh lemon juice
¼ cup Cointreau
Dash of cinnamon
Fresh mint leaves, garnish

1. Peel, seed, and coarsely chop cantaloupe.
2. Place cantaloupe in food processor fitted with steel blade. Process until smooth.
3. Add remaining ingredients and process just until blended. Chill.
4. When serving, garnish with a sprig of mint.

4 servings

A beach favorite! Cold fruit soups are a nice change in the summertime - on vacation or at home. Try this for a wonderfully refreshing taste.

GREAT GAZPACHO

There are dozens of versions of gazpacho soups existing today. Most people associate the soup with a Spanish flavor. It is such a versatile soup that it can be served at anytime during a meal. Using fresh herbs and vegetables can only enhance the flavor of this soup. As stated in **The Art of Eating** (New York: Vintage, 1976) "Above all, it should be tantalizing, fresh, and faintly perverse as are all primitive dishes eaten by worldly people."

4 cups cold V-8 juice
1 small onion, minced (Vidalia best)
2 cups fresh, diced tomatoes
1 cup minced green pepper
1 teaspoon honey
1 cucumber, peeled and diced
2 scallions, chopped
Juice of 1 lime
Juice of ½ lemon
2-3 tablespoons wine vinegar, optional

1 teaspoon dried tarragon (scant)
1 teaspoon dried basil or 1 tablespoon chopped fresh basil
¼ teaspoon ground cumin
¼ cup minced fresh parsley
Dash of Tabasco sauce or cayenne pepper
2 tablespoons olive oil
Salt and freshly ground pepper to taste

Combine all ingredients and chill at least 2 hours.
6 servings

CHILLED AVOCADO
AND CUCUMBER SOUP

3 cups chicken stock
2 scallions, chopped
3 very ripe avocados, peeled, pitted, and mashed
1 cucumber, peeled, seeded, and chopped

3 cups half and half
1 cup sour cream
2 tablespoons fresh lemon juice
White pepper to taste
Salt to taste

1. Place stock and scallions in a saucepan and heat until mixture is hot. Remove from heat and stir in the avocado and cucumber.
2. In a blender or food processor, purée the mixture in batches and transfer the purée to a large ceramic or glass bowl.
3. Stir in half and half, sour cream, and lemon juice. Add white pepper and salt to taste.
4. Cover soup and chill at least 1 hour.
5. Serve in chilled bowls.

8 servings

Hint: Top with one of these garnishes:
1. Chives, bacon, and chopped tomato
2. Chopped parsley and a sprinkle of lemon pepper
3. A sprig of fresh dill

Avocados and cucumbers make one think of summer. A chilled soup at this time of year is quite refreshing for lunch or as a prelude to the evening meal. This appetizing soup will make the palate realize the "lazy, hazy days of summer" are truly here.

AUNT FLORINE'S CURRY SANDWICHES

A great conversational sandwich. The ingredients are a mystery but the compliments are many.

1	cup ripe, pitted olives, chopped	½	cup mayonnaise
½	cup thinly sliced green onion tops	½	teaspoon salt
1½	cups grated sharp Cheddar cheese	½	teaspoon curry powder, or to taste
			Toast

1. Heat the first six ingredients in top of double boiler.
2. Serve over toast.

6 servings

Hint: Serve from chafing dish with small pieces of toast as an hors d'oeuvre.

SPRING GARDEN SANDWICH SPREAD

Put your processor to use! Try a light refreshing sandwich for those hot days of summer. Also can be used as a nutritious dip or spread for crackers. A great way to entice children to eat "veggies".

2	cucumbers, peeled and finely chopped	½	green pepper, finely chopped
2	carrots, peeled and finely chopped	1	teaspoon lemon juice
1	cup finely chopped celery	1	teaspoon salt
1	small onion, finely chopped	2	cups mayonnaise
		1	envelope unflavored gelatin
		¼	cup cold water

1. Combine the finely chopped vegetables in a large colander. Drain overnight in the refrigerator.
2. Place drained vegetables in a large bowl. Add lemon juice, salt, and mayonnaise to vegetables. Toss gently until thoroughly mixed.
3. Combine gelatin and cold water. Dissolve mixture over hot water in a double boiler.
4. Combine vegetables with gelatin mixture and chill.

6 cups

Hints: Keeps tightly closed in refrigerator for several days.
Makes lovely finger sandwiches for luncheon or tea.
Can be put in a mold and served with crackers as an hors d'oeuvre.

DILLED HAVARTI POCKET SANDWICHES

Per Sandwich:
1 whole wheat pita bread
1-2 large leaves of leaf lettuce, washed and patted dry
2 ounces Havarti cheese with dill, sliced or grated

2-3 slices ripe fresh pear
1-2 tablespoons Thousand Island dressing
Alfalfa sprouts
Sliced black olives

1. Remove a 1-inch slice from top of pita bread and open to form "pocket".
2. Line bread with lettuce leaves.
3. Fill with cheese and pear slices; spoon dressing over filling.
4. Top with sprouts and olives.

1 serving

Hint: Sandwiches may be assembled ahead of time and refrigerated. Spoon dressing over filling when ready to serve. Add 1 ounce julienned, cooked ham for a heartier sandwich.

A truly original sandwich—the unusual combination of ingredients produces a delightful change from ordinary luncheon fare. With the substitution of a low calorie dressing, even weight-watching can be a treat.

HAM AND CHEESE BISCUITS

½ cup butter, softened
2 teaspoons prepared mustard
2 tablespoons poppy seeds
2 teaspoons Worcestershire sauce

1 small onion, chopped
1 package of 20 small rolls (Pepperidge Farm party rolls)
4-6 slices baked ham
4-6 slices Swiss cheese

1. Preheat oven to 300° (if serving immediately). Place butter, mustard, poppy seeds, Worcestershire sauce, and onion in food processor fitted with steel blade. Process until blended.
2. Cut rolls in half lengthwise and spread each side with butter mixture.
3. Cut ham and cheese to fit rolls and place a slice of each on bottom half. Place tops on rolls.

There are so many uses for this quick and simple recipe, that it is a must! Make them ahead and freeze - use at football picnics, cocktail parties, or wedding receptions. Make them in a larger roll to serve with a fresh spinach salad for lunch.

4. Wrap in aluminum foil.
5. Heat in oven for 20 minutes or until cheese is melted.

20 biscuits

Hints: May refrigerate in foil for heating later.
May spread one side of roll with butter, the other side with combination of mustard and mayonnaise and sprinkle of poppy seeds.
These sandwiches freeze beautifully.

BARBECUED HAM SANDWICHES

How could something so easy be so good! Make this in quantity when serving teenagers—the football team will love it for a pre-game dinner. In fact, it will be popular with the whole family!

¼ cup vinegar	6 ounces chili sauce
2 tablespoons grape jelly	2 tablespoons water
½ teaspoon paprika	1 pound chipped or
½ teaspoon dry mustard	shaved ham (from deli)
3 tablespoons brown sugar, firmly packed	Sandwich buns

1. In a saucepan, blend together the first seven ingredients and heat thoroughly. Stir in ham.
2. Serve on warm buns.

6 servings

Hint: Makes a nice, quick Sunday night supper.

STROGANOFF SANDWICH

A "take-off" on a true stroganoff but much quicker and easier. After a busy and tiring day, having these ingredients on hand solves the dinner dilemma.

4 French rolls	2-4 tablespoons margarine
1 pound ground beef	1 ripe tomato, sliced
¼ cup chopped onion	1 green pepper, sliced
1 cup sour cream	1 cup grated Cheddar
2 tablespoons milk	cheese
⅛ teaspoon garlic powder	

1. Preheat oven to 350°.
2. Wrap rolls in foil and heat in oven for 15 minutes.
3. In skillet, brown beef and onions. Add sour cream, milk, and garlic powder. Stir to heat but do not boil.

4. Remove rolls from foil, split lengthwise and spread with margarine. Spread bottom halves with meat mixture. Top the meat with alternate slices of tomato and green pepper. Sprinkle cheese on top.
5. Place sandwiches, without tops, on cookie sheet. Heat in oven for 5 minutes, or until cheese melts and sandwich is hot.
6. Place the tops on sandwiches and serve.

4 servings

Hint: May be served open-face.

GYRO SANDWICHES

Patties:
1¼ pound ground beef
1¼ pound ground lamb
2 tablespoons dried oregano
1½ tablespoons onion powder
1 tablespoon garlic powder
¾-1½ tablespoons black pepper
1 teaspoon dried thyme
¾ teaspoon salt

Sauce:
½ cup plain yogurt
½ cup sour cream
¼ cup finely chopped cucumber
¼ cup finely chopped onion
2 teaspoons olive oil
Garlic powder
Salt and freshly ground pepper
4-6 large pita bread rounds, cut in half
Thinly sliced onion rings

"Gyro" is the Greek word for circle. Serve this highly seasoned meat in pita topped with a sauce and your circle will be complete!

1. For patties: Combine all ingredients in bowl.
2. Shape into hamburger patties and refrigerate.
3. Cook over medium charcoal fire or grill to desired degree of doneness.
4. For sauce: Combine first 5 ingredients in small bowl. Add garlic powder, salt, and pepper to taste.
5. To assemble: Place 1 meat patty in each pita half. Top with yogurt sauce.
6. Garnish with thinly sliced onion rings.

4-6 servings

Hints: May use all ground beef.
Serve in pita bread with tomato and cucumber slices and chopped parsley.
Serve on English muffin with sour cream and fresh chives or parsley.

FLANK STEAK SALAD SANDWICHES

A simple, light supper on a summer evening can be such fun for your family and friends. Try these delightful sandwiches which can be prepared earlier in the day, and when ready to serve, let your guests assemble their own.

2 flank steaks, about 1 pound each
Seasoned salt or garlic salt
Lemon pepper
Dressing:
1 8-ounce carton sour cream
½ teaspoon dried dill weed
¼ cup chopped green onion
Vegetable Toss:
½ cup vegetable oil
½ cup dry white wine
2 tablespoons vinegar

2 teaspoons sugar
1 teaspoon dried basil
½ teaspoon salt
1 pint fresh mushrooms, sliced
2 large tomatoes, coarsely chopped
½ cup sliced green onions
8 ounces fresh spinach, torn
Sandwich rounds:
1 13-ounce package hot roll mix
1 cup warm water, 110°-115°

1.   Flank steak: Sprinkle each side with salt and pepper and rub into surface of meat. Let stand 30 minutes. Grill over medium hot fire until desired doneness, about 5 minutes per side for medium rare. Cover and chill in refrigerator for 3-24 hours.
2.   Dressing: Combine all ingredients, mixing well. Cover and chill 3-24 hours.
3.   Vegetable Toss: Combine first 6 ingredients in a jar. Cover and shake well. Pour over next 3 ingredients and toss. Cover and chill 3-24 hours. Before serving, toss vegetable mixture with spinach.
4.   Sandwich Rounds: In a large bowl, stir yeast from roll mix and water until dissolved. Stir in flour from the roll mix. Turn out onto a floured surface and knead for 2 minutes. Cover and let rest 15 minutes. Divide dough into 8 portions and roll each portion into a smooth ball. Cover and let rest 10 minutes. On a floured surface, using fingers, gently flatten one ball. Then lightly roll dough with rolling pin into a 7-inch circle (turning over once). Do not stretch or crease dough. Place on a baking sheet. Repeat with other balls. Bake 2 at a time in a 450° oven for 4 minutes. Turn over and bake 3-4 minutes longer. Place in a paper bag immediately to soften. (Wrap individually in plastic wrap to freeze, if desired.) Makes 8 rounds.

5. Before serving: Thinly slice beef into bite-size strips. For each sandwich, spread some dressing on one side of sandwich round. Place some sliced beef and vegetable toss on one half of round and fold. Pass the remaining dressing.

8 servings

Hints: Recipe is easy, it just has many parts. They may be done in advance: make bread ahead and freeze, do vegetable toss and dressing the day before, and prepare steak early on day it will be served.
Could use packaged pita bread and serve as pocket sandwiches.
May use ½ cup plain yogurt and ½ cup sour cream for dressing.

BARBECUE SANDWICHES

¼ cup vinegar	2 medium onions, sliced
1½ cups water	½ cup margarine
¼ cup granulated sugar	4 cups 2-inch strips
4 teaspoons prepared	cooked beef (left over
mustard	roast such as chuck,
¼ teaspoon pepper	shoulder, etc.)
1 tablespoon salt	1 cup chili sauce
¼ teaspoon cayenne	3 tablespoons
pepper	Worcestershire sauce
2 thick slices lemon	Kaiser or onion rolls

1. Early in the day, combine vinegar and next 9 ingredients in a Dutch oven. Simmer uncovered for 20 minutes.
2. Add meat, chili sauce, and Worcestershire sauce. Refrigerate.
3. Before serving, simmer slowly 45 minutes and place on buns.

8-10 servings

Recipes which call for leftovers are great. This recipe uses leftover roast such as chuck or shoulder to create a nice sandwich for family and friends. Most of the work is done ahead of time, so enjoy it after a football game when a chill is in the air.

Tailgate

Mushroom Caviar

Wintergreen Special   Herbed Tomato Soup

Flank Steak Salad Sandwiches

Double Fudge Brownies   Peanut Squares

DANCE FESTIVAL FAVORITE

The hot months call for light evening meals, especially ones that can be prepared ahead and served with little or no fuss at mealtime. Salads that can stand alone as a main course are a perfect solution. Instead of tossing spinach with the salad, try serving pasta-chicken mixture on a bed of spinach leaves. Serve with a well-made Mâcon or a California Sauvignon Blanc.

6 ounces rotini or other pasta twists
⅛ cup sesame seeds
½ cup oil
⅓ cup soy sauce
⅓ cup white wine vinegar
2 tablespoons sugar
½ teaspoon salt
¼ teaspoon pepper
3 cups chopped cooked chicken, chilled
½ cup chopped fresh parsley
½ cup thinly sliced green onions
8 cups lightly packed torn spinach leaves
Fresh sprouts or mushrooms, optional

1. Cook pasta in a large pot of boiling salted water until barely tender (al dente). Drain, rinse with cold water, drain again. Turn into a large bowl.
2. In small frying pan, combine sesame seeds and ¼ cup oil. Cook over medium low heat, stirring until seeds are golden (2 minutes). Cool.
3. Combine sesame seeds, remaining ¼ cup oil, soy sauce, vinegar, sugar, salt, and pepper. Pour over cooked pasta.
4. Add chicken and toss gently. Cover and chill for at least 6 hours.
5. To serve, add parsley, onion, and spinach. Toss lightly.

8 servings

Hint: Serve with crunchy bread sticks.

SEAFOOD AND PASTA PRIMAVERA SALAD

Pasta:
1 pound sea shell pasta
⅓ cup olive oil
¼ cup red wine vinegar
Salt and freshly ground
   pepper to taste
Seafood:
2 pounds bay or sea
   scallops
2 pounds large raw
   shrimp, in the shell
⅓ cup olive oil
3 tablespoons wine
   vinegar
1 clove garlic

Vegetables:
15 very thin asparagus
   stalks
3 cups broccoli florets
1 pound sugar snap peas,
   trimmed
1 pint cherry tomatoes
1 head leaf lettuce
Dill mayonnaise:
2 eggs
1 teaspoon dry mustard
1½ teaspoons salt
3 tablespoons vinegar
3 tablespoons lemon
   juice
½ cup fresh dill
⅔ cup salad oil
1½ cups olive oil

Fresh herbs are simple and inexpensive to grow. The enhancement that they bring to many foods is irreplaceable. This dish is flavored with a mayonnaise made with fresh dill combined with the best of summer's bounty. The result is a perfect entrée for summer buffets. Serve with a good Mâcon or any light red wine.

1. Cook pasta al dente. Drain and rinse with cold water. Drain again. Transfer to large bowl. Add oil and vinegar. Season with salt and pepper.
2. If using sea scallops, cut in half. Gently poach scallops in simmering water about 2 minutes. Drain and rinse with cold water.
3. Poach shrimp in their shells until they turn pink. Rinse with cold water. Shell and devein. Cut in half lengthwise.
4. Combine all seafood in a large bowl and toss with oil, vinegar, and garlic.
5. Separately steam asparagus and broccoli until just crisp-tender. Rinse immediately with cold water and drain.
6. Wash sugar snaps, tomatoes, and lettuce leaves.
7. Make dill mayonnaise: Combine all ingredients except olive oil in blender or processor. Blend on high. With machine running, slowly dribble in olive oil.
8. To assemble salad: Gently toss pasta with half the dill mayonnaise and all vegetables except lettuce. Arrange in center of lettuce-lined large platter. Make a well in center of pasta and mound seafood in it.
9. Refrigerate 6-24 hours for flavors to blend.
10. Serve with remaining mayonnaise on the side.

8 servings

Hints: If sugar snaps are unavailable, substitute thinly sliced zucchini.
For a variation, add red or green peppers, cut into small squares.

LINGUINE MEDITERRANEAN

Clams add a subtle seafood flavor to this pasta dish, but for a bolder taste, substitute anchovies. Take your pick and don't be afraid to try this delicious medley of ingredients. If using clams, serve with a fresh, young Valpolicella. If using anchovies, try cold beer.

6 slices bacon, cut into 1-inch pieces
1 medium onion, chopped
1 medium green pepper, cut in strips
½ pound mushrooms, sliced
2 6-ounce cans whole baby clams, undrained
1 cup chopped, pitted black olives
½ cup minced fresh parsley
1 teaspoon crushed red hot pepper
Salt and pepper to taste
1 pound linguine, cooked al dente
½ cup butter
Freshly grated Parmesan cheese

1. Sauté bacon until crisp in a skillet. Drain on paper towels.
2. Add onion and green pepper to skillet and sauté until soft.
3. Stir in mushrooms and clams with their broth. Cook over moderate heat for 10 minutes, stirring occasionally.
4. Stir in olives, parsley, bacon, and red hot pepper. Season with salt and pepper.
5. In a large bowl, toss the cooked linguine with the butter.
6. Pour the sauce over the linguine and serve with freshly grated Parmesan cheese.

6 servings

PASTA WITH ASPARAGUS AND CRAB

¾ pound fresh asparagus, cut into 1-inch diagonals
4 tablespoons butter
1½ cups heavy cream
¾ pound crabmeat
2 chopped scallions

½ cup minced fresh parsley
1 teaspoon dried basil
Salt and pepper to taste
1 pound flat noodles, cooked al dente
Freshly grated Parmesan cheese

1. Steam asparagus 5 minutes.
2. Melt butter in saucepan. Add asparagus and stir to coat with butter.
3. Add cream and cook until slightly thickened.
4. Add the crab, scallions, and seasonings, and simmer 10 minutes.
5. Serve over cooked noodles. Garnish with freshly grated Parmesan cheese.

4 servings

A seasonal must when fresh asparagus is available. With the addition of crabmeat and noodles, this dish is pure heaven for pasta and seafood lovers alike. Be traditional and serve a Sauvignon Blanc or try something innovative like a Pinot Noir Blanc from California.

SPAGHETTI VERDI

2 cups spinach leaves (washed but not dried and firmly packed)
½ cup fresh parsley leaves (washed but not dried and firmly packed)
3 cloves garlic
½ cup butter
¼ cup olive oil
½ cup pine nuts

¼ cup walnuts
1 teaspoon dried basil, or 1 tablespoon chopped fresh basil
½ cup freshly grated Romano cheese
½ cup freshly grated Parmesan cheese
1 pound spaghetti, cooked al dente

1. Combine all ingredients except pasta in food processor.
2. Blend until mixture is almost puréed, but still has flecks of spinach and parsley.
3. If too thick, add small amount of water.
4. Toss with cooked spaghetti. The heat from the spaghetti warms the sauce.

6-8 servings

A winter version of a classic summer dish, this pesto sauce does not require fresh basil. The robust flavor comes from the use of fresh spinach and parsley leaves. In season, don't overlook fresh basil.

PASTA PRIMAVERA

After sampling this dish, it is easy to understand the popularity of combining vegetables and pasta. It's especially good with lots of freshly grated Parmesan cheese. The vegetables are so visually appealing that they coax everyone to the table.

¼ cup butter
1 small onion, chopped
1 clove garlic, minced
3 ounces cauliflower, in pieces
½ carrot, sliced
½ zucchini, sliced
½ pound fresh asparagus, cut in ¼-inch pieces
¼ pound fresh mushrooms, sliced
½ cup heavy cream

¼ cup chicken stock
1 teaspoon dried basil
Salt and pepper to taste
½ cup frozen peas, thawed
2 scallions, thinly sliced
12 ounces vermicelli or linguine, cooked al dente
Freshly grated Parmesan cheese

1. In large skillet, melt butter and sauté onion and garlic.
2. Add cauliflower and carrot; cook 3 minutes.
3. Add zucchini, asparagus, and mushrooms to skillet and cook 2 minutes more.
4. Add cream, stock, and seasonings, and cook until liquid is slightly reduced.
5. Add peas and scallions and cook briefly.
6. Serve sauce over cooked and drained noodles. Sprinkle with lots of fresh Parmesan cheese.

4 servings

FETTUCINE À LA MONA LISA

This easy, versatile pasta recipe is rich enough for a main course but can also double as a side dish. For a hearty entrée, add ½ pound chopped ham, prosciutto, or cooked bacon; 8 ounces fresh mushrooms, sliced; or 8 ounces fresh peas, blanched.

6 tablespoons butter
2 cups heavy cream
3 egg yolks, beaten
2 cups freshly grated Parmesan cheese

24 ounces spinach or egg fettucine noodles, cooked al dente
Freshly ground black pepper

1. In a saucepan over low heat, melt butter (don't let foam).
2. Stir cream into butter and heat through.
3. Add butter-cream mixture to beaten yolks a little at a time. Return to saucepan and reheat without bringing to a boil.
4. Blend in cheese slowly.
5. When cheese is well incorporated into cream mixture, pour over hot noodles.
6. Garnish with freshly ground pepper.

6 servings

THE BEST SPAGHETTI SAUCE

2 pounds ground chuck
1 onion, chopped
1 green pepper, chopped
1 32-ounce can whole
  tomatoes, chopped
1 12-ounce can tomato
  paste
3 10-ounce cans tomato
  soup

3 tablespoons
  Worcestershire sauce
¼ cup sugar
1 tablespoon salt
1 teaspoon chili powder
Pepper to taste

1. Brown meat in 4-5 quart Dutch oven. Spoon off excess fat.
2. Add all other ingredients.
3. Simmer uncovered 2 hours. Stir occasionally.
4. Serve over cooked spaghetti or linguine noodles.

8 servings

Hints: Freezes very well.
May add mushrooms.
May substitute 2 15-ounce cans tomato sauce for 3 cans tomato soup.

A spaghetti sauce with Worcestershire sauce and chili powder? What's the world coming to? And stranger yet, leftovers can be used on hot dogs! Don't be turned off. This is an excellent, unusual recipe.

MEXICAN SPAGHETTI

6 links mild Italian
  sausage
6 ounces vermicelli,
  broken into quarters
2 tablespoons oil
1 16-ounce can tomatoes
1 cup chicken broth
1 medium onion,
  chopped
1 clove garlic, minced
½ teaspoon salt

⅛ teaspoon pepper
½ teaspoon dried oregano
¼ teaspoon sugar
¼ teaspoon dried red
  pepper, optional
2 tablespoons freshly
  grated Parmesan
  cheese
½-1 canned green chili
  pepper, rinsed, seeded,
  and chopped, optional

1. Peel the thin casing off sausage links and discard. Break up meat in large skillet and cook 10-12 minutes or until browned. Drain and set aside.

File this under husband pleaser! It's a nice change from most spaghetti sauces; the red pepper and mild green chilies give it a different twist.

2. Add oil to skillet. Add noodles and cook until browned.
3. Add tomatoes and break into chunks. Stir in chicken broth, onion, garlic, salt, pepper, oregano, sugar, and red pepper.
4. Arrange sausage on top of tomato mixture. Cook, covered, about 10 minutes or until noodles are tender.
5. Sprinkle with cheese and chili pepper before serving.

4 servings

LASAGNA

When you have some spare time, make this lasagna and freeze it. Though preparation time is lengthy, cooking time is relatively short. Serve it on a snowy evening or during bowl games and score your own points!

2 **16-ounce cans tomatoes (Italian style preferred)**	2 **pounds lean ground beef**
3 **8-ounce cans tomato sauce**	2 **teaspoons Accent, optional**
½ **teaspoon salt**	6 **whole lasagna noodles**
3 **teaspoons dried oregano**	1½ **pounds ricotta or creamed cottage cheese**
¼ **teaspoon pepper**	2 **eggs**
⅓ **cup salad oil**	1 **pound mozzarella cheese, sliced**
2 **cups minced onions**	
2 **garlic cloves, minced**	1 **cup freshly grated Parmesan cheese**

1. In a saucepan, simmer the tomatoes, tomato sauce, salt, oregano, and pepper uncovered.
2. In a large skillet, sauté onions and garlic in the oil until slightly brown.
3. Add beef (and Accent) to skillet. Cook until meat is brown.
4. Add meat mixture to tomato sauce. Simmer 2½ hours until thickened. Skim off fat.
5. Cook lasagna noodles according to package directions. Cool on tea towel.
6. Mix ricotta and eggs.
7. In 9x13 inch casserole dish, make layers as follows: ⅓ of the meat sauce, 3 noodles (should cover the whole dish), ½ of the cheese-egg mixture, ½ of the mozzarella cheese, ½ of the Parmesan cheese.
8. Repeat layers, making meat sauce final layer.
9. Cover with a towel and let stand 1 hour.
10. Bake 30 minutes at 350°. Turn off oven and let stand in oven at least 1 hour.

8-10 servings

HOMEMADE PIZZA

1 tablespoon active dry yeast
½ teaspoon sugar
1¼ cups warm water (115°)
1½ cups unbleached flour
1½ cups whole wheat flour
1½ teaspoons salt
2-3 cups tomato sauce (recipe follows)
½ pound mozzarella cheese, grated
¼ cup freshly grated Parmesan cheese

Sauce:
1 onion, chopped
1 clove garlic, minced
2 tablespoons oil
1 small green pepper, chopped
1 bay leaf
1 teaspoon dried oregano
½ teaspoon dried thyme
2 tablespoons dried parsley
2 cups fresh or canned tomatoes
1 6-ounce can tomato paste
1 teaspoon salt

Show someone you care - make a homemade pizza! Your boundaries are unlimited. Try smoked turkey and broccoli on top. This recipe yields 2 crusts. Freeze one to take out for a quick supper on a busy night.

1. Sprinkle yeast and sugar into warm water. Allow to stand 10 minutes until bubbly.
2. Combine flours and salt in a large bowl. Make a well in the center and pour in yeast mixture. Gradually work in flour to form a stiff dough.
3. Turn dough onto lightly floured surface. Knead until smooth and elastic (about 5 minutes) using only enough extra flour to keep dough from sticking. Place in lightly oiled medium size bowl. Turn dough to coat with oil.
4. Cover with clean towel. Let rise in warm place for about 45 minutes or until doubled.
5. Punch dough down and divide in half. Spread each piece onto a well greased 12-inch pizza pan, pinching dough to form an outside edge. Let sit 20 minutes.
6. Preheat oven to 425°.
7. Spread each crust with tomato sauce and sprinkle with Parmesan cheese.
8. Bake for 15 minutes.
9. Remove from oven and sprinkle with grated mozzarella cheese. Return to oven and bake until cheese melts.

Tomato Sauce:
1. Sauté onion and garlic in oil until onion is soft.
2. Add green pepper, bay leaf, and herbs. Stir well.
3. Blend in tomatoes, tomato paste, and salt.
4. Simmer 30 minutes. Discard bay leaf.

4-8 servings

Hint: Can sprinkle optional toppings such as pepperoni, mushrooms, or cooked sausage onto pizza with the mozzarella cheese.

NOODLES ROMANOFF

When a change of pace is in order, try this unusual side dish. The yogurt gives it a tangy taste and marries well with the thyme for a delectable combination.

4   chicken or beef
    bouillon cubes
4   cups boiling water
8   ounces egg noodles
1½ cups cottage cheese
½ cup sour cream

½ cup plain yogurt
1   small onion, minced
½ teaspoon salt
¼ teaspoon garlic salt
¼ teaspoon dried thyme
½ cup bread crumbs

1. Dissolve bouillon cubes in boiling water.
2. Cook noodles in broth until tender - do not drain.
3. Preheat oven to 350°.
4. Stir cottage cheese, sour cream, yogurt, onion, and seasonings into hot undrained noodles. Stir to combine ingredients.
5. Pour into shallow 10-cup baking dish.
6. Top with bread crumbs. (May be prepared ahead to this point and refrigerated. Bring to room temperature before baking.)
7. Bake uncovered for 25 minutes.

6 servings

NOODLE PUDDING (KÜGEL)

This traditional German dish is slightly sweet and a perfect accompaniment to a spicy entrée such as brisket.

8   ounces broad noodles
1   cup raisins
6   tablespoons butter,
    melted
3   eggs, beaten
½ cup sugar
1   cup sour cream
1   cup cottage cheese

⅛ cup orange juice
¾ teaspoon vanilla
2   tablespoons cornflake
    crumbs, optional
    topping
2   tablespoons melted
    butter, optional
    topping

1. Cook noodles according to package directions. Drain well.
2. Preheat oven to 350°.
3. Combine noodles and all other ingredients in a large bowl. Mix well and pour into a greased 1½-quart baking dish.
4. Sprinkle topping on noodles, if desired.
5. Bake, uncovered, for 45 minutes.

6-8 servings

Hint: May be assembled up to 3 days ahead.

LASAGNA SWIRLS

2 8-ounce cans tomato sauce	2 tablespoons freshly grated Parmesan cheese
1 small onion, chopped and sautéed	½ pound ricotta cheese
½ teaspoon dried basil	¼ teaspoon nutmeg
Salt and pepper to taste	6 lasagna noodles, cooked and drained
1 16-ounce can tomatoes	
1 10-ounce package frozen chopped spinach, cooked and well-drained	

1. Place tomato sauce, onion, basil, salt, pepper, and tomatoes in saucepan. Simmer while preparing remainder of recipe.
2. Mix spinach, Parmesan cheese, ricotta, nutmeg, salt, and pepper.
3. Preheat oven to 350°.
4. Spread spinach mixture on noodles and roll up. Place in greased casserole dish. Cover with sauce. Bake 20 minutes.

4 servings

Everyone has at least one friend who is a vegetarian. Here's a dish to try when inviting him to dinner. Don't expect to spend much time in the kitchen; this dish can be assembled ahead of time.

SHRIMP AND SPINACH SOUFFLÉ

⅓ cup butter	1 pound shrimp, cooked, peeled, and chopped
⅓ cup all-purpose flour	1½ cups cooked, chopped fresh spinach (cook and drain before measuring)
½ teaspoon salt	
1¼ cups milk	
¾ cup freshly grated Parmesan cheese	
⅓ cup dry white wine	8 eggs, separated

1. Melt butter in large saucepan. Add flour and blend until smooth. Add salt and milk. Cook, stirring until thick.
2. Remove sauce from heat. Add cheese and wine.
3. Fold in shrimp and spinach.
4. In separate bowl, beat egg yolks 5 minutes. Stir into shrimp mixture.
5. Preheat oven to 325°.
6. Wash beaters. Beat egg whites into soft peaks. Carefully fold into shrimp mixture until white "blotches" disappear.

Don't be intimidated by the word soufflé. Just be careful with the eggs - the rest is simple. This soufflé is an especially nice combination of shrimp, fresh spinach, and Parmesan cheese. Try a fresh but full-flavored Chardonnay from California or an Italian Trebbiano.

7. Turn mixture into ungreased 2-quart soufflé dish.
8. Bake 50 minutes or until knife inserted into middle comes out clean.
9. Serve immediately.

6-8 servings

ROULADE DE SAVOIE

A roulade is a flat soufflé baked in a rectangular shape, then rolled up to enclose a filling. Serve this one as a first course for dinner, or as a main course for luncheon or supper accompanied by a green salad and a chilled white wine.

4 eggs
½ teaspoon salt
¼ teaspoon freshly ground pepper
¼ teaspoon nutmeg
2 tablespoons flour
3 tablespoons butter, divided
1 small zucchini, julienned

4 ounces mushrooms, thinly sliced
Salt and freshly ground pepper to taste
1 pint heavy cream
6 ounces Gruyère cheese, grated
2 ounces cooked ham, julienned
¼ cup minced fresh parsley

1. Preheat oven to 350°.
2. Separate eggs, reserving whites. Add salt, pepper, and nutmeg to yolks. Beat until thick (approximately 10 minutes) in electric mixer. Add flour to yolks.
3. Beat whites until stiff and fold into egg mixture.
4. Using 1 tablespoon of butter, grease waxed paper and place on jelly roll pan or cookie sheet. Using a spatula, spread egg mixture onto paper-lined pan to a thickness of about ½ inch. Bake for 8-9 minutes.
5. Turn baked egg mixture over onto second sheet of waxed paper and peel off first sheet.
6. Sauté zucchini and mushrooms in 1 tablespoon butter for 2-3 minutes. Season with salt and freshly ground pepper.
7. Heat cream. Dribble generous amounts of hot cream over roulade. Add 1 tablespoon of shaved butter; sprinkle with ¾ cup Gruyère, sautéed zucchini, mushrooms, and julienned ham.
8. Roll egg sheet from long side to enclose filling (forming a long roll).
9. Place seam side down in shallow baking dish. Pour remaining hot cream over and around roulade in order for it to be absorbed. (At this point, roulade can sit for 1-1½ hours, if desired before baking.)
10. Preheat oven to 375°.
11. Sprinkle remaining ¾ cup Gruyère on top. Bake for 8-12 minutes or until golden. Garnish with parsley before serving.

6 servings

Midnight Supper

Herbed Boursin with Melba Toast Rounds

Spring Soup   Roulade de Savoie

Fresh Mushroom Salad   Honey Wheat Muffins

Raspberry Cream

ARTICHOKE FRITTATA

½ pound fresh
mushrooms, sliced
1 cup chopped onions
1 tablespoon oil
5 large eggs
1 10-ounce package
frozen spinach, thawed
and well-drained

2 6-ounce jars marinated
artichoke hearts,
drained
1½ cups grated New York
Cheddar cheese

1. Preheat oven to 350°.
2. In skillet, sauté mushrooms and onions in oil until limp. Remove from heat.
3. Beat eggs in large bowl. Add mushroom mixture and all remaining ingredients.
4. Pour into buttered 1½-quart casserole.
5. Bake covered 45 minutes.

6 servings

Artichoke hearts are such a treat and so is this frittata. Try it for a brunch or combine it with a menu of fruit and bran muffins for a light supper.

VEGETARIAN QUICHE

2 9-inch deep dish pie
shells, unbaked
2 tablespoons unsalted
butter
3 medium carrots,
chopped
2 small onions, chopped
3 small yellow squash,
chopped

1 large head broccoli,
chopped into florets
8 ounces Swiss cheese,
grated
1½ cups half and half
4 beaten eggs
½ teaspoon paprika
Salt and pepper to taste

1. Preheat oven to 400°.
2. Prick bottom of pie shells and bake 5 minutes at 400°. Reduce oven temperature to 350°.

Sometimes it's hard to find a good meatless entrée. This flavorful quiche is good for brunches, luncheons, or light suppers. Even children may eat their vegetables with this one!

3. Melt butter and sauté vegetables until tender, about 7 minutes.
4. Spoon half of vegetable mixture in bottom of each pie shell.
5. Sprinkle cheese evenly over vegetables.
6. Whisk together eggs, half and half, and seasonings. Pour over vegetables and cheese.
7. Bake 50 minutes.

12 servings

Hints: Can be frozen after cooking.
Any vegetable may be used.

ZUCCHINI QUICHE

An excellent way to use zucchini that ripens in the garden all at once. In fact, it is as easy to make two quiches as it is to make one. This quiche has more zip than most because of the herbs. As a time saver, try using crescent rolls for the crust.

1 **9-inch pie crust, unbaked**	½ **teaspoon salt**
2 **teaspoons Dijon mustard**	½ **teaspoon pepper**
6 **tablespoons butter**	¼ **teaspoon garlic powder**
4 **cups thinly sliced zucchini**	¼ **teaspoon dried basil**
1 **cup chopped onion**	¼ **teaspoon dried oregano**
½ **cup minced fresh parsley (or 2 tablespoons dried parsley)**	2 **eggs**
	8 **ounces mozzarella cheese, grated**

1. Preheat oven to 375°.
2. Spread mustard onto unbaked pie crust.
3. Melt butter in a large skillet. Add zucchini and onion and sauté until soft.
4. Add all spices and herbs; mix thoroughly.
5. Combine eggs and cheese in a separate bowl. Stir into zucchini mixture. Pour into crust.
6. Bake about 30 minutes or until set. Let stand a few minutes before serving.

6 servings

Hint: Use fresh herbs whenever they are available.

CRUSTLESS QUICHE

4 eggs
1½ cups milk
½ teaspoon salt
Dash cayenne pepper

2 cups shredded Swiss, Monterey Jack and/or Cheddar cheese
2 tablespoons all-purpose flour

1. Preheat oven to 350°.
2. Grease and flour a 9-inch pie pan.
3. In blender, mix eggs, milk, salt, and pepper. Skim off foam.
4. Toss cheese with flour and place in prepared pie plate.
5. Pour egg mixture over cheese.
6. Bake 40-45 minutes. Let stand 10 minutes before serving.

6 servings

Hints: Can add chopped sautéed mushrooms, peppers, ham, shrimp, etc.
Can make in 9-inch square pan, cut into squares, and serve as appetizers.

Talk about easy! Here's a basic crustless quiche that enables you to use your imagination. The sky is the limit. Be safe with simple cheeses or combine your favorite ingredients for that personal touch!

SMITHFIELD HAM SAUSAGE QUICHE

1 9-inch deep dish pie shell, unbaked
1 package Smithfield ham sausage
1 medium green pepper, chopped
1 medium onion, chopped
8 ounces Swiss cheese, grated

4 eggs
¾-1 cup half and half
2 tablespoons unsalted butter, melted
1 tablespoon all-purpose flour
½ teaspoon salt
1 teaspoon nutmeg
1 teaspoon ground red pepper

1. Preheat oven to 375°.
2. Brown pie shell very lightly in oven. Remove to a rack to cool.
3. Brown sausage in medium frying pan and drain well. Transfer to a large mixing bowl.
4. Sauté green pepper and onion in same frying pan. Add them to sausage.

If a brunch is on your agenda, try this quiche. It has an unusual combination of textures and flavors that is bound to receive compliments. Prepare it ahead of time; the hostess should enjoy herself, too!

5. Add grated Swiss cheese to sausage mixture and blend.
6. Spoon sausage mixture into pie crust.
7. Blend eggs, half and half, melted butter, flour, salt, nutmeg, and red pepper with a whisk. Pour over sausage mixture.
8. Bake for 40-50 minutes. Quiche is done when filling appears to be set.

6 servings

Hints: To reheat, cover with foil and heat at 350° for 30 minutes.
May be frozen.

BROCCOLI AND FETA CHEESE TART

Phyllo dough is growing in popularity - especially among those who have discovered how easy it is to work with! Always brush phyllo with melted butter and keep it moist. Even the novice will feel comfortable trying this recipe.

3 **10-ounce packages chopped broccoli, thawed and drained**	½ **pound feta cheese, crumbled**
8 **whole phyllo leaves (sheets)**	¼ **cup dried parsley**
¼ **cup butter**	2 **tablespoons dried dill weed**
½ **cup finely chopped onion**	1 **teaspoon salt**
3 **eggs**	⅛ **teaspoon white pepper**
	½ **cup melted butter**

1. Preheat oven to 350°.
2. Drain broccoli very well.
3. Allow phyllo to come to room temperature, covered with damp towel.
4. In a large skillet, sauté onion in ¼ cup butter until golden. Add broccoli and mix with onion. Remove from heat.
5. Beat eggs in a large bowl. Stir in feta cheese, parsley, dill, salt, pepper, and broccoli-onion mixture.
6. Brush the top of each of 4 phyllo leaves with melted butter.
7. Line the inside of a 9-inch springform pan with 4 buttered phyllo leaves (one on top of another).
8. Pour filling in pan on top of the leaves.
9. Fold phyllo, overlapping the edge of the filling.
10. From the remaining 4 sheets of phyllo, cut 4 circles the diameter of the springform pan. Brush each with butter and place in layers over the filling.
11. With scissors, cut through top pastry to make desired number of servings (8 sections).
12. Pour remaining butter over the top.

13.   Place pan on cookie sheet. Bake 40-45 minutes or until the top is puffy and golden.
14.   Remove outer ring from springform pan. Serve tart warm.

8 servings

Hints: Tart may be frozen before cooking.
Always thaw frozen phyllo dough in refrigerator (for 1-2 days) before using.

PROVENÇAL PIE

⅔ **cup bread crumbs, divided**
¼ **cup freshly grated Parmesan cheese**
3 or 4 **medium tomatoes**
1   **medium onion, thinly sliced**

½ **cup grated mild Cheddar cheese**
2   **eggs**
½ **teaspoon salt**
¼ **teaspoon dried oregano**
Pepper to taste
3   **strips bacon, partially cooked**

1.   Preheat oven to 350°.
2.   Put ⅓ cup bread crumbs in bottom of a 9-inch pie pan. Mix Parmesan cheese with remaining crumbs.
3.   Layer half the tomatoes, onion, and Cheddar cheese in pie pan atop crumbs. Repeat for second layer.
4.   Beat eggs with salt, oregano, and pepper; pour over layers.
5.   Sprinkle with rest of bread crumb-Parmesan mixture.
6.   Top with 3 strips bacon.
7.   Bake 30 minutes.

6 servings

Great side dish when summer tomatoes are plentiful.

RICOTTA CRÊPES WITH MEAT-MUSHROOM SAUCE

These crêpes are so luscious that you might want to increase the recipe to allow for seconds! No freezer should ever be without this meat and mushroom sauce. Serve over noodles for fast delicious family fare or over crêpes for a more sophisticated dish.

Ricotta Crêpes:
1 pound ricotta cheese
¼ pound Monterey Jack cheese or domestic Muenster, shredded
¼ teaspoon nutmeg
⅛ teaspoon salt
Freshly ground black pepper to taste
1 dozen prepared crêpes
2 tablespoons butter
1 tablespoon freshly grated Parmesan cheese
6 cups hot meat-mushroom sauce

Meat-Mushroom Sauce:
1 pound pork sausage
2 pounds ground beef round

4 very large onions, chopped
1 cup minced fresh parsley
4-6 large cloves garlic, minced
¾ pound fresh mushrooms, thinly sliced
3 15-ounce cans tomato sauce
1 fifth dry red table wine
2 teaspoons salt
1 teaspoon ground sage
1 teaspoon dried rosemary
½ teaspoon dried marjoram
½ teaspoon dried thyme
½ teaspoon freshly ground black pepper

Crêpes:
1. Preheat oven to 350°.
2. Stir together ricotta, Monterey Jack cheese, nutmeg, salt and fresh pepper.
3. Divide mixture among 12 crêpes, putting it in center of crêpe and folding in sides.
4. Arrange filled crêpes in single layer in shallow buttered baking tray.
5. Dot with butter and sprinkle with Parmesan cheese.
6. Bake 12 minutes or until bubbly.
7. Serve topped with heated sauce.
Sauce:
1. In large Dutch oven slowly brown sausage.
2. Add ground round and brown.
3. Add onions and sauté until limp.
4. Add garlic, parsley, and mushrooms and stir to coat with meat drippings.
5. Stir in remaining ingredients. Partially cover and simmer, stirring occasionally, 3 hours or until reduced and thickened.
6. Skim off any excess fat. Yields 3 quarts sauce.

6 servings

Hints: Delicious served with spinach salad and crusty bread. Can be assembled in morning and cooked before serving. Sauce freezes beautifully.

FRENCH TOAST SOUFFLÉ

¼ cup butter	6 tablespoons sugar
3 eggs	¾ cup all-purpose flour
1½ cups milk	¼ teaspoon salt

1. Preheat oven to 425°.
2. Put butter in 8-inch shallow pan and heat in oven until butter melts and bubbles.
3. Combine eggs, milk, sugar, flour, and salt until smooth.
4. Pour into hot pan over butter.
5. Bake for 30 minutes.

6 servings

This mock French Toast is not only fun but delicious. Serve with warm maple syrup, sour cream, or fresh berries.

BREAKFAST CASSEROLE

1½ pounds bulk pork sausage (hot)	1 teaspoon salt
9 eggs, slightly beaten	3 slices white bread, cubed
3 cups milk	1½ cups grated sharp
1½ teaspoons dry mustard	Cheddar cheese

1. Break up sausage in a skillet and cook thoroughly. Drain.
2. Grease a 9x13 inch pan.
3. In a large bowl, mix eggs, milk, and mustard.
4. Stir in remaining ingredients. Pour into prepared pan and refrigerate overnight.
5. Bake uncovered for 1 hour at 350°. Let stand 10-15 minutes before serving.

9 servings

Hint: Serve with fresh fruit and muffins.

House guests for the week-end? Assemble this simple breakfast casserole a day ahead and enjoy an extra hour of sleep.

POULTRY AND SEAFOOD

HERBED ROAST CHICKEN WITH VEGETABLES

A simple supper that could be low in calories if the butter were eliminated. Baking the chicken breast-side-down produces a wonderfully moist bird; the finished product makes a lovely platter. Serve with a green salad, fresh popovers, and a full-bodied Chardonnay or perhaps a chilled light red such as Valpolicella.

1 2½-3 pound fryer, whole
1 clove garlic
1 teaspoon dried tarragon
¼ teaspoon dried savory
⅛ teaspoon dried marjoram
½ teaspoon salt
4 shallots, minced
1 pound new potatoes, unpeeled, cut into 1x1½x¼ inch pieces
½ pound pearl onions, peeled (or other small onions)
½ pound carrots, peeled, cut into 1-inch diagonal chunks
½ cup dry white wine
2-4 tablespoons unsalted butter, melted
Fresh parsley, garnish

1.   Preheat oven to 325°.
2.   Wash chicken inside and out. Pat dry. Cut off tail fat.
3.   Rub chicken inside and out with split garlic clove, then place garlic inside.
4.   Combine herbs. Sprinkle cavity of chicken with herb mixture and rub rest of mixture into skin on outside.
5.   Place chicken breast-side-down in shallow roasting pan and sprinkle with shallots. Bake at 325° for 30 minutes.
6.   Steam or blanch vegetables for 10 minutes. They should remain crunchy.
7.   When chicken has baked 30 minutes, place vegetables in pan around chicken. Pour wine and melted butter over all and continue baking until chicken is done, basting every 20 minutes with pan juices. Turn chicken breast-side-up for browning during last 20 minutes. Allow approximately 30-35 minutes per pound.
8.   Let chicken stand 10-15 minutes before carving. Cut into serving pieces and arrange on serving platter, surrounded by vegetables. Pour pan juices over all. Garnish with fresh parsley.

4-6 servings

Hint: If vegetables are not done when bird is, remove chicken to hot platter, cover, turn oven to 400°, baste vegetables, and continue cooking until done.

ORIENTAL VELVET CHICKEN

2 teaspoons cornstarch
1 tablespoon soy sauce
⅛ teaspoon pepper
1 tablespoon oil
4 chicken breast halves, boned
1 4-ounce can mushrooms

1 tablespoon cornstarch
3 tablespoons oil
2 cloves garlic, minced
½ teaspoon ground ginger, or 1 tablespoon chopped fresh ginger

1. Combine 2 teaspoons cornstarch, soy sauce, pepper, and 1 tablespoon oil.
2. Cut chicken into match-like pieces, toss with soy sauce mixture, and let stand at least 30 minutes.
3. Drain mushrooms, reserving liquid.
4. Whisk mushroom liquid with 1 tablespoon cornstarch.
5. Heat 3 tablespoons oil in skillet over medium-high heat. Add chicken, garlic, and ginger, and stir-fry until just done. Do not brown.
6. Add mushrooms and mushroom liquid-cornstarch mixture. Cook and stir until thickened.
7. Serve immediately.

4 servings

This simple chicken dish must be prepared at the last minute. It employs the stir-fry cooking method which ensures moistness and discourages over-cooking. Use your imagination to create fried rice, a perfect accompaniment to this dish.

CHICKEN DIANE

6 chicken breast halves, boned
Flour, for dredging
¼ cup unsalted butter
3 tablespoons brandy
2 teaspoons minced shallots

¼ pound fresh mushrooms, sliced
½ cup heavy cream
2 tablespoons Dijon mustard
2 teaspoons minced fresh parsley

1. Dredge chicken breasts in flour, shaking to remove excess.
2. Melt butter in large skillet. Sauté chicken in butter 3-4 minutes on each side.
3. Warm brandy slightly. Ignite brandy and pour over chicken. Shake skillet until flames die out. Remove chicken and set aside.

Definitely a last-minute dish, this one is fun to prepare for an audience of friends. If you've never cooked with flaming brandy, practice on your family—children find this magical and entertaining.

4. In same skillet with pan juices, sauté shallots and mushrooms until tender, about 5 minutes.
5. Add cream and stir. When thickened, add parsley and mustard.
6. Return chicken to skillet and simmer, uncovered, over low heat for 5 minutes.

4 servings

Hint: Nice served with brown rice.

CHICKEN BREASTS PARMIGIANA

This recipe has its origins in Northern Italy. Expand the Italian theme by serving this dish with rice florentine, an Italian salad, and Broccoli-Stuffed Tomatoes.

6 **chicken breast halves, skinned and boned**	¾ **cup dry Marsala or sherry**
½ **cup all-purpose flour**	½ **cup chicken stock**
1 **cup unsalted butter, melted**	½ **cup shredded mozzarella cheese**
1½ **cups sliced mushrooms**	½ **cup freshly grated Parmesan cheese**

1. Preheat oven to 450°.
2. Pound chicken breasts and dredge them in flour.
3. Melt butter in large skillet. Brown chicken over medium-low heat.
4. Place browned chicken in buttered baking dish, with edges overlapping.
5. Sauté mushrooms in skillet used to brown chicken. Sprinkle over chicken.
6. Add wine and stock to skillet drippings and cook 10 minutes, stirring to deglaze pan. Add salt and pepper to taste. (May be prepared ahead to this point and refrigerated.)
7. Spoon half of sauce over chicken. Sprinkle cheeses over chicken. Bake 10 minutes.
8. Turn on broiler for 2 minutes to brown chicken. Add remaining sauce.

4-6 servings

CHICKEN FLORENTINE IN RAMEKINS

4 whole chicken breasts, skinned and boned
Salt and freshly ground pepper to taste
2 tablespoons plus 2 teaspoons unsalted butter
1 tablespoon minced shallots
¼ pound fresh mushrooms, sliced, optional
½ cup dry white wine
½ cup chicken broth
2 sprigs of fresh parsley
2 tablespoons flour
1 cup heavy cream
1 egg yolk, lightly beaten
2 10-ounce packages fresh or frozen spinach, cooked and drained
Nutmeg
1-2 tablespoons grated Gruyère and/or Parmesan cheese

The presence of spinach in a dish is usually designated by the word "florentine". This is a great do-ahead dish that looks elegant yet is simple to prepare. Try a full-bodied Italian white wine such as Est! Est!! Est!!! or a somewhat fruitier white such as Chenin Blanc.

1. Open up chicken breasts on a flat surface, skinned side down. Sprinkle with salt and pepper. Fold together each whole chicken breast skinned side out.
2. Butter the bottom of a large skillet with 2 tablespoons butter and sprinkle with shallots and optional mushrooms. Add the breasts, flat side down. Add wine, broth, salt and pepper to taste, and parsley. Bring to a boil. Reduce heat, cover, and simmer 15-20 minutes until breasts are just cooked through. Remove from heat.
3. Drain and reserve all the cooking liquid from the breasts (about 1½ cups). Cover chicken breasts and keep warm.
4. Preheat oven to 350°.
5. Heat the remaining 2 teaspoons butter in a saucepan. Add the flour, stirring with a whisk until blended. Whisk in the reserved cooking liquid. When thickened and smooth, simmer about 5 minutes. Add cream and cook 2 minutes. Remove from heat and add egg yolk, stirring briskly.
6. Divide spinach and layer in the bottom of 4-6 ramekins or individual casserole dishes. Sprinkle with nutmeg. Arrange chicken breasts on top of spinach. Spoon sauce over all. Sprinkle cheese on top. (Recipe may be prepared ahead to this point and refrigerated. Bring to room temperature before baking.)
7. Bake, uncovered, until hot and bubbly.

4-6 servings

Hint: Can also be assembled in large casserole dish.

HERBED CHICKEN BREASTS

The irresistible combination of herbs and lemon gives this chicken a flavor similar to piccata. It is a versatile entrée that is simple to prepare.

1 tablespoon salt
¼ teaspoon freshly ground pepper
1 teaspoon dried rosemary
1 teaspoon dried marjoram
1 teaspoon dried oregano

8 chicken breast halves, skinned
6-8 tablespoons butter or margarine
¼ cup fresh lemon juice
½ cup chicken broth
½ cup white wine

1. Mix together salt, pepper, and herbs. Roll chicken breasts in herb mixture.
2. Melt butter in large skillet or electric frypan. Sauté chicken in butter until browned. Add lemon juice, broth, and wine.
3. Cover and simmer 30-45 minutes, or until chicken is tender.

6-8 servings

Hint: A whole fryer, cut into serving pieces, may be substituted for chicken breasts. Cook chicken 45 minutes to 1 hour, or until tender and juices run clear when chicken is pricked with a fork.

CHICKEN IN WINE
AND CLAM SAUCE

12 chicken breast halves,
   skinned and boned
Salt and freshly ground
   pepper to taste
4 tablespoons finely
   minced shallots,
   divided
½ cup unsalted butter,
   divided
1 teaspoon dried thyme
½ cup dry white wine
½ clove garlic, finely
   minced

¼ cup flour
½ cup light cream
1 pint fresh clams,
   cooked and chopped, or
   2 10-ounce cans whole
   clams
1 cup chicken stock
1 teaspoon sugar
½ cup buttered bread
   crumbs
2 tablespoons freshly
   grated Parmesan
   cheese

*The versatility of
chicken is unlimited.
The use of fresh clams,
when available,
enhances its flavor.
Serve with a fresh pasta
such as linguine and a
green vegetable.*

1.   Preheat oven to 375°.
2.   Season chicken with salt and pepper.
3.   In a large skillet, sauté 2 tablespoons shallots in ¼ cup
butter until tender. Add chicken breasts and brown on all
sides. Add thyme and wine. Cover and bring to a boil.
Reduce heat and cook gently until chicken is tender, about
10-15 minutes.
4.   Transfer chicken to shallow 2-quart casserole and keep
warm. Reserve liquid in which chicken was cooked.
5.   Sauté garlic and remaining 2 tablespoons shallots in ¼
cup butter. Blend in flour. Slowly add cream, stirring
constantly.
6.   Drain clams; reserve juice. Combine clam juice and
liquid in which chicken was cooked to make 1½ cups.
(Chicken broth may be used if necessary to make 1½ cups.)
Gradually stir this mixture into cream sauce.
7.   Bring sauce to a boil, stirring constantly, and cook 5
minutes. Add sugar, salt and pepper to taste, and clams.
Cook 2 minutes.
8.   Pour sauce over chicken, top with crumbs mixed with
cheese, and bake 20-30 minutes or until hot, bubbly, and
golden brown.

8-10 servings

*Hint: Can be totally prepared ahead and refrigerated. To bake,
cover with foil for 30 minutes. Uncover and continue cooking
until sauce is hot and bubbly, about 15-20 minutes.*

CHICKEN AND BROCCOLI IN PHYLLO

This recipe is a bonus for the novice who has never worked with phyllo pastry. It is simple to prepare, and the end result is as impressive in appearance as it is in taste. The rich, elegant filling surrounded by the crispy, light pastry makes it a first choice for entertaining. Serve with a full-flavored California Chardonnay or white Burgundy.

6   chicken breast halves, bone in
1   large bunch broccoli, stems removed
1   pint dairy sour cream
Salt and freshly ground pepper to taste

8-10 sheets phyllo pastry
1   cup unsalted butter, melted
8   slices bread, processed to fine crumbs
1   cup freshly grated Parmesan cheese

1.   Poach chicken in water to cover, 20-30 minutes, or until tender. Remove, skin, and bone breasts. Shred the meat into small strips.
2.   Steam broccoli in microwave for 3-4 minutes (or on top of stove in steamer) until crisp-tender. Do not overcook. Cool and chop into small pieces.
3.   Combine chicken and sour cream. Add salt and pepper to taste.
4.   Lay out one sheet of phyllo. Brush with melted butter and sprinkle with bread crumbs. Place next sheet of phyllo on top of first and repeat butter and bread crumbs until you have used 4 or 5 phyllo sheets. Butter and sprinkle crumbs on last one.
5.   Leaving a 2-inch border around the layered phyllo rectangle, spread half the chicken mixture, half the broccoli, and half the Parmesan cheese on phyllo. Fold in a 1-inch border on all sides of the rectangle and butter the fold.
6.   Starting with short end of rectangle, roll up phyllo jelly-roll style. Brush outside of roll with melted butter.
7.   Repeat steps 4, 5, and 6 to assemble second roll.
8.   Place both rolls on a well-buttered cookie sheet. Bake at 375° for 20-25 minutes or until lightly browned. Let stand 10 minutes before serving.
9.   Using a serrated knife, slice into 1½-2 inch thick slices and serve immediately.

10-12 servings

Hints: Recipe may be prepared one day ahead and refrigerated. Bring to room temperature before baking.
One large (3½-4 pound) fryer may be substituted for chicken breasts.

TWIN PEPPER CHICKEN

2 pounds boneless chicken breasts
5 tablespoons vegetable oil, divided
6-8 small dried whole red peppers
1-2 red bell peppers, thinly sliced and halved crosswise
½ pound fresh mushrooms, thinly sliced
3-4 green onions, sliced diagonally into 1-inch lengths

1 tablespoon cornstarch
¾ cup chicken broth
2 tablespoons sesame oil (the dark, Oriental variety)
Marinade:
2 cloves garlic, minced
2 tablespoons dark soy sauce
2 tablespoons dry sherry
2 tablespoons vegetable oil
1 tablespoon cornstarch

A beautiful dish that was created when unexpected dinner guests appeared. A raid of refrigerator and pantry yielded these ingredients. This dish is spicy but not overpowering. When fresh snow peas are available, be sure to include them.

1. Slice chicken breasts crosswise into ¼-inch strips, being careful to remove white tendon that runs through "fillet" on bottom. Stir marinade ingredients into chicken and let sit at room temperature while preparing vegetables (or cover and refrigerate for an hour).
2. Heat wok or large skillet over high heat. When hot, add 3 tablespoons oil and heat 30 seconds or until very hot. Drop whole red peppers into oil and press with back of spoon, swirling in oil until dark. For less spicy dish, remove peppers before continuing. (Do not allow guests to eat these if you leave them in!)
3. Scatter chicken pieces in hot oil and stir-fry rapidly until done, about 3-5 minutes. Remove chicken from pan, scraping bits.
4. Add 2 tablespoons oil to wok. When hot, scatter in sliced sweet red bell pepper strips. Stir-fry 30 seconds. Add mushrooms and onions. Stir-fry 1 minute. Add cooked chicken to pan. Stir to blend with vegetables. Dissolve cornstarch in chicken broth and add to wok. Stir and cook until slightly thickened, about 1 minute. Add sesame oil, stir to blend, and remove from heat.

6-8 servings

Hint: Garnish with a ring of fresh snow peas that have been lightly stir-fried. A beautiful dish.

LEMON GARLIC CHICKEN

These well-seasoned chicken breasts are a wonderful choice when entertaining as they can be assembled ahead of time.

½ cup plus 2 tablespoons unsalted butter, melted
1 small clove garlic, crushed
¾ cup dry bread crumbs
½ cup freshly grated Parmesan cheese
1½ tablespoons minced fresh parsley
1 teaspoon salt
Pepper to taste
6 chicken breast halves, boned and skinned
Juice of one lemon
Paprika

1. Preheat oven to 325°.
2. Combine ½ cup butter and garlic; set aside.
3. Combine bread crumbs, cheese, parsley, salt, and pepper; stir to blend.
4. Dip each chicken breast in butter mixture and coat with breadcrumb mixture.
5. Roll tightly, starting at narrow end, and secure with wooden pick.
6. Arrange rolls in a shallow baking dish. Drizzle with remaining butter and lemon juice. Sprinkle with paprika.
7. Bake for 50 minutes.

4-6 servings

INDIAN CHICKEN CURRY

With the addition of the condiments, this becomes such fun to serve to guests. Everyone will enjoy experimenting with flavors, and a unique and special evening will unfold.

½ pound butter
2 medium onions, chopped
2 cloves garlic, minced
2 stalks celery, chopped
3 tablespoons minced fresh parsley
1 large cucumber, peeled and chopped
2 apples, peeled and chopped
4 tablespoons flour
1 teaspoon ground nutmeg
1 teaspoon dry mustard
3 tablespoons curry powder (or more, to taste)
2 cups chicken broth
2 cups light cream
1 cup coconut milk
1½ teaspoons salt
1 tablespoon fresh lemon juice
12 chicken breast halves, skinned, cooked, and cubed

1. In a large skillet, melt the butter over medium heat and sauté the onion, garlic, celery, parsley, cucumber, and apples until tender, about 3-5 minutes.

2. Add the flour, nutmeg, mustard, and curry powder, and cook an additional 5 minutes, stirring often.
3. Add the chicken broth, cream, coconut milk, and salt. Bring the mixture to a boil over high heat, reduce the heat, and simmer partially covered for one hour.
4. Pour the mixture through a sieve into a bowl, squeezing all juice from cooked fruits and vegetables.
5. Discard the fruits and vegetables, return the juices to the skillet, add lemon juice, and correct seasonings if necessary. If adding curry powder, dissolve in a small amount of juice before adding.
6. Add the chicken and simmer about 15 minutes, or until chicken is heated through, stirring well.

8 servings

Hint: Serve with rice and condiments. Any or all of the following are suggested: chopped scallions, raisins, crumbled bacon, chopped hard-cooked eggs, shredded coconut, chopped peanuts or cashews, grapes, sliced bananas, chutney.

LEMON BARBECUED CHICKEN

1 cup vegetable oil, or ½ cup olive oil and ½ cup vegetable oil	2 teaspoons onion salt
	2 teaspoons dried basil
	1 teaspoon dried thyme
½ cup fresh lemon juice (about 5 lemons)	¼ teaspoon garlic powder
1 teaspoon seasoned salt	8 chicken breast halves, bone-in
1 teaspoon paprika	

1. Mix first 8 ingredients and pour over chicken. Marinate at least 10 hours, preferably overnight, in refrigerator.
2. Drain chicken and reserve marinade.
3. Grill over low to medium coals. Baste often with marinade.

8 servings

Hint: Can be partially baked in 350° oven for 30 minutes and finished on grill.

Some of the most memorable chicken dishes are cooked over a charcoal fire. The mild flavor of chicken is the perfect foil for highly-flavored marinades such as this one.

CHICKEN BREASTS WITH DIJON MUSTARD SAUCE

This mustard sauce is delicious yet subtle in flavor. Rice or noodles are perfect accompaniments.

4 whole chicken breasts, halved, skinned, and boned	2 tablespoons flour
	1 cup chicken broth
	½ cup light cream
3 tablespoons unsalted butter	3 tablespoons Dijon mustard

1. In large skillet, sauté chicken in butter for 15 minutes, turning occasionally.
2. Remove chicken and add flour to pan juices, stirring well.
3. Add broth, cream, and mustard; stir and cook until thickened.
4. Return chicken to pan and continue cooking until chicken is tender, about 10 minutes.

4-6 servings

CHICKEN BREASTS À L'ORANGE

This sauce does double duty: it adds a pleasant citrus tang as well as a pretty glaze to chicken. Also try it with turkey.

4 large chicken breast halves, bone-in	Sauce:
4 tablespoons butter or margarine, melted	½ cup sugar
Salt and pepper to taste	1½ tablespoons cornstarch
Flour, for dredging	½ teaspoon salt
¾ cup boiling water	½ teaspoon cinnamon
	½ teaspoon ground cloves
	1 cup orange juice

1. Preheat oven to 375°.
2. Brush chicken with butter. Salt and pepper chicken, then dust lightly with flour.
3. Place skin side up in baking pan. Add boiling water.
4. Cover and bake for 30 minutes.
5. Remove cover and bake 1 hour longer or until chicken is tender and crust is golden brown.
6. Make sauce: Combine dry ingredients, and add orange juice. Stir over low heat until smooth, thickened, and clear. Serve in gravy boat.

4 servings

TARRAGON CHICKEN

½ cup butter or
  margarine
½ cup flour, for dredging
1 chicken, cut into
  serving pieces
1 medium onion, thinly
  sliced
¼-½ pound fresh
  mushrooms, sliced

Salt to taste
½ teaspoon freshly
  ground pepper
1 tablespoon dried
  tarragon or 8-10 sprigs
  fresh tarragon
3 tablespoons minced
  fresh parsley
¾ cup dry white wine

1. Preheat skillet to medium-high and melt butter.
2. Dust chicken lightly with flour and brown in butter.
3. Add onions and mushrooms, and cook until vegetables are tender, but not browned.
4. Add salt, pepper, tarragon, parsley, and wine.
5. Cover and cook over medium heat 15-20 minutes or until chicken is tender.

4 servings

Tarragon has a mild anise flavor, and the French call it the King of Herbs. This chicken is a favorite because it is easy to prepare and makes an excellent party dish.

CHICKEN CRANBERRY CASSEROLE

1 6-ounce package long
  grain and wild rice
  with herb seasoning
1 16-ounce bag frozen
  French-style green
  beans
8 chicken breast halves,
  skinned and boned
Paprika
1 cup freshly grated
  Parmesan cheese
½ cup butter or
  margarine

½ cup chopped onion
1 cup chopped celery
1 cup sliced mushrooms
1½ cups fresh cranberries
  or 2 16-ounce cans
  whole berry cranberry
  sauce
1 cup dry white wine
½ cup slivered almonds
¼ cup butter or
  margarine

1. Preheat oven to 350°.
2. Prepare rice according to package directions.
3. Cook green beans in small amount of boiling water for 4-5 minutes; drain.
4. If using canned cranberry sauce, drain in colander until most of liquid is drained, leaving berries.

Reminiscent of Thanksgiving dinner, this recipe combines all the flavors traditionally associated with that annual feast. Do use fresh cranberries when available and be prepared—guests will ask for seconds.

5. Sprinkle chicken with paprika. Roll in cheese.
6. Melt ½ cup butter in large skillet. Add onion, celery, and mushrooms; sauté until soft. Stir in rice and cranberries.
7. Place green beans and almonds in shallow 3-quart casserole. Place chicken breasts on top in single layer in the center. Spoon rice mixture around edge of casserole. Pour wine over all. Dot chicken with ¼ cup butter or margarine. (May be prepared ahead to this point and refrigerated.)
8. Bake 45-50 minutes.

6-8 servings

SOUTHERN CHICKEN PIE

The crust and the topping make this special, but the filling is also tasty in a frozen pie crust when time is limited. If using frozen pie crust, bake at 325° for 8 minutes or until lightly browned before adding filling.

Crust:
1 cup all-purpose flour
Dash of salt
⅓ cup plus 1 tablespoon shortening
½ cup grated Cheddar cheese
3 tablespoons cold water
Filling:
3-4 cups cubed cooked chicken
1 cup chopped celery
1 cup chopped green pepper
2 tablespoons grated onion

1 tablespoon fresh lemon juice
1 4-ounce jar chopped pimento
1 cup mayonnaise
½ teaspoon salt
½ teaspoon freshly ground black pepper
Grated Cheddar cheese, optional
Optional topping:
4 tablespoons butter, melted
½ cup milk
½ cup all-purpose flour
1 teaspoon baking powder
¼ teaspoon freshly ground black pepper

1. Make crust: In a food processor fitted with steel blade, mix flour and salt. Add shortening, cheese, and water, and mix until dough forms a ball. Wrap in waxed paper and chill 1 hour.
2. Preheat oven to 475°.
3. Roll out dough and fit into 9-inch deep dish pie (or quiche) pan. To blind-bake, line crust with parchment paper or aluminum foil and fill with pie weights or dried beans. Bake 8-10 minutes; remove foil and pie weights. (Crust may be prepared ahead.)
4. Lower oven temperature to 350°.
5. Combine ingredients for filling and pour into partially baked shell.
6. Top with grated Cheddar cheese or mix optional topping ingredients and pour evenly over pie.
7. Bake pie 30-40 minutes.

6 servings

CASSOULET

Step 1:
1 pound Great Northern beans
1 16-ounce can tomatoes, chopped, with liquid
1 onion, sliced
1 carrot, sliced
1 bay leaf
½ teaspoon dried thyme
5 cups water
2 teaspoons salt
1 teaspoon freshly ground black pepper

Step 2:
1 2½-3 pound chicken
3 tablespoons butter
Salt to taste
1 small onion, sliced
2 stalks celery, with leaves
1 carrot, sliced
¼ cup minced fresh parsley
1 bay leaf
1 cup dry white wine

Step 3:
¾ pound pork shoulder, cut in small pieces
2 tablespoons unsalted butter
1 cup dry white wine
Chicken stock
3 slices bacon
1 cup dry bread crumbs
1 pound smoked sausage, thinly sliced

1. Soak beans overnight in 3 quarts water. Drain and rinse.

2. Combine beans with remaining ingredients listed in "Step 1", bring to a boil, and cook, partially covered, for 1 hour. Let cool.

3. Place onion, celery, carrot, parsley, bay leaf, and wine in roasting pan. Sprinkle salt and dot butter inside and outside of chicken. Roast chicken at 350° for 1 hour or until done, basting frequently with pan juices. Let cool and shred meat into small pieces.

4. In medium skillet, brown pork shoulder in butter. Remove, drain, and reserve fat. Add wine to skillet and deglaze. Reserve this mixture. Drain bean mixture reserving liquid. Add enough chicken stock to bean liquid to make 2 cups.

5. Arrange bacon, halved, at bottom of deep 3½-quart ovenproof casserole. Layer as follows (salt and pepper each layer): ⅓ bean mixture, ½ pork shoulder, ½ chicken pieces, ½ sausage slices, ⅓ bean mixture, ½ pork shoulder, ½ chicken pieces, ½ sausage slices, ⅓ bean mixture. Pour bean liquid and wine over casserole. Top with bread crumbs.

6. Bake, uncovered, at 350° for 1¼ hours. Break crust and baste with cooking mixture twice.

8 servings

Hint: Prepare separate ingredients 1-2 days ahead and assemble just before baking. When serving, be sure to include some of each layered ingredient for guests.

This hearty winter entrée requires a deep casserole dish in order to achieve a layered effect. Serve with a green salad, crusty French bread, and a spicy, full-bodied red wine such as Côtes du Rhône or an Italian Barolo. Another great companion to this dish is a warm fire!

COUNTRY CAPTAIN

A special southern
party dish appreciated
by well-known folks
such as General George
Patton, who upon
arrival in Columbus,
Georgia, would say,
"Bring on the Country
Captain."

3½-4 pounds chicken
   pieces, skinned
Flour, for dredging
Salt and pepper
Vegetable oil
2 onions, finely chopped
2 green peppers, finely
   chopped
1 small clove garlic
1 teaspoon salt
½ teaspoon white pepper

1-2 teaspoons curry
   powder, or to taste
2 16-ounce cans tomatoes
½ teaspoon minced fresh
   parsley
½ teaspoon dried thyme
3 heaping tablespoons
   currants or raisins
¼ pound toasted almonds
Fresh parsley sprigs,
   garnish
Cooked rice

1.   Roll skinned chicken pieces in flour, salt, and pepper.
Fry in hot oil in large skillet until brown. Remove chicken
pieces from pan but keep chicken hot (this is the secret of
this recipe's success).
2.   Preheat oven to 350°.
3.   Into the oil in which the chicken has been fried, put
onions, green pepper, and garlic clove. Cook very slowly,
stirring constantly. Season with salt, pepper, and curry
powder. Add tomatoes, chopped parsley, and thyme.
4.   Place chicken in roaster and pour tomato mixture over
it. If the sauce does not cover the chicken, add water to
skillet in which chicken was cooked and pour over chicken.
Tightly cover roaster with lid or foil. Place in oven and cook
45 minutes or until chicken is tender.
5.   Remove chicken from sauce and place in middle of
large serving platter. Surround with 2 cups or more of
cooked rice.
6.   Drop currants or raisins into sauce mixture and pour
over rice. Scatter almonds on top. Garnish with fresh
parsley sprigs.

4-6 servings

MEXICAN CHICKEN CASSEROLE

1 3½-4 pound fryer
1 medium onion, sliced
1 pound Velveeta cheese, sliced
1 8-ounce package tortilla chips, crushed

1 cup chicken broth (reserved from cooking chicken or made with bouillon cubes)
2 10¾-ounce cans cream of chicken soup
1 10-ounce can tomatoes with green chilies

Rich and spicy! Serve this family favorite over rice or accompany with fresh corn on the cob and a green salad.

1. Place chicken in Dutch oven; add water to cover. Season with salt and pepper. Bring to a boil; cover, reduce heat, and simmer until chicken is tender, about 1 hour. Cool. Remove meat from bones. Reserve 1 cup broth.
2. Preheat oven to 350°.
3. Place chicken in 2½-quart casserole. Layer onions on top of chicken. Then layer half of cheese slices, then half of crushed tortilla chips.
4. Combine broth, soup, and tomatoes. Pour over top.
5. Add remaining cheese. End with layer of tortilla chips. (May be prepared ahead to this point and refrigerated.)
6. Bake until cheese is lightly browned on top, about 20 minutes.

8 servings

South of the Border

Mexican Salsa

Black Bean Dip   Tortilla Chips

Chicken in Lime & Basil   Stuffed Red Peppers

Cheddar Corn Muffins

Caramel Flan

CHICKEN QUESADILLAS

Mexican food is as rewarding as any in the world. Its popularity has increased tremendously in recent years, and many ingredients essential to Mexican cuisine are now widely available. Quesadillas, the Mexican version of a turnover, can hold an endless variety of fillings. Start with this one using chicken and next time create your own.

2 small onions, thinly sliced	4 10-inch flour tortillas
1 tablespoon unsalted butter	2 cups cooked chicken, shredded
1 large ripe avocado	1 4-ounce can diced green chilies
2 tablespoons fresh lime juice or lemon juice	4 ounces Monterey Jack cheese, grated
Salt and freshly ground pepper	Picante sauce
½ tablespoon unsalted butter	Sour cream

1. In small skillet, sauté onion slices in 1 tablespoon butter until translucent. Reserve.
2. Peel and seed avocado. Mash with a fork and stir in lime juice. Season with salt and pepper. Reserve.
3. Preheat a large griddle or electric frypan to medium-high heat. Butter, using ½ tablespoon.
4. Place tortillas on buttered griddle and heat for 1-2 minutes. Turn tortillas over.
5. Layer chicken, onion, chilies, and cheese on one half of each tortilla, dividing ingredients evenly among tortillas.
6. Quickly fold unfilled half of each tortilla over filling, and heat until cheese is melted and filling is hot.
7. Serve immediately, topping each folded tortilla with guacamole, sour cream, and picante sauce.

4 servings

CHICKEN IN LIME AND BASIL

A versatile chicken dish that can be served hot or cold. Chicken thighs are great buffet or picnic fare, but this unique marinade works well on any cut of chicken.

¾ cup fresh lime juice	1 teaspoon freshly ground pepper
¾ cup mild olive oil	12 chicken thighs
2-3 cloves garlic, minced	Lime slices
½ cup minced fresh basil leaves	Fresh basil leaves
1½ teaspoons salt	

1. Whisk together first 6 ingredients in medium bowl.
2. Place chicken thighs in sturdy plastic bag and pour marinade over chicken. Refrigerate at least 6 hours or overnight, turning bag occasionally.

3. Preheat oven to 350°.
4. Drain chicken and place in single layer on baking sheet.
5. Bake for 30 minutes. (May be prepared ahead to this point and refrigerated. Bring to room temperature before continuing.)
6. Preheat gas or charcoal grill to medium heat.
7. Grill chicken thighs until skin is crisp and chicken juices run clear when pierced with a fork. Serve immediately, garnished with lime slices and fresh basil leaves.

4-6 servings

Hint: Any cut of chicken will work; adjust cooking times accordingly.

ASPARAGUS CHICKEN SALAD

6   chicken breast halves, skinned and boned
24 asparagus tips
Fresh spinach, garnish
Marinade:
7   tablespoons oil
1   medium onion, chopped
1   bay leaf
1   teaspoon white pepper
4   tablespoons fresh lemon juice

2   tablespoons Herbes de Provence (basil, thyme, and rosemary)
Blender vinaigrette:
1   clove garlic, peeled, sliced
½   cup fresh lemon juice
1   teaspoon salt
½   teaspoon freshly ground black pepper
2   heaping teaspoons Dijon mustard
1   cup safflower oil

1. Combine ingredients for marinade; pour over chicken and marinate in refrigerator 8 hours or overnight.
2. Discard marinade. Steam or poach chicken breasts just until tender. Slice into thin strips and reserve.
3. Boil asparagus tips until crisp-tender. Drain.
4. While asparagus is cooking, prepare blender vinaigrette: Combine all vinaigrette ingredients in blender or processor and pulse to combine.
5. Thirty minutes before serving, toss sliced chicken with blender vinaigrette and mound on serving platter lined with fresh spinach. Arrange asparagus tips around chicken and spoon remaining vinaigrette over all.

4-6 servings

Unusual - and delicious! Garnish the salad with cherry tomatoes, black olives, and fresh basil leaves. And for dessert, why not a sinfully rich "chocolate something"!

CHICKEN SALAD MOLD

Serve this salad for a springtime luncheon. Place individual portions on lettuce cups garnished with tomato wedges and blanched fresh asparagus.

1 envelope unflavored gelatin
1 cup cold water
1 cup chicken stock, heated to boiling
1 cup slivered almonds, lightly toasted
4 cups cubed cooked chicken
4 hard-cooked eggs, chopped
1 cup finely chopped celery
1 7½-ounce can green peas, drained
2 cups mayonnaise
4 heaping tablespoons India sweet relish
Cayenne pepper

1. In a large bowl, soften gelatin in cold water; add boiling chicken stock and stir to dissolve.
2. Add nuts, chicken, eggs, celery, peas, mayonnaise, and relish. Sprinkle with cayenne and stir.
3. Put into 3-quart rectangular glass dish or mold and chill until firm.
4. To serve, cut into squares or wedges.

12 servings

Hints: One large hen (about 4½-5 pounds) will yield 4 to 5 cups cooked chicken; may also substitute 8 chicken breasts. When cooking chicken be sure to reserve stock for salad.

CHICKEN SALAD IN A CREAM PUFF

This chicken salad is dressy enough to attend a wedding brunch, to be the overture for an evening concert, or the guest speaker at a luncheon. A very visually appealing dish.

Chicken Salad:
2 cups cubed, cooked chicken
1 cup seedless green grapes, halved
½ cup (2 ounces) shredded Swiss cheese
½ cup sliced celery
3 tablespoons sliced green onions
½ cup dairy sour cream
¼ cup mayonnaise
¼ cup toasted sliced almonds

Cream Puff:
½ cup margarine
1 cup boiling water
1 cup all-purpose flour
¼ teaspoon salt
4 eggs
Leaf lettuce, garnish

1. Combine chicken, grapes, cheese, celery, onion, sour cream, and mayonnaise. Chill until ready to serve.
2. Preheat oven to 400°.
3. Add margarine to boiling water and stir until melted; add flour and salt all at once. Stir until well blended and a ball forms. Set aside to cool for 10 minutes.
4. Add eggs to flour mixture, one at a time. Stir after each addition until thoroughly blended.
5. Butter a 9-inch pie pan. Spread batter evenly in bottom and on sides.
6. Bake 30-35 minutes, or until puffed and lightly browned.
7. When ready to serve, line pastry with lettuce leaves and fill with chicken salad. Sprinkle toasted almonds on top.
8. To serve, cut into wedges.

4-6 servings

Hints: Cream puff may be made one day ahead and re-crisped in moderate (325°) oven for 5 minutes.
Chicken salad may be prepared 1-3 days ahead.

CHICKEN WITH FRUIT AND CURRY

2 cups cooked, diced chicken	1 cup diced cantaloupe
1¼ teaspoons curry powder	1 cup seedless white grapes
½ teaspoon salt	½ cup walnuts, optional
Freshly ground black pepper to taste	¼ cup sour cream or plain yogurt
1 tablespoon fresh lemon juice	½ cup mayonnaise

1. Toss chicken with curry powder, salt, and pepper.
2. Add lemon juice. Refrigerate until cold.
3. Combine with remaining ingredients. Chill briefly and serve.

4 servings

This refreshing chicken salad makes a super summer lunch served in melon halves and accompanied by fresh bread.

SAUSAGE-STUFFED CORNISH GAME HENS

One special form of chicken that is not always thought of as such is Rock Cornish hens. These little birds are a cross of two small breeds of chicken, the Plymouth Rock and the Cornish. Their weight averages one pound each, so allow one bird per person. Any leftover stuffing may be served as a main dish over rice without the hens.

8   Rock Cornish game
    hens
Salt and pepper to taste
Soft butter or margarine
Paprika to taste
¼   cup melted butter
1   10-ounce jar currant
    jelly
Fresh parsley sprigs for
    garnish

Stuffing:
1   pound bulk pork
    sausage, crumbled
4   tablespoons butter or
    margarine
1   cup chopped onion
1   cup chopped green
    pepper
1   pound fresh
    mushrooms, sliced

1.   If hens are frozen, thaw overnight in refrigerator.
2.   On serving day, remove giblets from hens.
3.   Wash and dry hens. Sprinkle with salt and pepper inside and out.
4.   Preheat oven to 425°.
5.   Prepare stuffing: In large skillet, cook crumbled sausage; drain and set aside. Sauté onions, green peppers, and mushrooms in butter. Combine vegetables and sausage.
6.   Loosely fill hen cavities with stuffing.
7.   Rub outside of hens with soft butter. Sprinkle with paprika. Place in large shallow roasting pan. (May be prepared ahead to this point and refrigerated.)
8.   Roast hens 1 hour, basting with melted butter until well-browned.
9.   Melt currant jelly in small saucepan or microwave oven.
10.   Pour melted jelly over hens and garnish with parsley.

8 servings

Hints: Delicious with wild rice! Spoon wild rice on attractive serving platter; arrange hens around rice and garnish with parsley sprigs.

FLOUNDER WITH BLUE CHEESE STUFFING

½ cup unsalted butter
¼ cup minced fresh parsley
1 medium tomato, chopped
½ cup minced celery
¼ cup firmly packed blue cheese

3 cups fresh (soft) breadcrumbs
1 egg, well beaten
½ teaspoon salt
1½-2 pounds flounder fillets
Juice of 1 lemon

1. In a large skillet, melt ¼ cup of the butter.
2. Add parsley, tomato, and celery and sauté for 10 minutes, stirring frequently. Remove from heat.
3. Crumble cheese into butter mixture. Add bread crumbs, egg, and salt. Mix gently but well.
4. Preheat oven to 350°.
5. Divide mixture and spread evenly on fillets. Roll and fasten with a wooden toothpick.
6. Butter a large baking dish. Place fillets in dish, seam side down.
7. Melt remaining ¼ cup butter and combine with lemon juice. Pour mixture over fish rolls.
8. Bake for approximately 30 minutes or until fish flakes easily with a fork.

4-6 servings

Hints: Serve with rice pilaf.

When selecting fish, reject any that have a fishy odor. A truly fresh fish will have a mild, almost sweet smell. The fine-textured delicate flesh of flounder is a natural foil for savory stuffings. The following two recipes can be easily assembled for family and guests. Select either one and you'll have a winner.

FLOUNDER STUFFED WITH SHRIMP

¼ cup chopped onion
¼ cup butter
1 3-ounce can chopped mushrooms, drained and liquid reserved, or 4 ounces fresh mushrooms, thinly sliced and lightly sautéed
½ pound shrimp, peeled, cooked, and chopped coarsely
½ cup saltine crackers, coarsely crumbled

2 tablespoons minced parsley
½ teaspoon salt
Dash pepper
2 pounds flounder fillets, skinned
3 tablespoons butter
3 tablespoons flour
¼ teaspoon salt
1-1½ cups milk
⅓ cup dry white wine
4 ounces shredded Gruyère or Swiss cheese
½ teaspoon paprika

1. In a skillet, cook onion in butter until translucent. Stir drained mushrooms into pan with shrimp, cracker crumbs, parsley, ½ teaspoon salt, and dash pepper.
2. Place flounder, skinned side out, on counter and spread mixture over fillets, dividing evenly among them. Roll fillets up and place seam side down in 12x8 inch baking dish. (Recipe may be prepared to this point early in the day and refrigerated.)
3. Sauce: In a saucepan, melt 3 tablespoons butter. Add 3 tablespoons flour and stir until bubbly. Add enough milk to reserved mushroom liquid to yield 1½ cups (or use all milk if using fresh mushrooms). Add milk, ¼ teaspoon salt, and white wine to saucepan, whisking until smooth. Cook and stir until mixture is bubbly and thick. Pour over fillets.
4. Bake 20-25 minutes in 400° oven. Sprinkle with cheese and paprika. Return to oven and bake until fish flakes easily with fork, approximately 10 minutes.

6-8 servings

FLOUNDER SUPREME

6 flounder fillets,
preferably fresh
1 lemon
3 tablespoons unsalted
butter

Salt and freshly ground
pepper to taste
½ pound fresh
mushrooms, thinly
sliced
½ cup heavy cream

1. Preheat oven to 350°.
2. Place fillets in shallow glass baking dish.
3. Squeeze lemon juice over fillets. Dot with butter.
Sprinkle with salt and freshly ground pepper. Scatter
mushrooms on top. Drizzle cream over all.
4. Bake 20 minutes.

4-6 servings

*This recipe ranks as one
of cooking's triumphs of
simplicity. Angel hair
pasta or pecan rice
makes a wonderful
partner for the
accumulated
pan juices.*

GRILLED SALMON STEAKS

4 salmon steaks, 1 inch
thick
⅓ cup unsalted butter,
softened
2 tablespoons chopped
green onion
1 clove garlic, minced

1 teaspoon dried dill
weed or 1 tablespoon
chopped fresh dill
1 teaspoon salt
¼ teaspoon freshly
ground pepper

1. Dry steaks with paper towel.
2. Combine remaining ingredients and spread generously
on one side of steaks.
3. Grill over medium heat, buttered side down, 5-6
minutes. Butter top side, turn, and grill 5-6 minutes or until
firm.
4. Serve any remaining butter mixture on top. Garnish
with lemon wedges.

4 servings

*With the popularity of
gas grills, outdoor
cooking is no longer
limited to summer
months. This recipe is
"exceptional"—
exceptionally quick,
exceptionally easy, and
exceptionally delicious.
In summer, it's great
with corn on the cob
and a green salad; in
winter, accompany with
a rice dish and add a
green vegetable.*

SEEFOOD IN PHYLLO PASTRY

Working with phyllo dough can be an exacting process, so tackle this recipe when time is not a factor. The most valid recommendation came from one of our category chairmen: "This is the best recipe I have tested — perhaps one of the best I have ever cooked!" A "buttery" California Chardonnay or a rich white Burgundy from France would be nice with this dish.

Cream Sauce:
2 tablespoons unsalted butter
2 tablespoons all-purpose flour
½ teaspoon Dijon mustard
Salt and freshly ground pepper to taste
Dash of cayenne pepper
¾ cup milk
2 tablespoons heavy cream

Bread crumbs:
1 cup fresh bread crumbs
¼ cup freshly grated Parmesan cheese
¼ teaspoon dry mustard

Herbs:
¼ cup minced fresh parsley
¼ cup chopped shallots
2 tablespoons chopped chives
1 large clove garlic, minced
½ pound phyllo sheets
1 cup unsalted butter, melted
1 pound bite-size seafood (your choice)
½ cup grated Swiss cheese
2 hard-cooked eggs, chopped
¾ cup dairy sour cream
¾ cup unsalted butter, melted (for basting)

1. Make sauce: Melt 2 tablespoons butter, stir in flour to make paste; stir until it bubbles. Remove from heat and add mustard, salt, pepper, and cayenne pepper. Gradually stir in milk. Cook over medium heat until thickened. Add cream. Cover and chill until firm.
2. Combine bread crumbs, Parmesan cheese, and dry mustard. Set aside.
3. Mix parsley, shallots, chives, and garlic. Set aside.
4. Spread damp towel on counter; cover with waxed paper. Unfold phyllo sheets on waxed paper, then fold phyllo in half. Turn back one sheet at a time, brushing with melted butter and sprinkling with bread crumb mixture. Continue until the center of the "book" of sheets is reached. Close the "book" of sheets and repeat procedure on other side until you reach the center again.
5. Layer ingredients in lower third of phyllo lengthwise: seafood, Swiss cheese, chopped eggs, sour cream, herb mixture, and cream sauce.
6. Fold ends in toward the center and roll sheets lengthwise as jelly roll using towel and waxed paper to help roll.
7. Place seam side down on baking sheet. Brush with ¼ cup melted butter.
8. Preheat oven to 375°.
9. Bake 12 minutes. Cut diagonal slices 1½ inches thick almost through "loaf".
10. Return to oven 30-40 minutes, basting frequently. Remove. Baste again with ½ cup butter.
11. Cool 10 minutes. Transfer carefully to serving platter.

12 servings

COQUILLES ST. JACQUES PROVENÇALES

1 tablespoon unsalted butter, melted
2 tablespoons olive oil
¼ cup chopped shallots or green onions
1 cup chopped green pepper
2 cloves garlic, minced
½ pound mushrooms, sliced
1 tablespoon unsalted butter, melted
2 tablespoons olive oil
1½ pounds scallops, washed, salted, and dredged in flour

⅔ cup dry white wine
2 large fresh tomatoes, chopped, or 1 16-ounce can whole tomatoes, well drained
1 bay leaf
1 teaspoon dried basil, or 1 tablespoon chopped fresh basil
Salt and pepper to taste
¼ cup grated Jarlsberg or Swiss cheese
2 tablespoons freshly grated Parmesan cheese

1. Preheat broiler.
2. In large skillet, sauté shallots, green pepper, and garlic in 1 tablespoon butter and 2 tablespoons olive oil over low heat for 10 minutes or until slightly tender. Add mushrooms and sauté briefly. Remove mixture from skillet.
3. Brown scallops in 1 tablespoon butter and 2 tablespoons olive oil over medium-high heat for 2 minutes. Reduce heat.
4. Add wine, tomatoes, herbs, and shallot mixture to skillet and simmer at low heat about 2-3 minutes, just until mixture thickens. Add salt and pepper to taste.
5. Place scallop mixture in au gratin serving dish or individual shells; top with cheeses. Heat briefly under broiler until cheese is melted.

4-6 servings

Scallops are as tasty as shrimp or crabmeat but usually not as expensive. The unique combination of ingredients in this recipe makes it truly elegant. Be prepared; guests will want seconds.

FRUIT OF THE BAYOU

This dish is not an inexpensive one to serve, but there are always those times when one wants something extra special and cost takes a back seat. The aromatic bitter-sweet flavor of fennel is an excellent accompaniment to seafood. This recipe has it all! Serve with a fine "buttery" Chardonnay from California or a well-aged Burgundy or Chablis from France.

½ cup butter
8 ounces fresh or frozen scallops
8 ounces fresh or frozen crabmeat, picked
8 ounces fresh or frozen shrimp, peeled and deveined
8 ounces fresh or frozen lobster, cut into chunks
1 cup sliced mushrooms
¼ cup dry white wine
1 tablespoon chopped shallots
¼ cup flour
1-1¾ cups light cream
1½ teaspoons dried rosemary
½ teaspoon Worcestershire sauce
½ teaspoon salt
¼ teaspoon pepper
¼ teaspoon dried basil
¼ teaspoon fennel seed
Few drops hot pepper sauce
1 avocado, for garnish
Lemon juice

1. In a large skillet, melt butter. Add seafood, mushrooms, wine, and shallots. Cook over medium-low heat for 7 minutes. Stir in flour. Add cream to skillet and cook until thickened, stirring continuously. Add rosemary, Worcestershire, salt, pepper, basil, fennel seed, hot pepper sauce, and stir.
2. Place in a 2-quart casserole. (May be prepared ahead to this point and refrigerated.) Bake at 350° for 30 minutes or until bubbly.
3. Top with avocado slices that have been sprinkled with lemon juice.
4. Serve immediately.

6-8 servings

Hint: Serve with rice.

FILLET OF SOLE WITH WHITE WINE AND WALNUTS

1 pound fillet of sole, fresh or frozen
Cayenne pepper to taste
½ cup chicken broth
½ cup dry white wine
½ cup chopped walnuts

2 tablespoons minced fresh parsley
1 tablespoon unsalted butter
1 tablespoon fresh lemon juice
Lemon slices

1. Thaw fillets if frozen. Pat dry.
2. Preheat oven to 325°.
3. Put fillets in single layer in a shallow greased baking dish. Sprinkle with cayenne. Add broth and wine.
4. Cover and bake 15-20 minutes until fish is opaque.
5. Remove from oven and pour liquid in a small saucepan. Reserve fish and keep warm while preparing sauce.
6. Boil liquid over moderately high heat until reduced to ⅓ cup. Stir in walnuts, parsley, butter, and lemon juice.
7. Pour sauce over fish, garnish with lemon slices, and serve.

3-4 servings

Hint: Substitute perch or flounder fillets.

Nuts contain concentrated protein and very little starch, but it is their oils that carry the flavor. Walnuts are the secret to the success of this dish. They are a pleasing accompaniment to the other ingredients and make for an out-of-the-ordinary entrée.

Hot Off The Grill

Mexican Salsa   Tortilla Chips
Grilled Grouper
Grilled New Potatoes with Onions & Peppers
Fresh Grilled Corn-in-the Husk
Squash Kebabs
Pioneer Lettuce Salad
Rich Vanilla Ice Cream & Fresh Blueberry Sauce

GRILLED GROUPER

Hellmann's mayonnaise
Fresh lemon juice

Fresh grouper (about ⅓-½ pound per person)

1.   Brush grouper with a light coating of mayonnaise. Refrigerate 3 to 4 hours.
2.   Using equal amounts of mayonnaise and lemon juice, prepare sauce, whisking to blend.
3.   Grill grouper over charcoal fire, basting with sauce each time fish is turned. Cook until fish flakes easily when tested with fork.

Hints: Swordfish steaks may be substituted.
Substitute lime juice for lemon juice.

SEAFOOD FEAST

This recipe was confiscated from an "old salt". Splurge at the seafood market and share his secret—you'll be hooked!

2   1-pound mackerel steaks
½   pound oysters
½   pound scallops
½   pound raw shrimp, peeled and deveined
4   medium white potatoes, unpeeled and thinly sliced

¼   cup butter
Garlic powder to taste
Salt and pepper to taste
8   strips bacon
Lemon slices, garnish
Minced fresh parsley, garnish

1.   Preheat oven to 425°.
2.   In a large broiler pan lined with aluminum foil, place mackerel steaks, oysters, scallops, shrimp, and sliced potatoes on top of one another in that order.
3.   Dot potatoes with butter and season with garlic powder, salt, and pepper.
4.   Place strips of bacon on top and seal securely in foil.
5.   Bake 35 minutes at 425° and then broil on high for 6-10 minutes with foil opened.
6.   Garnish with lemon slices and parsley.

4 servings

LOUIS' FAVORITE FISH

½ cup butter or margarine
1 package Good Seasons Italian dressing mix
1 teaspoon lemon juice

4 mackerel steaks or large fillets
Fresh lemon slices, optional
Fresh parsley, optional

1. Melt butter or margarine. Add dry Italian dressing mix and combine well. Add lemon juice.
2. Coat both sides of mackerel with butter mixture.
3. Grill over low coals, basting occasionally with remaining butter mixture.

4 servings

Don't be fooled by the simplicity of this recipe. Garnished with lemon slices and fresh parsley, it is a worthwhile addition to your seafood recipe file.

SCALLOPS IN LIME SAUCE

3 pounds fresh scallops
½ cup melted butter or margarine
2 tablespoons lime juice
3 teaspoons salt

½ teaspoon dried thyme or oregano
½ teaspoon pepper
2-3 drops hot sauce
½ pound bacon strips, cut in half

1. Place scallops in bowl. Combine remaining ingredients except bacon, and pour over scallops. Marinate in refrigerator 30 minutes to 1 hour.
2. Preheat broiler.
3. Drain scallops, reserving marinade. Divide scallops equally among 6 ramekins. Spoon a little marinade over each. Cover with bacon strips.
4. Broil, until scallops and bacon are done, about 5 minutes.

6 servings

Hint: For grilled scallops, wrap bacon around each scallop and thread on skewers. Grill about 4 minutes over medium coals, basting and turning occasionally.

Versatility is a plus with this recipe. The scallops can either be served in ramekins or grilled on skewers. Try this easy recipe often.

SHRIMP CREOLE

Shrimp Creole can be a lifesaver if you have lots of hungry folks to feed. Prepare the sauce ahead and add the shrimp at the last minute for an easy yet sure-to-please main dish.

½ cup minced onion
2 tablespoons butter or margarine
2 tablespoons flour
1 bay leaf
¼ cup diced celery
1 teaspoon minced fresh parsley
½ cup minced green pepper
Dash cayenne pepper
¼ teaspoon hot pepper sauce
½ teaspoon salt
1 6¼-ounce can tomato paste
3 cups water
1½ pounds shrimp, shelled and deveined

1. In large skillet, sauté onion in butter until soft. Do not brown.
2. Add remaining ingredients, except shrimp. Cook slowly, stirring occasionally, for 30 minutes.
3. Stir in shrimp and cook until shrimp are done, about 5 minutes.

4-6 servings

Hint: Serve over rice.

SHRIMP TEMPURA WITH SWEET AND HOT SAUCE

This tangy sauce, spicier than commercial duck sauce, is outstanding. It can be prepared ahead—a real plus. Peeling shrimp doesn't have to be a chore. Invite a friend over to help. You won't have to twist her arm to stay for dinner - the aroma will do that!

Sweet and Hot Sauce:
8 ounces orange marmalade
1 tablespoon Chinese hot mustard
1 tablespoon freshly grated ginger root
2 tablespoons prepared horseradish
2 tablespoons fresh lemon juice

Tempura:
1½ pounds large raw shrimp, shelled (except for tail section) and deveined
2 cups all-purpose flour
1 teaspoon salt
1 tablespoon paprika
1 teaspoon freshly ground black pepper
12 ounces beer, room temperature
All-purpose flour, for dredging shrimp
Vegetable or peanut oil for deep frying

1. One day in advance, mix ingredients for sweet and hot sauce in processor fitted with plastic blade. Chill in refrigerator overnight to allow flavors to blend.

2. Combine 2 cups flour, salt, paprika, pepper, and beer. Let stand at room temperature for 15-20 minutes.
3. Heat 2-3 cups oil in deep fryer or wok. Oil should be very hot, 375°-400°.
4. Dredge shrimp in flour, dip in beer batter, and fry in hot (400°) oil in wok until lightly brown. Drain on tempura rack or paper towel.
5. Serve with sweet and hot sauce for dipping.

3-4 servings

CRAB CRÊPES

Crêpes:
1 **cup all-purpose flour (sifting not necessary)**
3 **large eggs, lightly beaten**
1½ **cups milk**
Dash salt
1 **tablespoon butter, melted**
1 **teaspoon cognac, optional**
1 **tablespoon confectioners' sugar, optional**

Filling:
6 **tablespoons butter**
1 **teaspoon minced shallot**
4 **ounces white wine**
1 **pound fresh crabmeat**
½ **cup heavy cream**
1 **teaspoon salt**
1 **teaspoon pepper**
Sauce:
2 **tablespoons butter**
3 **tablespoons flour**
2 **cups milk**
¼ **teaspoon salt**
¼ **cup grated Swiss cheese**
Nutmeg
Salt
Freshly ground pepper

This crêpe recipe is a very basic one for entrées or desserts. The beauty of crêpes is their versatility and ability to be kept frozen for long periods of time. Crêpes can have a variety of fillings, and this one is especially easy and delicious. Prepared a day ahead, it can be a wonderful Sunday brunch venture.

Crêpes:
1. Measure flour and salt into mixing bowl. Gradually stir in eggs, melted butter, and milk to make a thin batter just thick enough to coat the spoon. If desired, add cognac and sugar. Let batter stand for 20-30 minutes before cooking. Pour batter into pitcher or 1-quart measure with pouring lip.
2. Heat crêpe pan or small 8-inch frying pan over moderately high heat. Put ½ teaspoon butter in pan and swirl to coat bottom and sides. After butter melts, pour in about 2 tablespoons of crêpe batter. Tilt pan in circular motion to spread batter evenly over the bottom.
3. Cook crêpe for about 1 minute or until set and brown on under side. Carefully turn crêpe with spatula, and cook for about ½ minute longer, or until brown on under side.
4. Serve immediately, or stack with waxed paper between crêpes, wrap tightly in foil, and freeze.
Filling:
1. Melt butter in 1-quart saucepan; add shallots and wine. Cook slowly until reduced to half.

2. Add crabmeat, cream, salt, and pepper, and cook over low heat for 10 minutes.

Sauce:

1. Melt butter over low heat. Blend in flour until frothy. Cook roux 2 minutes. Remove from heat.

2. Heat milk and salt and add all at once to roux beating with wire whisk. Return to heat and cook for 1 minute, stirring constantly.

3. Add ¼ cup grated Swiss cheese, nutmeg, salt, and pepper. Stir until cheese is melted.

Assembly:

1. Preheat oven to 350°.

2. Place 1-2 tablespoons of crab mixture on each crêpe and roll up.

3. Butter a large casserole dish and place crêpes, seam side down in bottom of dish.

4. Cover with cheese sauce and bake 25 minutes. If desired, garnish with minced parsley before serving.

20 crêpes: 8-10 servings

FILLETS AU FROMAGE

Try this delicious topping for fish fillets. Serve with broccoli, boiled new potatoes or corn on the cob, and fresh tomatoes.

1 pound fish fillets (flounder, grouper, catfish, or sole recommended)	**4 ounces Muenster cheese, sliced**
Salt and pepper to taste	**1 tablespoon dry bread crumbs**
	¼ teaspoon paprika

1. Preheat oven to 425°.

2. Place fillets in a single layer in a greased shallow baking dish. Sprinkle with salt and pepper.

3. Top each fillet with cheese slices.

4. Combine bread crumbs and paprika. Sprinkle over fillets.

5. Bake 15-20 minutes or until fish flakes easily with a fork.

4 servings

GRILLED SWORDFISH

4   swordfish steaks, cut 1
    inch thick
¼   cup vegetable oil
2   tablespoons fresh
    lemon juice

1   teaspoon dried dill
    weed or 1 tablespoon
    chopped fresh dill
1   tablespoon paprika
1   teaspoon salt
¼   teaspoon pepper

1.   Place fish in shallow glass dish.
2.   Combine remaining ingredients and pour over fish.
Cover and marinate 4 hours in refrigerator or 1 hour at
room temperature.
3.   Grill over medium fire, basting with marinade, about 15
minutes, turning once. Fish will flake easily with a fork
when done. Do not overcook.

4 servings

The flavor of dill enhances most any fish. This recipe calls for swordfish but any thick fish steak will do. Fresh dill is very easy to grow; it will tolerate almost any soil as long as it is well drained. Harvest the seeds and leaves as well for a special treat to use all summer.

CRAB IN A SHELL

1   pound crabmeat,
    picked
2   tablespoons unsalted
    butter
2   tablespoons minced
    onion
3   tablespoons butter
2   tablespoons flour
¾   cup milk
½   teaspoon dry mustard
1   teaspoon
    Worcestershire sauce

1   tablespoon fresh lemon
    juice
Salt and pepper to taste
Dash cayenne pepper
1   egg, beaten
2   tablespoons minced
    fresh parsley
¼   cup dry bread crumbs
2   tablespoons unsalted
    butter, melted

1.   In large skillet, sauté onion in 2 tablespoons butter.
Remove and reserve.
2.   In the same skillet make white sauce: Melt 3
tablespoons butter, add 2 tablespoons flour, and cook until
flour browns very slightly. Add milk and cook, stirring until
thick as mayonnaise. (Stir with wire whisk to remove
lumps.)
3.   Add mustard, Worcestershire, lemon juice, salt, pepper,
and cayenne. Remove from heat.

Serving this dish in shells is pretty as well as practical. Assemble this ahead of time, and add bread crumbs just before baking. A green salad and stuffed tomatoes complete this menu.

4. In a small bowl, beat egg slightly. Temper the egg by adding a small amount of white sauce to the bowl and stirring to blend. Add tempered egg mixture to white sauce. Stir in crabmeat, onions, and parsley.
5. Prepare crust: Add dry bread crumbs to 2 tablespoons melted butter.
6. Put crab mixture in greased shells. Sprinkle crumb mixture on top. (May be prepared ahead to this point and refrigerated or frozen.)
7. Bake 15-20 minutes in 350° oven.

4-5 servings

CRAB AND SHRIMP CASSEROLE

A dinner party hit! For a lovely presentation, sauté ½ pint whole cherry tomatoes in 2 tablespoons unsalted butter for 3-5 minutes. Spoon tomatoes as a border around inside edge of casserole dish before serving.

1 cup cooked white rice	½ cup chopped onion
½ pound fresh mushrooms, sliced	1 cup chopped celery
3 tablespoons butter	1 cup mayonnaise
1 pound raw shrimp, shelled and deveined	¾ cup light cream
1 pound crabmeat, fresh or frozen	1 tablespoon Worcestershire sauce
½ medium sweet red or green pepper, chopped	⅛ teaspoon pepper
	½ teaspoon salt

1. Cook shrimp in boiling salted water just until they turn pink. Drain well and set aside.
2. Preheat oven to 375°.
3. Sauté mushrooms in 3 tablespoons butter until tender, 5 to 8 minutes.
4. Combine shrimp, mushrooms, and all remaining ingredients. Pour into large ungreased casserole dish. (May be prepared ahead to this point and refrigerated.)
5. Bake, uncovered, for 30 minutes or until hot and bubbly.

6-8 servings

MARYLAND CRAB CAKES

1 pound backfin
  crabmeat
1 egg, lightly beaten
1 teaspoon prepared
  mustard

1½ teaspoons mayonnaise
¾ cup crushed cornflakes
Salt and freshly ground
  pepper
¼-½ cup butter

1. Place crabmeat in a large bowl and with fingers, remove any shell pieces.
2. Add egg, mustard, mayonnaise, cornflakes, salt and pepper to taste, and mix gently with your hands. Divide mixture into 6 portions and form into cakes.
3. Cover and refrigerate at least one hour to allow flavors to blend.
4. Melt butter in a large skillet over medium heat.
5. Brown crab cakes on both sides. Serve immediately.

6 large cakes

No one will ask "Where's the crabmeat?" The use of very few extras in this recipe enhances the delicious sweet flavor of fresh crabmeat.

SHRIMP AND CASHEWS WITH RICE

1½ tablespoons cornstarch
¼ teaspoon sugar
¼ teaspoon baking soda
1¼ teaspoons salt, divided
⅛ teaspoon pepper
2 pounds raw shrimp,
  peeled and deveined
1 cup regular rice,
  uncooked

½ cup vegetable oil
1 cup chopped onion
1 clove garlic, minced
1 teaspoon minced fresh
  ginger
1 cup cubed, unpeeled
  zucchini
½ cup diced sweet red or
  green pepper
½ cup salted cashews

1. Combine cornstarch, sugar, baking soda, ¼ teaspoon salt, and pepper in medium bowl. Cut shrimp in half lengthwise. Stir shrimp into cornstarch mixture, toss to coat, and let stand at room temperature 15 to 20 minutes.
2. While shrimp is marinating, prepare rice according to package directions.
3. Heat oil in wok or skillet until very hot. Add shrimp gradually. Cook and stir over high heat until shrimp turn pink (2-3 minutes). Remove and reserve shrimp.

Stir-frying is one of the best ways to retain the color and flavor of food. This recipe is superb in taste and appearance. Serve it the next time a shrimp-lover comes to dinner. Be sure to include the sweet red pepper. It makes the dish dazzling!

4. Drain all but 2-3 tablespoons of oil. Sauté onions, garlic, and ginger in oil until transparent. Add zucchini and pepper. Cook and stir 2 minutes. Stir in cooked rice, cashews, and shrimp. Toss gently until heated.
5. Serve immediately.

4-6 servings

AVOCADO AND SHRIMP SALAD

The combination of avocados and apples makes this recipe. Don't be timid! Try this unusual medley of flavors with a fruity white wine such as Chenin Blanc or Riesling.

2 **pounds raw shrimp, unshelled**	1 **cup mayonnaise**
4 **tablespoons finely chopped onion**	¼ **cup catsup**
4 **medium apples, unpeeled and cubed (Granny Smith recommended)**	1 **tablespoon fresh lemon juice**
	4-6 **drops Tabasco sauce, or to taste**
4 **ripe avocados**	2 **tablespoons cognac**
	2 **tablespoons dry sherry**

1. Cook shrimp in boiling salted water until they turn pink (5-8 minutes).
2. Shell, devein, and cut each shrimp into 2-3 pieces. Set aside in a mixing bowl. Add finely chopped onion and cubed apples.
3. Carefully slice each avocado in half, separating without bruising. Discard pit. Scoop out avocado meat with a spoon in chunks as large as possible, leaving the shell intact. Cube avocado meat, and add to shrimp and apple mixture.
4. In a separate bowl, whisk together remaining ingredients in proportions recommended or to taste.
5. Gently toss salad with dressing and serve in reserved avocado half on a bed of lettuce.

8 servings

Hints: Minced onion, cooked shrimp, and dressing may be prepared ahead of time. However, apples and avocados discolor and therefore should be prepared just before serving.

SCALLOPS IN CHEESE SAUCE

5 tablespoons unsalted butter	1 pound raw fresh scallops
5 tablespoons flour	½ cup minced celery
1½ cups milk	¼ cup diced pimento
1 teaspoon salt	Dash of cayenne pepper, optional
½ teaspoon freshly ground black pepper	3 tablespoons unsalted butter or margarine, melted
1½ cups grated sharp Cheddar cheese	
½ teaspoon dry mustard	¾ cup fine breadcrumbs

1. Preheat oven to 350°.
2. Melt 5 tablespoons butter in heavy saucepan over low heat. Add flour, stirring until smooth. Stir and cook 1 minute. Gradually add milk; cook, stirring, over medium heat until thick and bubbly. Season to taste with salt and pepper. Add cheese and stir until cheese is melted. Add mustard, scallops, celery, pimento, and cayenne to sauce.
3. Spoon mixture into a lightly greased 1½-quart shallow casserole. Combine melted butter and breadcrumbs. Sprinkle on top.
4. Bake uncovered for 30 minutes.

4-6 servings

Hint: Serve these scallops in their sauce over rice or toast points.

When selecting scallops (or any seafood), let your nose be your guide. Test for freshness by making sure they have a sweetish odor. Sea or bay scallops may be used in this recipe. If using sea scallops, which are larger, remove small white muscle at the side of each and cut horizontally into 2 pieces.

CRABMEAT DIVAN

1 bunch fresh broccoli or 1 10-ounce package frozen broccoli	⅓ cup mayonnaise
	1½ teaspoons lemon juice
½ pound backfin crabmeat or 1 6-ounce package frozen king crab meat, thawed and drained	½ teaspoon prepared mustard
	1 teaspoon grated onion
	¼-½ cup grated Cheddar cheese

1. Preheat oven to 350°.
2. Cut fresh broccoli into small florets and cook in boiling salted water until crisp-tender. Drain. (Or cook frozen broccoli according to package directions.)

A first cousin of chicken divan, this dish is just as easy to prepare. The crabmeat offers an elegant rendition of an old favorite.

3. Arrange broccoli on oven-proof platter. Cover with pieces of crabmeat.
4. Combine mayonnaise, lemon juice, mustard, and onion. Spoon over crabmeat. Top with cheese.
5. Bake 20 minutes.

2-4 servings

CRAB SALAD

This is a true delight—the ultimate in crab salads. It blends the delicate flavor of crab with avocado and spices, then incorporates a creamy dressing. Keep the wine simple: a crisp, dry white such as Muscadet or French Chablis.

3 large avocados, peeled and pitted	Lettuce
2½ pounds lump crabmeat, picked	Tomato quarters for garnish
½ cup finely chopped celery	Dressing:
½ cup thinly sliced red radishes	1 cup mayonnaise
¼ cup lemon juice	¼ cup chili sauce
¼ cup vinegar	2 tablespoons minced fresh parsley
3 tablespoons olive oil	1 tablespoon finely chopped onion
2 tablespoons finely chopped shallots	1 tablespoon finely chopped chives
¼ teaspoon cayenne pepper	Dash cayenne
Salt to taste	¼ cup heavy cream, whipped

1. Cut the avocados into cubes. In a large bowl combine avocado cubes with crab, celery, radishes, lemon juice, vinegar, olive oil, shallots, cayenne pepper, and salt.
2. Make dressing: Combine first six ingredients. Fold in cream.
3. Mound the salad on a serving dish. Garnish with lettuce, tomato quarters, and lemon slices, decoratively cut. Spoon dressing over salad.

10-12 servings

SHRIMP WITH FETA CHEESE

1 pound raw shrimp, shelled and deveined	1½ cups canned Italian plum tomatoes
2 tablespoons lemon juice	½ cup clam juice
¾ cup minced scallions	3 tablespoons butter
2 tablespoons minced fresh parsley	1 tomato, peeled
2 garlic cloves, minced	½ teaspoon dried oregano
¼ cup olive oil	¼ cup dry white wine
	½ pound feta cheese, crumbled

1. Sprinkle shrimp with lemon juice; set aside.
2. In large skillet, sauté scallions, parsley, and garlic in oil until soft.
3. Add canned tomatoes to scallion mixture and bring to a boil. Reduce heat to moderately low and simmer, covered, for 20 minutes. Stir in clam juice and cook for another 5 minutes.
4. Preheat oven to 400°.
5. Sauté shrimp in butter for 4 minutes or until pink.
6. Pour tomato mixture into 1½-quart shallow baking dish. In center put peeled tomato. Surround with shrimp. Sprinkle oregano over shrimp. Pour wine over all. Sprinkle with cheese.
7. Bake 15-20 minutes.

3-4 servings

Hint: Serve with lemon rice.

Feta cheese makes this recipe noteworthy. The blend of herbs, spices, and wine combines elegantly with the shrimp and tomatoes to make the whole dish come alive with flavor. Serve with a chilled, light red wine such as Beaujolais or possibly a fruity white like Riesling or California Chenin Blanc.

CURRIED SHRIMP CASSEROLE

1½ cups raw rice	2½ pounds shrimp, cooked, peeled, and deveined
1 small onion, grated	½ cup slivered almonds
¾ cup butter or margarine	¾ cup raisins
1 teaspoon curry powder	6 slices cooked bacon, crumbled
1 teaspoon ground white pepper	
1 teaspoon celery salt	

An economical way to serve shrimp to a crowd—as good as shrimp curry but a lot less trouble.

1. Cook rice according to package directions. Reserve.
2. Preheat oven to 350°.
3. In a large skillet, sauté onion in butter until translucent. Add curry, pepper, and celery salt.
4. Add rice and shrimp. Stir in almonds and raisins. Season to taste with salt and pepper.
5. Place in a 2-quart casserole and bake until heated thoroughly, about 20 minutes.
6. Top with crumbled bacon before serving.

8-10 servings

ORIENTAL SKEWERED SHRIMP

Ever thought of grilling shrimp? This oriental marinade is first-rate and allows the shrimp to retain moisture. Rice pilaf or fried rice is a tasty accompaniment.

⅔ cup dry sherry
⅓-⅔ cup soy sauce
⅔ cup olive or peanut oil
½ teaspoon powdered ginger
½ teaspoon freshly grated lemon zest
1 clove garlic, crushed
Fresh lemon juice

1 pound raw shrimp, shelled and deveined
¾ pound fresh mushrooms, stemmed
1 6½-ounce can whole water chestnuts
¼ pound bacon, cut into 2-inch lengths

1. In a 2-quart bowl, combine sherry, soy sauce, oil, ginger, lemon zest, and garlic.
2. Sprinkle a little lemon juice over shrimp. Place shrimp in bowl with marinade and refrigerate no longer than one hour.
3. On metal skewers, alternate shrimp with mushroom caps, water chestnuts, and bacon.
4. Cook over medium coals, turning frequently and basting with the marinade, until shrimp are pink, 6-8 minutes.

4 servings

GUS'S CRAB PIE

1	pound crabmeat	1	teaspoon horseradish
4	eggs	½	teaspoon
1	cup chopped celery		Worcestershire sauce
2	tablespoons chopped green pepper	½	teaspoon Tabasco sauce
1	cup grated Cheddar cheese		Salt and pepper to taste
3	tablespoons mayonnaise	6	tablespoons butter
		1½	cups dry stuffing mix

1. Preheat oven to 350°.
2. Combine crabmeat, eggs, celery, green pepper, Cheddar cheese, mayonnaise, horseradish, Worcestershire sauce, Tabasco, salt, and pepper. Place in a well greased 13x9 inch baking dish.
3. Sauté stuffing mix in butter. Spread evenly over crab mixture.
4. Bake 25-30 minutes.

4-6 servings

Make a pound of crabmeat go a long way—serve this on a buffet or cut into squares as a delicious appetizer. Every morsel will be devoured eagerly.

SALMON SOUFFLÉ

3	tablespoons unsalted butter or margarine	¼	teaspoon dried rosemary
2	tablespoons flour	2	eggs, separated
1	8-ounce carton plain non-fat yogurt or 1 cup buttermilk	1	7½-ounce can salmon, drained and bones removed, mashed
	Dash pepper		Finely crumbled bacon, optional
	Dash salt, if desired		
	½-1 teaspoon dried basil		

1. Preheat oven to 350°.
2. Melt butter in saucepan; stir in flour. Mix in yogurt and cook, stirring constantly, until thick and smooth. Add pepper and salt to taste. Stir in basil and rosemary.
3. Cool sauce for a few minutes and stir in 2 well-beaten egg yolks.
4. Beat 2 egg whites with mixer until stiff, but not dry. Reserve.
5. Fold salmon into yogurt cream sauce.
6. Gently fold in beaten egg whites. Turn into buttered 1-quart soufflé dish and sprinkle with bacon if desired.
7. Bake 35 minutes. Serve immediately.

2-4 servings

A great way to prepare something special using canned salmon. Serve it on a summer night when a light seafood dish is in order.

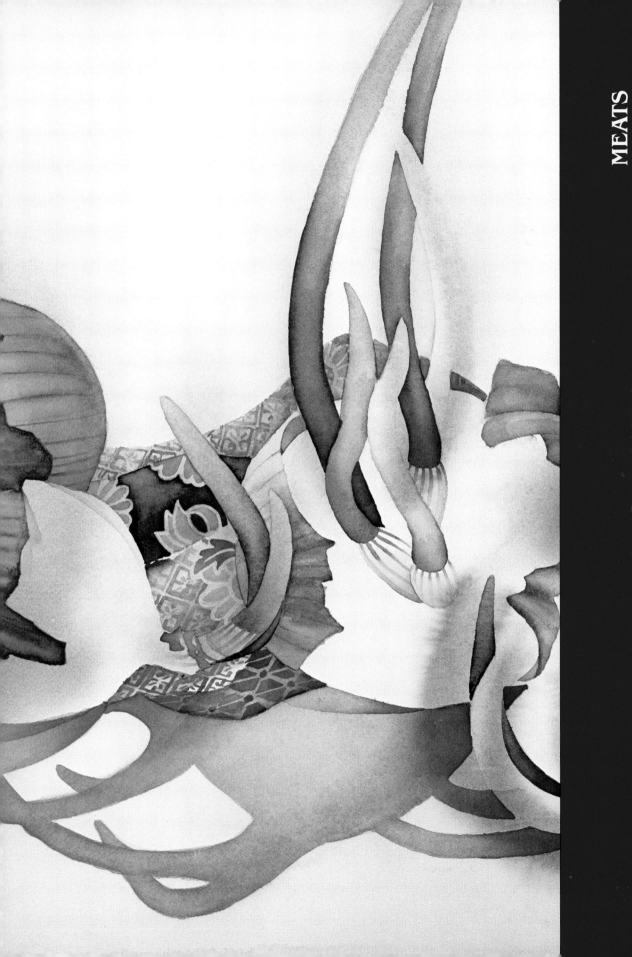

TEXAS BRISKET

A hearty beef dish with a suggestion of the smoked flavor so popular in the Southwest. Can easily be prepared ahead and reheated, although it would be a shame to rob your guests of the wonderful aroma present during baking time. Any leftovers freeze beautifully.

1 large fresh beef brisket, 4-7 pounds
1 cup double strength coffee
Sauce:
2 cups catsup
10 ounces cola
¼ cup Worcestershire sauce
3 tablespoons brown sugar
2 tablespoons liquid smoke
2 tablespoons prepared mustard
2 teaspoons Knorr Swiss Aromat meat seasoning
¼ teaspoon Tabasco, or more to taste

1. Preheat oven to 200°.
2. Place brisket in large shallow roasting pan, fat side up.
3. Pour coffee over brisket and cover tightly with heavy duty aluminum foil. Cook for 24 hours.
4. Check occasionally to make sure brisket remains tightly covered and there is still liquid in the pan. If liquid should evaporate, add 1 cup hot water and continue cooking, covered.
5. After 24 hours, drain any liquid from pan.
6. Remove brisket and trim fat from top; return meat to pan.
7. Combine ingredients for sauce and pour over meat. (May be prepared ahead to this point and refrigerated. Bring to room temperature before continuing.)
8. Bake for 1 hour, uncovered. Check occasionally to be sure sauce does not evaporate. If so, cover for remainder of cooking time.
9. Slice thinly across grain. Serve sauce on top or in heated bowl on side.

10-12 servings

Hint: Serve with Potato Nachos or Noodle Kügel, a green salad, and Cheddar Muffins.

Tex-Mex Buffet

Mexican Layered Dip

Tortilla Chips   Spicy Beef Brisket

Potato Nachos   Marinated Fresh Vegetables

Cheddar Muffins

Mocha Pie with Pecans

SPICY BEEF BRISKET

1 large beef brisket, 5 pounds	1 teaspoon dried red pepper flakes
Sauce:	1 tablespoon salt
1 10-ounce bottle Worcestershire sauce	1¾ cups white vinegar
½ cup butter	Heavy aluminum foil
1 tablespoon Tabasco sauce, optional	1½ cups commercial barbecue sauce (your own favorite)
1 tablespoon coarse black pepper	

1. In saucepan, combine ingredients for sauce and simmer 10 minutes. Cool before pouring on meat.
2. For smoker: Make a large boat from aluminum foil, using 3-4 layers, to hold brisket and sauce.
3. Place brisket in foil, fat side up. Pour sauce over and smoke 4-5 hours or until tender.
4. Remove ½ cup of meat juices from foil and combine with barbecue sauce in a small pan. Simmer for 10 minutes.
5. Slice beef thinly across the grain and serve with heated sauce.
6. For oven: Line large roasting pan with foil. Place meat in pan fat side up. Cover with sauce; fold foil over meat.
7. Bake at 325° 4-5 hours. Then uncover and cook approximately 1 more hour. Serve with sauce as above.

8-10 servings

Hint: Good for buffet. Serve with au gratin potatoes and salad.

This sounds too hot to eat but the meat absorbs the sauce and acquires a zing that's wonderful. (Eliminate the Tabasco, if desired.) The whole brisket can be prepared ahead and reheated after slicing. It freezes beautifully and any leftovers make great sandwiches!

RICH BEEF STEW

A colorful winter dish. It is unique because rather than including the vegetables in the stew, they are used as toppings. Use your imagination as to what toppings you might prefer - like making your own sundae! Great company idea.

4 pounds boneless lean beef, cut into 1½-inch cubes	2 tablespoons catsup
1 medium onion, chopped	2 tablespoons vinegar
1 clove garlic, minced	½ teaspoon dried oregano
3 tablespoons butter or oil	Cooked rice
½ cup soy sauce	Toppings: Sour cream, sliced green onions, chopped green peppers, chopped fresh tomato, sliced fresh mushrooms
½ cup dry red wine	

1. In a large Dutch oven, brown meat in oil a few pieces at a time. Remove all meat and reserve.
2. Sauté onion and garlic in Dutch oven adding more oil or butter if needed.
3. Return meat to pan and add all remaining ingredients except rice. Simmer until meat is tender, at least 1 hour.
4. Serve stew over rice and garnish with desired toppings.

8 servings

LEMON MARINATED CHUCK ROAST

A great alternative to pot roast. The marinade tenderizes the chuck roast as well as giving it a tangy, fresh flavor. So don't just think of a chuck roast for a winter meal - buy one this summer for the grill!

1 4-pound beef chuck roast, 1½ inches thick	4 teaspoons sugar
Marinade:	Dash garlic salt
1 teaspoon grated lemon zest	1 teaspoon Worcestershire sauce
½ cup lemon juice	½ teaspoon prepared mustard
⅓ cup cooking oil	⅛ teaspoon pepper
2 tablespoons sliced green onions with tops or 2 tablespoons chopped onion	

1. Score fat edges of roast.
2. Place meat in shallow baking dish. Combine ingredients for marinade and pour over roast. Marinate roast 24 hours, turning several times.
3. Remove roast from marinade, reserving marinade.
4. Pat excess moisture from roast with paper toweling.
5. Grill roast over medium hot coals approximately 10 minutes per side, or until cooked to desired degree of doneness.

6. Heat reserved marinade. Remove roast to serving platter. Carve across the grain into thin slices. Spoon marinade over.

6-8 servings

Hints: Good with green salad and Noodles Romanoff.
Can be cooked in the oven. Other cuts of beef can be used also.

STIFADO-GREEK STEW

3 pounds lean beef, cut into 1½-inch cubes	1 tablespoon brown sugar
Salt	1 clove garlic, minced
Pepper	1 bay leaf
½ cup butter	1 medium cinnamon stick
2½ cups small fresh onions, peeled	½ teaspoon whole cloves
1 6-ounce can tomato paste	¼ teaspoon ground cumin
⅓ cup red wine	2 tablespoons currants or raisins
2 tablespoons red wine vinegar	

1. Season meat with salt and pepper.
2. Melt butter in Dutch oven, heavy kettle, or crock pot with cover.
3. Add meat and coat with butter, but do not brown.
4. Arrange peeled onions over meat.
5. Mix tomato paste, wine, wine vinegar, sugar, and garlic. Pour mixture over meat and onions.
6. Add bay leaf, cinnamon, cloves, cumin, and currants.
7. Cover kettle or crock pot and simmer 3 hours or until done. Do not stir.
8. Stir gently to blend before serving.

6 servings

Hints: Great with garlic pita bread, noodles, and Greek tomato salad.
Good reheated - even better the day after it's prepared.

An easy, aromatic, delicious change of pace. The herbs and spices permeate the house and arouse everyone's curiosity as to the outcome of the pot on the stove. The jury won't deliberate long—all will agree that it's wonderful! Serve with a peppery red from the Rhone Valley of France or a Petite Syrah from California.

CHUCK ROAST WITH MUSHROOMS

Chuck roasts traditionally have a good flavor but are not always tender. This marinade makes an absolutely delicious chuck roast - one that's full of flavor and melts in your mouth.

5-6 pound chuck roast, 1½ inches thick
2 2½-ounce cans button mushrooms
Marinade:
¼ cup olive oil
¼ cup vegetable oil
1 teaspoon dried parsley
1 tablespoon salt
1 teaspoon black pepper

2 tablespoons honey
½ teaspoon dry mustard
½ teaspoon soy sauce
Dash Tabasco sauce
1 tablespoon lemon juice
2 tablespoons steak sauce
¼ cup wine vinegar
¼ cup cooking sherry
4 tablespoons catsup

1. Combine all ingredients for marinade in saucepan and heat thoroughly.
2. Place meat in a glass baking dish and pour heated marinade over it. Pierce meat with a fork; cover with plastic wrap and refrigerate for at least 3 hours. Turn meat several times while marinating.
3. Preheat oven to 350°.
4. Pour off most of marinade and reserve. Place meat in Dutch oven. Bake, covered, for 2½-3 hours. Baste occasionally.
5. Before serving, heat reserved liquid in saucepan; add mushrooms and cook for 5 minutes or until heated. Place mushrooms on and around roast before serving. Pass marinade.

4-6 servings

Hints: Can prepare as a pot roast and add carrots, celery, onions, and potatoes.
Fresh mushrooms may be substituted for canned.

BEEF STROGANOFF

1½ pounds beef tenderloin cut into ¼-inch thick strips
2 tablespoons flour
1 teaspoon salt
3 tablespoons butter
1 3-ounce can sliced mushrooms, drained, or ¼ pound fresh mushrooms, thinly sliced
½ cup chopped onion
1 clove garlic, minced
2 tablespoons butter
3 tablespoons flour
1 tablespoon tomato paste
1 10½-ounce can condensed beef broth
1 cup sour cream
2 tablespoons dry white wine
Salt and freshly ground black pepper to taste

1. Combine 2 tablespoons flour and 1 teaspoon salt. Coat meat strips with flour mixture.
2. Heat a large skillet to medium high. Add 3 tablespoons butter. When melted, add beef strips and brown quickly on both sides.
3. Add onion, mushrooms, and garlic. Cook 3-4 minutes until crisp-tender.
4. Remove meat mixture from the pan.
5. Add 2 tablespoons butter to pan drippings. Blend in 3 tablespoons flour. Add tomato paste and stir for one minute, or until smooth. Stir in beef broth.
6. Cook, stirring over medium heat until thickened and bubbly.
7. Return meat and mushrooms to pan along with any drippings that have accumulated.
8. Stir in sour cream and wine. Cook slowly until heated through. Do not boil. Season to taste with salt and freshly ground pepper.

4-5 servings

A less expensive cut of beef may certainly be used, but it is the tenderloin that makes this dish so outstanding. Serve atop hot buttered noodles or parsleyed rice. Any fresh green salad or vegetable would fill out the menu. Even people who do not prefer stroganoff find this recipe exceptional. A dish of this richness calls for an equally rich, full-bodied red Burgundy or Pinot Noir.

EASY BEEF TENDERLOIN

1 whole beef tenderloin	½ cup Worcestershire
2-3 tablespoons cracked	sauce
black pepper	Cotton twine
2-3 tablespoons garlic salt	Foil

1.   Preheat oven to 350°.
2.   Trim fat from tenderloin.
3.   Tie small end so roast will cook evenly.
4.   Mix cracked pepper and garlic salt together.
5.   Make a "boat" from 2-3 layers of aluminum foil to fit length of roast.
6.   Pour Worcestershire sauce over beef. Roll in garlic-pepper mixture and place in foil "boat."
7.   Bake in preheated oven, uncovered, for 45 minutes. Let rest 10 minutes before slicing.
8.   Serve with any sauce that suits you (i.e. mushroom, bearnaise, etc.).
9.   Beef will be medium rare regardless of size.

Yield depends on size of tenderloin.

ORIENTAL BEEF MARINADE

3-4 pounds beef: steak, roast, or cubes	1 tablespoon garlic powder
Marinade:	1 tablespoon ground ginger
½ cup soy sauce	1 cup salad oil
¼ cup plus two tablespoons honey	4 green onions, sliced
¼ cup red wine vinegar with garlic	

1.   Mix marinade ingredients in glass bowl using fork or wire whisk to ensure thorough blending.
2.   Pierce meat with fork. Place meat in plastic bag and add marinade. Secure tightly, making sure the marinade surrounds the meat.
3.   Refrigerate at least 4 hours or overnight for less tender cuts of meat.
4.   Drain meat and reserve marinade.
5.   Grill on charcoal or gas grill to desired doneness, basting frequently with marinade.

8-10 servings

Hints: Use skewers for cubes; cook roasts by indirect heat method in covered grill. Slice steaks or roasts thinly across grain.

GRILLED MARINATED CHUCK ROAST

1   3-pound chuck roast, 2
    inches thick
Marinade:
⅓ cup wine vinegar
¼ cup catsup
2   tablespoons oil
2   tablespoons soy sauce

1   tablespoon
    Worcestershire sauce
1   teaspoon prepared
    mustard
¼ teaspoon garlic powder
¼ teaspoon pepper
1   teaspoon salt

1.   Combine ingredients for marinade. Place meat in a
shallow pan and pour marinade over meat. Coat both sides
well. Cover and refrigerate for at least 3 hours. Turn
occasionally.
2.   Drain marinade from meat and reserve.
3.   Cook roast in a covered grill 10-15 minutes per side.
Baste frequently with marinade while cooking.

4 servings

*Hints: This marinade can be saved and used again. It is also
good on shish kebabs and can be made a day ahead. The longer
it marinates the better.*

*This is a great way to
use a less expensive cut
of beef. The aroma of a
marinated roast on the
grill is something
special on a hot
summer evening.*

BEEF BURGUNDY

3   pounds lean stew beef
2   potatoes, diced
2   onions, chopped
6   carrots, sliced
4   ribs of celery, sliced
2   4-ounce cans button
    mushrooms
1   tablespoon salt
1   tablespoon sugar

¼ teaspoon pepper
2   tablespoons quick-
    cooking tapioca
1   10½-ounce can tomato
    soup
1   soup can water
¼ cup Burgundy wine
1   cup sour cream

1.   Preheat oven to 300°.
2.   Combine all ingredients except sour cream in Dutch
oven.
3.   Cover and bake for 3 hours.

*With a loaf of
homemade bread, this
makes a meal. It is very
substantial, hearty fare.
A glowing winter fire
would set the mood for
this dish.*

4. Stir in sour cream, cover, and bake for an additional hour.

6 servings

Hints: Substitute fresh mushrooms for canned.
Omit potatoes and serve over noodles or rice.

SWEET AND SOUR BEEF STEW

1½ pounds beef, cut in 1-inch cubes	¼ cup brown sugar
2 tablespoons oil	¼ cup vinegar
1 cup chopped carrots	1 tablespoon Worcestershire sauce
1 cup sliced onions	1 teaspoon salt
1 8-ounce can tomato sauce	1¼ cups water, divided
	4 teaspoons cornstarch

1. In a heavy 4-quart saucepan, brown beef cubes in oil. Drain and add remaining ingredients except water, salt, and cornstarch.
2. Cook 2 hours, covered. During this time, add one cup water and the salt a little at a time.
3. After beef stew cooks, add ¼ cup cold water and 4 teaspoons cornstarch (which have been stirred together).
4. Simmer an extra 30 minutes.

6 servings

Hints: Can be made in the morning and reheated. An unusual but good "company" meal.
Good served with rice, a salad, and bread.

PHYLLO LEAVES AND GROUND BEEF

½ pound mushrooms, sliced	Oregano
⅓ cup chopped onion	1½ cups grated Swiss or Gruyère cheese
2 tablespoons butter	6 phyllo pastry leaves, thawed
1½ pounds ground beef	
Garlic salt	Unsalted butter, melted
Pepper	

1. Preheat oven to 400°.
2. Sauté onion and mushrooms in 2 tablespoons butter and remove from pan.

3. Cook ground beef and drain.
4. Return onion, mushrooms, and beef to the pan and add seasonings (garlic salt, pepper, and oregano) to taste.
5. Remove from heat, cool, and add the Swiss or Gruyère cheese. (May be prepared ahead to this point and refrigerated or frozen.)
6. Brush butter on bottom of cookie sheet or flat pan with edges. Place one sheet of phyllo on buttered surface and brush butter on top of sheet. Place second sheet of phyllo on top of buttered first sheet and repeat for six sheets.
7. Spread mixture on top of layers of phyllo.
8. Beginning with the shortest end of phyllo, roll up in jelly roll fashion. Pinch ends together. Brush entire roll with melted butter.
9. Bake for 30-40 minutes.
10. Slice and serve.

4 servings

Hint: This recipe can easily be doubled, and the entire dish may be frozen.

PIZZA CASSEROLE

1½ pounds ground chuck
Salt
Pepper
8 ounces thin noodles
8 ounces fresh
   mushrooms, sliced
1 small onion, chopped
2-4 tablespoons butter or
   margarine

1 16-ounce can tomato
   sauce
1 pound sharp Cheddar
   cheese, grated
½ pound mozzarella
   cheese, grated and
   divided

1. Preheat oven to 350°.
2. Brown ground chuck with salt and pepper. Drain and set aside.
3. Cook noodles al dente in boiling salted water.
4. Sauté mushrooms and onion in butter.
5. Combine meat, noodles, mushrooms, onions, tomato sauce, Cheddar cheese, and all but 1 cup of mozzarella cheese.
6. Pour into two greased 2-quart casseroles.
7. Top with the reserved cup of mozzarella cheese.
8. Bake for 30 minutes.

2 casseroles, 4-6 servings each

Hint: This casserole freezes well before cooking.

We are the casserole generation! And what better flavor for a casserole than pizza - especially for the smaller ones in the house. This is a different way to use ground beef - definitely not routine.

EDWINA'S ENCHILADA PIE

The popularity of Mexican food is now nationwide. Here is a very tasty Mexican dish that is not complicated or time consuming. Delicioso!

10 corn tortillas
Oil for frying
2 pounds ground beef
1 clove garlic, minced
1 medium onion, chopped
1 7-ounce can green chilies, chopped, diced, drained
1 10½-ounce can mushroom soup
1 16-ounce can stewed tomatoes
½ teaspoon chili powder
Salt to taste
Pepper to taste
1-1½ pounds longhorn cheese, shredded

1. Cut corn tortillas in quarters. Dip in small amount of hot cooking oil for just a few seconds until slightly crisp. Drain on paper towels.
2. Crumble beef into heated skillet. Add garlic and onion. Cook over medium heat, stirring occasionally, until meat loses its red color. Drain off grease.
3. Combine chilies, soup, and tomatoes. Add to meat mixture with chili powder, salt, and pepper. Mix well.
4. Arrange half of the tortilla quarters in overlapping rows in greased 9x13 inch baking dish. Spoon half of meat mixture on tortillas. Sprinkle half the cheese on meat mixture. Repeat layers ending with cheese.
5. Cover loosely with foil and bake at 350° for 45 minutes to 1 hour.

10-12 servings

Hints: Can be assembled ahead and refrigerated. Allow to come to room temperature before baking.
May be served with warm buttered flour tortillas.
Substitute packaged tortilla chips for corn tortillas.

CHIEF'S CHILI

The originator of this recipe has a large family (nine children) - thus the large quantity. The basil and cumin give this chili a unique twist. Recipe can easily be halved.

6 pounds ground beef
6 onions, chopped
9 15-ounce cans kidney beans
9 16-ounce cans tomatoes
3 15-ounce cans tomato sauce
3 tablespoons sugar
3 tablespoons ground cumin
2½ tablespoons chili powder
1 teaspoon black pepper
5 tablespoons dried basil

1. Sauté ground beef and onions. Drain thoroughly.
2. Return beef and onions to pot and add remaining ingredients.
3. Simmer for at least 2 hours. It is better the longer it cooks.

25 servings

FAN'S CHILI

2 pounds ground chuck
2 tablespoons corn oil
1 medium onion, chopped
1 cup chopped celery
½ cup chopped bell pepper
1 clove garlic, minced

2 cups fresh or canned tomatoes
1 cup tomato purée
2 teaspoons ground cumin
2 teaspoons chili powder
1½ teaspoons salt
1 16-ounce can kidney beans, undrained

1. In a 3-4 quart kettle, brown beef, drain, and set aside.
2. In same kettle, heat oil and brown onion, celery, green pepper, and garlic.
3. Add tomatoes, tomato purée, seasonings, and beef. Cover and cook for 45 minutes.
4. Add kidney beans and cook an additional 30 minutes.

2-3 quarts

Hint: Garnish top with any of the following: Sour cream, diced avocado, chopped scallions, grated sharp Cheddar.

Before football games, after football games— have people over or better yet, eat it all yourselves! This chili is great, and there are a lot of not-so-great chili recipes around. Try topping it with grated Cheddar cheese or a dollop of sour cream.

LIVER IN LEMON SAUCE

1 pound calf liver
4 strips bacon
Flour, for dredging
Salt and pepper to taste
3 tablespoons butter or margarine

2 tablespoons lemon juice
1 tablespoon fresh minced parsley

1. Fry bacon in skillet. Remove bacon, drain, and crumble. Retain bacon fat in skillet.
2. Combine flour, salt, and pepper. Dredge liver slices in this mixture.
3. Quickly fry liver in bacon fat according to your preference for doneness. Remove liver and keep warm.
4. Drain fat from skillet and add the butter or margarine. When melted, stir in lemon, parsley, and bacon bits.
5. Pour or spoon lemon mixture over warm liver slices.

4 servings

Try this simple recipe and be pleasantly surprised.

VEAL COLOGNE

There is no mystery about clarified butter. But since it is used in so many ways, here's how: melt butter over low heat. When completely melted, remove and let stand a few minutes to allow the milk solids to settle to the bottom. Skim the butter fat from the top and place in a container - this is the clarified, drawn butter.

6 veal cutlets, ¼ inch thick
6 eggs
1 cup freshly grated Parmesan cheese
¾ cup plus 2 tablespoons all-purpose flour
2 tablespoons dried parsley
2 tablespoons dried basil
1 teaspoon salt
1 cup milk
¼ cup clarified butter
24 asparagus stalks, cooked
12 ounces coarsely grated mozzarella cheese

1. In bowl beat eggs with Parmesan cheese, flour, parsley, basil, and salt. Beat milk into mixture a little bit at a time. Let batter stand covered for 1 hour.
2. Pound the cutlets between sheets of waxed paper and dust with flour.
3. Heat clarified butter in large skillet. Dip cutlets in batter and sauté them 3 at a time for 3 minutes on each side.
4. Place cutlets in a buttered au gratin dish. Top each with 4 cooked asparagus stalks.
5. Sprinkle cutlets with mozzarella, leaving asparagus tips uncovered. (May be prepared ahead to this point and refrigerated. Bring to room temperature before baking.)
6. Bake in a preheated 400° oven for 5-10 minutes, or until cheese is melted.

4-6 servings

Hints: Very good with fresh fruit and buttered noodles.
Could serve with a very rich dessert such as chocolate mousse or chocolate roll.

Company's Coming

Blue Cheese Ball with Crackers

Barley Soup

Veal Cologne   Spaghetti Verdi

Pioneer Lettuce Salad   Crispy White Braids

Mocha Pot de Crème

GRILLED LEMON VEAL

1 veal eye of round, 2-3 pounds
12-15 small new potatoes, unpeeled
1 large onion, cut in chunks
1 large red or green bell pepper, cut into 1-inch squares

Marinade:
⅓ cup oil
⅔ cup fresh lemon juice
1 teaspoon grated lemon zest
1½ teaspoons salt
½ teaspoon freshly ground pepper
1 teaspoon Worcestershire sauce
1 teaspoon Dijon mustard
2 green onion tops, sliced

1. Cut veal into 1-1½ inch cubes. Whisk together ingredients for marinade.
2. Place veal in a plastic bag. Pour marinade over meat and refrigerate 24-48 hours. Turn occasionally.
3. Drain meat. Reserve marinade.
4. Steam potatoes until almost done. Blanch onion and pepper squares 1 minute in boiling water.
5. Thread meat on skewers alternately with vegetables.
6. Grill meat over charcoal to desired doneness, 15-20 minutes.
7. Marinade is wonderful for basting or simply heat and serve on the side.

6 servings

Hints: Fettucine à la Mona Lisa and green salad are good as side dishes.
Any vegetables can be used on skewers. Try zucchini or cherry tomatoes in summer.

A favorite for special guests. The veal eye of round may have to be ordered ahead from the butcher. A veal roast may be substituted. The marinade is also wonderful on top sirloin if veal is not in the budget. If using veal, serve with a northern red Bordeaux or a Sonoma Valley Cabernet.

VEAL MARSALA

Make this on a special night when there are only two of you. A side dish of pasta really complements this delicious veal dish. The subtle but complex flavors of this dish call for a mellow, mature wine such as a well-aged Chianti Riserva or Amarone, a Pinot Noir, or even a right bank Bordeaux.

⅓ pound mushrooms, sliced
3 green onions, chopped
3 tablespoons butter or margarine
¾ pound veal (scallopini or cutlets) pounded thin

¼ cup flour (seasoned with a dash of salt and pepper)
1 tablespoon butter
1 tablespoon olive oil
⅓ cup Marsala cooking wine

1. In large skillet, sauté mushrooms and onions in 3 tablespoons of butter. Set aside.
2. Dredge veal in seasoned flour.
3. Heat 1 tablespoon butter and olive oil in skillet. Sauté veal until lightly browned on each side. Remove from pan and keep warm.
4. Return mushrooms and onions to hot skillet. Add Marsala and stir to deglaze pan.
5. Heat thoroughly. Pour over veal and serve.

2 servings

Hints: Fresh asparagus and spinach pasta tossed with garlic and Parmesan cheese are good accompaniments to this dish.

GRILLED LAMB CHOPS

Definitely one of the best lamb dishes of all. Try these chops with Parmesan Potatoes, Lemon Asparagus, and Cracked Wheat French Bread.

6-8 loin lamb chops, at least 1 inch thick
Marinade:
1 teaspoon dry mustard
5 tablespoons olive oil

3 tablespoons red wine vinegar
2 cloves garlic, minced
½ teaspoon salt
½ teaspoon paprika

1. Combine ingredients for marinade. Marinate lamb chops in refrigerator for at least 3 hours. Bring to room temperature before cooking.
2. Grill over medium hot grill for 5 minutes per side for medium rare. Baste with marinade while cooking.
3. Serve immediately and drizzle any remaining marinade over chops.

6-8 servings

LEG OF LAMB

1	4-pound leg of lamb	Salt
6	fresh garlic cloves, peeled	Pepper
		Rosemary leaves

1. Preheat oven to 300°.
2. With sharp knife, remove top layer of skin (fell).
3. Make six slits in top of lamb about ¼ inch deep. Place fresh garlic in the slits.
4. Using your hands, rub lamb with salt and pepper. Top with rosemary leaves.
5. Place in pan. Do not add water. Do not cover.
6. Cook 30 minutes per pound or until well-browned.
7. If desired, use pan drippings to make gravy.

4-6 servings

Hints: Also good recipe for a pork roast.
Serve with mint jelly.

Sometimes simplicity is best. Lamb is so good that one does not really need to jazz it up too much. "Keep it simple!" definitely applies here. Serve this lamb with a fine red Bordeaux or Cabernet Sauvignon, or an elegant French Burgundy.

LEG OF LAMB AU GRACE

1	small fresh leg of lamb (best if lamb is young, spring lamb)	Gravy:
¼	cup olive oil	½ cup butter
1	clove garlic, crushed	1 teaspoon salt
6	tablespoons dried rosemary	½ cup flour
2	tablespoons dried oregano	2 tablespoons sherry, optional
1	teaspoon black pepper	Meat juices
		Vegetable stock, optional

1. Preheat oven to 300°.
2. Brush leg of lamb with olive oil. Rub lamb with crushed garlic clove. Pierce lamb in two or three places; insert pieces of garlic clove in punctures.
3. Crush rosemary and oregano and mix with pepper. Coat leg with this mixture.
4. Place leg with fat side down on rack in roasting pan. Roast for 30 minutes per pound.

This recipe dates back to the early 1900's and is traditional Easter Sunday fare. Spring lamb is especially tender and succulent - thus the tradition. The gravy is worth the extra effort. An elegant, northern Bordeaux would be perfect with this dish. As an interesting alternative, serve a substantial Italian red like Montepulciano.

5. Gravy: Draw off fat from drippings and discard - use only the juices. Over medium heat in a skillet, melt butter. Stir in flour and salt to make paste. Stirring constantly, add meat juices and enough vegetable stock to bring gravy to desired consistency.

6-8 servings

Hints: Water or bouillon may be substituted for vegetable stock in gravy.
Nice with roasted small potatoes and salad.
Serve with mint jelly, of course!
Also good with pork roast.

HOFFMAN'S LAMB

This marinade is very complementary to lamb or pork. The thyme and rosemary blend well and the aroma is heavenly. Serve with broiled fruits such as apples and pears, an oil and vinegar salad, and plain rice for a meal that's sure to please.

3-5 pound leg of lamb
Marinade:
½ **cup Dijon mustard**
2 **tablespoons soy sauce**
3 **tablespoons olive oil**

½ **teaspoon dried thyme**
½ **teaspoon dried rosemary**
2 **large cloves garlic, minced**

1. Mix mustard and soy sauce. Beat in the rest of the ingredients for marinade and mix well. Let mixture stand for an hour or so.
2. Paint this mixture liberally over lamb. Allow to marinate for at least 1½ hours.
3. Bake at 400° for ½ hour then 350° for another hour for rare lamb.

4-6 Servings

Hints: May use fresh herbs but increase amount to 2 teaspoons.
Can also be used for pork roast.

TURKISH PILAF

2 pounds boneless lamb, cubed
4 tablespoons margarine
3 onions, chopped
¼ teaspoon cinnamon
¼ teaspoon pepper
1 teaspoon salt
1 cup rice, uncooked
2 cups water, salted with 1 teaspoon salt
¾ cup chopped and pitted prunes
½ cup raisins
1½ tablespoons butter
3 tablespoons lemon juice
1 tablespoon minced fresh parsley
½ cup slivered, toasted almonds

Put aside some extra time to make this pilaf. It's worth the effort when you need an exotic, special something to serve.

1. Place lamb pieces in heavy skillet with margarine and sauté lightly. Add onions, cinnamon, and pepper. Turn heat to low and cook, tightly covered, for 2½ hours. Add 1 teaspoon salt. Stir and cool.

2. Cook rice according to package directions.

3. Cover prunes and raisins with boiling water. Let stand 5 minutes. Drain.

4. When meat has cooled, spoon out juice, and reserve it in a small bowl. Discard congealed fat. Add fruit to meat.

5. Preheat oven to 300°.

6. Melt 1½ tablespoons butter in large casserole. Transfer fruit and meat mixture to casserole and cover with rice. Add 2 tablespoons water to reserved juice. Pour over rice.

7. Bake, covered, at 300° for 45 minutes. Check pilaf occasionally and add water if needed.

8. When ready to serve, toss and garnish with lemon juice, parsley, and nuts.

8 servings

Hint: Curried fruit is especially good with this.

LAMB CURRY

Even though lamb is
expensive, there are
times when nothing else
will do. This lamb curry
is unusually good. The
time spent to make it is
rewarded by the raves
from family and friends.
If you are
adventuresome, try a
fairly fruity red wine
like Beaujolais.
Otherwise, a European
style beer would be a
good choice.

3-4 **pounds lamb shoulder,
cut in 1½-inch cubes**
¼ **cup vegetable oil**
1 **cup thinly sliced
carrots**
3 **ribs celery, chopped
coarsely**
1 **cup coarsely chopped
onion**
2 **cups tart apples, cut in
½-inch cubes**
¼ **cup canned coconut**
½ **tablespoon minced
garlic**

2 **bay leaves**
½ **teaspoon dried thyme**
4 **tablespoons curry
powder**
¼ **cup flour**
4 **teaspoons tomato paste**
4 **cups chicken broth**
½ **cup chutney**
½ **cup cream**

1.   Preheat oven to 400°.
2.   Heat 2 tablespoons of oil in a large skillet. Brown meat
in batches and transfer to a large ovenproof Dutch oven.
3.   Add remaining 2 tablespoons of oil to skillet and sauté
carrots, celery, and onion.
4.   To meat in Dutch oven add: cooked vegetables, apples,
coconut, garlic, bay leaves, thyme, curry powder, flour, and
tomato paste. Stir until well blended.
5.   Add chicken broth and stir well.
6.   Add chutney, stir, and bring to a boil over medium
heat.
7.   Cover, place in oven, and bake for 1 hour.
8.   Remove from oven. Remove bay leaves and discard.
9.   Remove the meat and set aside.
10.   In a food processor or blender, purée the sauce.
11.   Return the meat and sauce to the pot, stir well, and
bring to a boil over medium heat.
12.   Add the cream; stir well.
13.   Serve over rice.

6-8 servings

*Hint: The traditional condiments for lamb curry are great with
this. Try peanuts, green onions, coconut, etc.*

PARTY PORK TENDERLOIN

1½-2 pounds pork
    tenderloin
Marinade:
1½ cups salad oil
¾ cup soy sauce
2 tablespoons dry
    mustard
1 tablespoon black
    pepper

⅓ cup fresh lemon juice
½ cup white wine
    vinegar
1½ teaspoons minced fresh
    parsley
1 clove garlic, crushed

1. Combine all ingredients for marinade and pour over meat. Cover and refrigerate 24 hours.
2. Preheat oven to 350° or prepare outdoor grill.
3. Drain marinade from pork and reserve.
4. Place tenderloin on rack in broiler pan or on grill.
5. Cook, basting frequently, for 30-45 minutes or to desired degree of doneness (165°F on meat thermometer).

4 servings

Hint: Serve with steamed green beans and fettucine.

An exotic twist to ordinary pork. This marinade could easily become your favorite for its simplicity and flavor. Also excellent on country pork ribs.

PORK À L'ORANGE

2 pounds pork tenderloin
2 tablespoons butter
½ cup chopped onion
1 teaspoon grated orange
    zest
⅔ cup orange juice

⅓ cup dry sherry
2 tablespoons sugar
2 teaspoons salt
Dash pepper
1 medium bay leaf
1 tablespoon cornstarch
1 tablespoon cold water

1. In a large skillet over medium-high heat, melt butter and brown meat on all sides. Remove meat and reserve.
2. In same skillet, cook onion until tender. Add orange zest and juice, sherry, sugar, salt, pepper, and bay leaf.
3. Return meat to pan and cover.
4. Simmer 1 hour 15 minutes or until tender, turning occasionally.
5. Remove meat to hot platter; slice.
6. Combine cornstarch and water. Stir into orange mixture. Bring to a boil and stir 1-2 minutes, or until thickened.

The orange juice and orange zest give this recipe an unusual flavor. It is simple to fix but has an elegant appeal. Even "picky" eaters will enjoy this very different way to serve pork tenderloin.

7. Drizzle some sauce over meat. Pass remainder.

4-6 servings

Hints: To make orange zest, grate only outer orange layer of skin. The white layer, known as the pith, has a bitter taste. Sauce is excellent over rice.
"Holds" well for a buffet.
Very good reheated.

PORK ROAST

Sometimes we get so carried away with fancy recipes that we forget the basics. This is a delicious, simple way to cook a pork roast. The herbs give gourmet flavor to a dish that's simple to prepare.

1 **4-5 pound pork roast**	1 **onion, sliced**
1 **teaspoon salt**	2-3 **stalks celery, sliced**
1 **teaspoon freshly**	**with leaves**
ground black pepper	**Fresh parsley**
1 **teaspoon dried thyme**	1 **bay leaf**
½ **teaspoon ground**	1 **10½-ounce can beef**
nutmeg	**consommé**
2 **carrots, peeled and cut**	¼ **cup dry white wine**
in 2-inch pieces	**Juice of ½ lemon**

1. Preheat oven to 450°.
2. Mix together salt, pepper, thyme, and nutmeg. Rub into roast, especially on the fat.
3. Put meat into roasting pan along with carrots, onion, celery, parsley, and bay leaf.
4. Pour consommé and wine over roast.
5. Brown at 450° for 20 minutes.
6. Reduce heat to 350° and bake, uncovered, for 3 hours, or until meat thermometer reaches 165°F.
7. During baking, prick and baste roast occasionally. If liquid evaporates, add water to the pan.
8. Pour lemon juice over the roast five minutes before removing it from the oven.

6 servings

Hint: This dish is also good cold.

SWEET AND SOUR PORK CHOPS

4   pork chops, 1 inch thick
½   cup flour
½   teaspoon salt
¼   teaspoon pepper
3   tablespoons oil
1   10½-ounce can beef broth
½   cup drained crushed pineapple
¼   cup catsup
¼   cup chopped green pepper
2   tablespoons wine vinegar
1   tablespoon brown sugar
1   teaspoon soy sauce
½   teaspoon dry mustard

1. Dredge pork chops in flour, salt, and pepper.
2. Heat oil in skillet and brown pork chops on both sides. Pour off excess fat.
3. Combine remaining ingredients and pour over pork chops.
4. Cook uncovered for 45 minutes on medium to low heat.

4 servings

Hint: Fried rice is a great side dish.

An excellent and simple sweet and sour pork recipe. The sauce can be made ahead so that you only need to brown the pork chops, pour the sauce over, and cook. The aroma coming from the kitchen will entice your family every time.

GRILLED PORK CHOPS

8   boneless pork chops, 1 inch thick
Marinade:
2   cloves garlic, minced
¼   cup vegetable oil
2   tablespoons red wine vinegar
1   teaspoon leaf sage, crumbled, or 1 tablespoon chopped fresh sage
1   teaspoon salt
½   teaspoon freshly ground pepper

1. Trim excess fat from chops, if necessary.
2. Combine ingredients for marinade. Place pork in large shallow dish and pour marinade over it. Cover with plastic wrap and marinate 4-6 hours (or all day) in refrigerator or 2 hours at room temperature. (If refrigerated, bring to room temperature before cooking.)
3. Grill over medium heat (or coals) no more than 8-10 minutes per side. Pork should be slightly pink inside. Do not overcook!.

4 servings

Hint: Nice with fruit and a green vegetable.

A great last minute, no-fuss dish, especially in summer. The marinade works well with any cut of pork. Be sure the meat is fairly thick to ensure a moist result.

SPANISH PORK CHOPS

Pork chops need not be boring. This slow cooking method enables the pork to absorb a south-of-the-border flavor. The result—a tender, juicy, and unusual entrée.

6 pork chops, medium thickness
2 tablespoons oil
½ teaspoon salt
⅛ teaspoon pepper
½ teaspoon herb seasoning

½ cup chopped onion
2 tablespoons sliced ripe olives
1 8-ounce can tomato sauce
1 4-ounce can sliced mushrooms, drained

1. In skillet over medium heat, brown pork chops in 2 tablespoons oil. Pour off drippings, reserving 2 tablespoons.
2. Season with salt, pepper, and herb seasoning. Cover tightly. Cook slowly for 90 minutes.
3. Combine onion, olives, mushrooms, tomato sauce, and reserved drippings. Pour over chops.
4. Cover tightly and cook 30 minutes.
5. Serve chops with a generous amount of sauce on top.

4-6 servings

Hint: Can substitute fresh mushrooms for canned.

ORIENTAL BARBECUED SPARERIBS

A good way to eat these spareribs is with your fingers! The marinade is equally good over chicken legs or wings, and this dish can be prepared in the oven or on an outdoor grill. All will agree they are "finger-lickin' good!"

3 pounds pork spareribs, cut into serving pieces
Marinade:
1 10-ounce jar plum jelly
⅓ cup dark corn syrup

⅓ cup soy sauce
¼ cup chopped green onions
2 cloves garlic, minced
2 teaspoons ground ginger

1. Preheat oven to 350°.
2. Heat ingredients for marinade in medium saucepan until hot.
3. Pour heated marinade over ribs and marinate for 1-2 hours.
4. Place ribs on a rack in a large foil-lined broiler pan.

5. Bake in oven for 1 hour, turning occasionally and basting with marinade.

4-6 servings

Hints: Save any leftover marinade to use again. It keeps in the refrigerator for a few days.
The marinade is especially hard to remove from pan, so be sure to line it with foil.

SWEET AND SOUR PORK

1 **pound pork, cut into 1-inch chunks**	2 **tablespoons soy sauce**
5 **tablespoons soy sauce**	2 **tablespoons cornstarch**
2 **tablepoons cornstarch**	⅓ **cup cold water**
½ **cup oil**	2 **tablespoons oil**
⅔ **cup sugar**	1 **green pepper, cut into 1-inch squares**
¼ **cup catsup**	1 **large onion, cut in wedges**
⅓ **cup pineapple juice (from chunks)**	1 **8-ounce can pineapple chunks**
½ **cup vinegar**	

1. Place pork in bowl with 5 tablespoons soy sauce and 2 tablespoons cornstarch. Let stand 30 minutes.
2. Mix together sugar, catsup, pineapple juice, vinegar, and remaining soy sauce in small saucepan. Heat to boiling. Add remaining cornstarch mixed with water. Allow sauce to thicken. Set aside.
3. Heat 2 tablespoons oil in wok or skillet. Stir-fry green pepper and onion for 2 minutes. Remove and set aside.
4. Heat ½ cup oil in wok or skillet. Fry pork chunks for 8 minutes. Drain oil from pan. Add green pepper, onion, and sauce. Heat until bubbly.
5. Add pineapple chunks and stir until heated.
6. Serve with rice.

4 servings

Hints: Stir-fried snow peas makes a good accompaniment for this dish.
Sauce can be made ahead.

This traditional dish can be assembled in no time on one of those hectic evenings when dinner needs to be quick and easy. With rice it makes a complete meal.

TRUDIE'S BRUNSWICK STEW

Grandmother Trudie's recipe could not be better. Make this in the summer when vegetables are fresh and chicken is inexpensive. It is wonderful to have in your freezer. It's good anytime but especially when the weather starts getting nippy in the fall.

2½ pound pork loin
4-5 pound hen
3 quarts canned tomatoes
3 onions, sliced
1 whole dried red pepper
2 10-ounce packages frozen baby lima beans
1 pound butter
2 16-ounce cans cream style corn
3 pounds Irish potatoes, peeled, cooked, and coarsely mashed
1 5-ounce bottle Worcestershire sauce

1. Cook meats in salted water until tender. Pull from bones. Strain broth and reserve 1 quart.
2. Place meat, reserved broth, tomatoes, onion, and pepper pod in large stock pot. Cook 1 hour, uncovered.
3. Add lima beans and butter. Cook ½ hour longer.
4. Add corn. Cook ½ hour longer.
5. Thicken with mashed potatoes until consistency suits you.
6. Stir in Worcestershire sauce.

7-8 quarts

Hint: Good with cole slaw and French bread or cornbread.

VEGETABLES IN HAM ROLLS

½ pound eggplant
5 tablespoons butter, divided
3 tablespoons flour
1 cup milk
1 cup cream
Salt and pepper to taste
½ teaspoon nutmeg (scant)
Pinch cayenne pepper

1 egg yolk
1 cup finely chopped celery
⅓ cup finely chopped onion
½ pound mozzarella cheese, cut in ¼-inch cubes
8 large thin slices cooked ham (approximately ¾ pound)
¼ pound Gruyère cheese, grated

An unusual entrée for a luncheon or light supper.

1. Peel eggplant and cut into ¼-inch cubes to yield approximately 2 cups. Set aside.
2. Melt 2 tablespoons butter in a medium saucepan. Add flour, stirring with a wire whisk. Slowly blend in milk, stirring continuously. As sauce thickens, add cream. When smooth and thickened, cook about 5 minutes more, stirring frequently. Blend in salt, pepper, nutmeg, cayenne, and egg yolk. Remove from heat and reserve.
3. Melt 2 tablespoons butter in skillet. Add eggplant, celery, and onion, and sauté for 5 minutes. Cool briefly and then add cheese cubes.
4. Preheat oven to 425°.
5. Arrange ham slices on flat surface and spoon equal portion of vegetable mixture on each. Roll slices, securing with toothpicks if necessary.
6. Butter 7¾x11½ inch baking dish with 1 tablespoon butter. Arrange ham rolls seam side down in dish. Spoon sauce over ham rolls and sprinkle with grated cheese.
7. Bake, uncovered, 10 minutes or until bubbling and lightly browned.

4-6 servings

FESTIVE ASPARAGUS

This recipe will please the asparagus aficionado in winter when fresh is not available.

2 **10-ounce packages frozen asparagus spears**
1 **cup sour cream**
½ **cup freshly grated Parmesan cheese**

1 **tablespoon lemon juice**
1 **teaspoon salt**
2 **tablespoons blanched, slivered almonds**

1.   Cook asparagus according to package directions; drain. Set aside and keep warm.
2.   In a saucepan, combine the sour cream, Parmesan cheese, lemon juice, and salt. Stir over low heat until blended and smooth; do not boil.
3.   Arrange the asparagus on serving platter. Pour sauce over asparagus and sprinkle almonds on top.
4.   Serve immediately.

4-6 servings

Hint: Fresh asparagus may be substituted. Cook asparagus just until tender.

LEMON ASPARAGUS

Asparagus at its best — simple and unadorned. No substitutes for fresh asparagus on this one please!

1 **pound fresh asparagus**
4 **tablespoons unsalted butter**
1 **tablespoon soy sauce**

2 **teaspoons fresh lemon juice**
Salt
Freshly ground pepper

1.   Trim tough ends from asparagus and slice diagonally into 1-inch pieces.
2.   Blanch asparagus in boiling water for 2-3 minutes or until crisp-tender. Do not overcook! Drain and run under cold water to stop cooking process. (May be prepared ahead to this point and refrigerated.)
3.   Melt butter in large skillet over medium-high heat. Add soy sauce, lemon juice, and asparagus. Stir-fry 3-5 minutes or until heated through.
4.   Season to taste with salt and pepper. Serve immediately.

4 servings

Hint: This simple recipe works very well with broccoli.

BAKED ASPARAGUS

1 pound fresh asparagus
2 tablespoons minced
  fresh parsley
Salt and freshly ground
  pepper to taste

1 tablespoon unsalted
  butter, melted
1 tablespoon olive oil

1. Preheat oven to 400°.
2. Wash, drain, and snap off the woody ends of asparagus.
3. Arrange asparagus in single layer in a 9x13x2 inch glass baking dish.
4. Sprinkle with parsley, salt, and pepper.
5. Combine the melted butter and olive oil, and drizzle over asparagus.
6. Cover with foil and bake for 15 minutes.

4 servings

Hint: No substitutions—fresh asparagus only!

Never fear overcooking asparagus when it is prepared this way. Use this recipe when something else on the menu requires last minute attention.

WATERCRESS HOLLANDAISE

½ cup unsalted butter
2 egg yolks
1 tablespoon lemon juice
⅛ teaspoon salt

Pinch cayenne pepper or
  dash Tabasco sauce
⅓ cup finely chopped
  watercress

1. Heat butter in saucepan until hot and bubbling.
2. Place egg yolks, lemon juice, salt, and cayenne pepper in blender. Blend quickly at high speed.
3. Remove blender cover and drizzle hot butter into eggs while blender is on high speed.
4. Add watercress and blend at low speed just to mix.

1 cup

Hint: Great topping for any fresh vegetable.

Try this no-fail blender version of hollandaise with steamed artichokes as a first course.

FRESH MUSHROOM SOUFFLÉ

Superb! An obvious choice for luncheon or a light supper, complete the menu with a green salad and fresh fruit. Don't overlook this as a delicious side dish with beef or pork.

8   tablespoons butter, divided
1   tablespoon freshly grated Parmesan cheese
1½ cups (⅓ pound) finely chopped fresh mushrooms
½   cup chopped onion
1   teaspoon dried thyme
6   tablespoons flour
1¼ teaspoons salt, divided
Pepper to taste
1¼ cups hot milk
½   cup grated Swiss cheese
6   eggs room temperature, separated
¼   teaspoon cream of tartar

1. Preheat oven to 350°.
2. Using 1 tablespoon butter, grease a 1½-quart soufflé dish and dust the bottom and sides with the Parmesan cheese.
3. In a skillet, melt 2 tablespoons butter over medium heat and sauté the mushrooms and onion for 5 minutes. Add thyme.
4. In a saucepan over low heat, melt 5 tablespoons butter; stir in the flour, 1 teaspoon salt, and a dash of pepper. Gradually stir in hot milk and continue to cook, stirring constantly, until thick and smooth.
5. Stir the Swiss cheese, mushrooms, and onions into the white sauce.
6. Beat the egg yolks and add to the sauce gradually. Cook 1 minute. Remove from heat and pour into a bowl.
7. Add ¼ teaspoon salt and cream of tartar to egg whites, then beat the egg whites until stiff but not dry.
8. Stir ⅓ of the whites into the cheese sauce, then fold in the remaining whites.
9. Spoon into the soufflé dish and bake for 55 minutes.
10. Serve immediately.

4 servings

STUFFED RED PEPPERS

4 large red peppers
½ cup butter
1 cup chopped onion
1 cup chopped celery
½ pound chopped mushrooms
1 fresh hot pepper, seeded and chopped
1 clove garlic, minced

4 ounces seasoned stuffing mix
1½ cups grated mozzarella cheese (reserve 2 tablespoons)
½ cup freshly grated Parmesan cheese
¼-½ cup pine nuts

1. Preheat oven to 350°.
2. Wash the red peppers and split lengthwise. Remove seeds and blanch peppers in a large pot of boiling water for 2-3 minutes. (The peppers should not be limp.) Remove and plunge peppers into ice water to stop cooking process. Drain and set aside.
3. Over medium heat, melt the butter in a skillet; add the onions and sauté until tender.
4. Add the celery, mushrooms, hot pepper, and garlic; sauté 3-5 minutes.
5. Add the stuffing, cheeses, and nuts and cook all ingredients 3-5 minutes.
6. Stuff the peppers with the mixture and sprinkle reserved 2 tablespoons mozzarella cheese on top. (At this point, the peppers may be frozen or refrigerated for later use.)
7. Place in a greased 13x9x2 inch baking dish and bake, uncovered, for 30 minutes.

6-8 servings

Peppers are a healthy indulgence for the dieter. One large bell pepper (red or green) contains less than 25 calories. This stuffed version is meatless, and therefore versatile— serve it as a side dish with grilled meats, a luncheon entrée or Lenten dish.

GRILLED NEW POTATOES WITH ONIONS AND PEPPERS

2 pounds small new potatoes
1 large sweet onion, Vidalia or Walla Walla
1 large green or red sweet pepper
2-3 large red or green banana peppers

½ cup unsalted butter, divided
Salt and freshly ground pepper
Fresh herbs to taste (rosemary, chives, marjoram, thyme, or oregano)

1. Steam new potatoes, unpeeled, until just crisp-tender. Cut in half, and reserve.

A simple treatment of summer's best vegetables, this combination will enhance most any menu.

2. Slice onion and green or red pepper into ¼-inch thick rings.

3. Slice banana peppers in half horizontally. Remove seeds and cut into ½-inch chunks.

4. In a large skillet, melt 3 tablespoons butter over medium heat. Sauté onions and all peppers until crisp-tender. (No longer than 10 minutes.)

5. Preheat charcoal or gas grill to medium heat.

6. Layer 3 pieces of heavy duty aluminum foil (at least 16 inches square) on top of each other.

7. Place half the potatoes in the center of foil sheet. Cover with half the onion-pepper mixture. Dot with butter and season liberally with salt, pepper, and fresh herbs. Repeat layers once more. Season again. Close foil packet securely. (May be prepared ahead to this point and refrigerated. Bring to room temperature before grilling.)

8. Grill vegetable packet for 15-20 minutes, or until heated through.

9. Serve directly from foil packet or transfer to heated platter.

4-6 servings

Hint: Use other vegetables in season, such as squash.

PARMESAN POTATOES

4 large baking potatoes	**½ cup minced fresh**
½ cup unsalted butter, melted	**parsley**
	Salt
½ cup freshly grated Parmesan cheese	**Freshly ground pepper**

1. Preheat oven to 350°.

2. Slice potatoes ⅛ inch thick. Do not peel.

3. Layer in 9x13 inch casserole dish and drizzle melted butter over slices.

4. Sprinkle salt and pepper on top and cover with foil.

5. Bake 30 minutes covered. Remove foil; sprinkle cheese and parsley on top. Bake uncovered for remaining 30 minutes. Serve immediately.

4-6 servings

These potatoes are simple to prepare yet always delicious. The crispness comes from baking uncovered in the last 30 minutes and will remind you of the adage, "You can't eat just one!"

NEW POTATOES WITH SNOW PEAS

14 small new potatoes
4 tablespoons unsalted
butter
½ teaspoon salt
1 teaspoon sugar

2 teaspoons minced fresh
parsley
2 cups snow peas
1-2 tablespoons cooking
oil

1. Scrub new potatoes and place the unpeeled potatoes in a steamer basket in a pot filled with a few inches of water.
2. Cover, bring to a boil, and steam until the potatoes are just tender, about 15 minutes.
3. In a small pan melt the butter; add the salt, sugar (if desired), and parsley.
4. Meanwhile, wash and remove any strings from fresh snow peas.
5. Using a wok or skillet, heat the oil, add the snow peas, and sauté for 2 minutes.
6. Add the potatoes and toss gently.
7. Place in a serving dish and pour butter mixture over all.

6 servings

Hint: Frozen snow peas may be used if fresh are not available. Substitute 2 boxes (6 ounces each) and follow the package directions.

Cook the new potato in its jacket—it's prettier, easier, and retains more vitamins. Cooked separately then served together, new potatoes and snow peas are a perfect combination. In summer, season with fresh herbs to taste.

POTATO NACHOS

6 medium baking
potatoes
3 tablespoons butter,
melted
Garlic salt to taste
Freshly ground pepper to
taste
4 ounces Cheddar
cheese, grated

4 ounces Monterey Jack
cheese, grated
1 4-ounce can diced
green chilies
Optional fillings:
Cooked crumbled bacon
Chopped cooked ham
Refried beans
Minced green onions

1. Preheat oven to 375°.
2. Scrub potatoes and bake until done (about 45 minutes to an hour). Cool slightly.
3. Cut potatoes in half lengthwise, scoop out ½-⅔ of potato pulp and reserve for another use.
4. Brush the interior of the remaining "shells" with the melted butter.

The potato was once called the Apple of Love. This stuffed version is wonderful with any meat, especially steak. Try any (or all) of the optional fillings for a heartier potato to serve in winter with soup. Smaller potatoes may be used to create hearty appetizers.

5. Generously sprinkle the shells with garlic salt and pepper. Top with the cheeses, followed by the chilies. (At this point, the nachos may be refrigerated for reheating later.)
6. Heat on a cookie sheet until cheese is bubbly, about 20 minutes.

6 servings

Hints: Mild pepper rings or sliced jalapeño pepper rings may be substituted for the green chilies.
For a heartier potato, add any of the optional fillings.

SPINACH MORNAY

A spinach lover's delight, this mornay is well-received by non-spinach lovers as well. It can be prepared casserole style or the filling spooned into tomato cases* (shells) and baked as individual servings.

3	10-ounce packages frozen chopped spinach	1	teaspoon dry mustard
		1	cup milk
		3	tablespoons grated Swiss cheese
Salt and pepper to taste			
4	tablespoons butter	¼	cup freshly grated Parmesan cheese
3	tablespoons flour		
Cayenne pepper		4	tablespoons light cream
1½	teaspoons Dijon mustard		

1. In a heavy saucepan, cook spinach over low heat slowly without additional water (check package directions for length of cooking time).
2. Drain thoroughly, season with salt and pepper, and set aside.
3. In a separate saucepan, melt butter, then remove from heat and stir in the flour.
4. Season the butter-flour mixture with additional salt, cayenne pepper, Dijon mustard, and dry mustard. Add the milk and blend well.
5. Return the sauce to heat, stirring until it boils. Add the Swiss and Parmesan cheeses, and light cream. Simmer 5 minutes.
6. Combine the sauce with the spinach and pour into greased ovenproof casserole dish. (May be prepared ahead to this point and refrigerated or frozen. If prepared ahead, bring to room temperature before baking.)
7. Bake in preheated 350° oven for 15-20 minutes. Remove from oven. Five minutes before serving sprinkle generously with additional grated Parmesan cheese.

8-10 servings

Hints: *See Broccoli-Stuffed Tomatoes for instructions to prepare tomato cases.

SPINACH ARTICHOKE CASSEROLE

2 10-ounce packages frozen chopped spinach	1 16-ounce can artichokes, drained and cut in half
4 tablespoons butter	1 pint sour cream
½ cup finely chopped onion	Salt and pepper to taste
	¼ cup freshly grated Parmesan cheese

1. Preheat oven to 350°.
2. Cook spinach as directed on package; drain well.
3. Melt the butter over medium heat in skillet and sauté the onions until tender.
4. Mix the spinach with the onions, artichokes, sour cream, salt, and pepper.
5. Place in a greased 2-quart casserole, stir in Parmesan cheese (reserve some to sprinkle on top), and bake for 20-30 minutes.

6-8 servings

Variation:

4 10-ounce packages frozen chopped spinach	½ cup butter, softened
	1 8-ounce can sliced water chestnuts
2 8-ounce packages cream cheese, softened	1 cup bread crumbs
	1 14-ounce jar marinated artichoke hearts

1. Preheat oven to 350°.
2. Cook the spinach as directed on package; drain well.
3. Cream together the softened cream cheese and butter; add to spinach and mix well.
4. Add water chestnuts and pour into greased 4½-quart casserole.
5. Sprinkle the bread crumbs over the spinach mixture and top with the drained artichoke hearts.
6. Bake for 30 minutes.

14-16 servings

The combination of spinach and artichokes makes this casserole an elegant luncheon or dinner choice. Recipe may easily be doubled to serve a crowd.

FRESH GRILLED CORN IN-THE-HUSK

This corn was first sampled on a riverboat ride in the mountains of West Virginia. It requires the freshest corn possible—preferably just picked. Once you've tried this method, you may never eat it any other way!

8 ears sweet corn, such as Silver Queen	Unsalted butter
Ice water	Salt, freshly ground black pepper

1.   In a very large bowl or stockpot, soak corn (in the husk) in ice water to cover for 1½-2 hours in refrigerator.
2.   Preheat charcoal or gas grill to high heat.
3.   Drain corn and place on grill. Cook, covered, for approximately 20-30 minutes, turning frequently. Corn will be tender when done and outer layer of husks will be charred.
4.   To serve, peel husks back and use them as "handles" for corn, or remove them if desired. Serve with butter, salt, and pepper.

4 servings

TURNIPS IN DIJON SAUCE

An unusual vegetable dish that is also very good cold.

2 medium turnips, peeled and diced	1 stalk celery, diced
1 medium potato, peeled and diced	Freshly ground black pepper to taste
1 carrot, peeled and diced	½ cup mayonnaise
1 onion, peeled and diced	1 tablespoon Dijon mustard
	1 tablespoon fresh lemon juice

1.   Steam vegetables until tender.
2.   Combine the pepper, mayonnaise, mustard, and lemon juice in small saucepan and heat gently.
3.   Add the vegetables to the sauce, stir, and serve immediately.

4-6 servings

LEMON BASIL CARROTS

1   pound carrots, peeled
    and cut into 2½-inch
    lengths
2   tablespoons unsalted
    butter
½   tablespoon fresh lemon
    juice, or to taste

½   teaspoon garlic salt
½   teaspoon dried basil, or
    1 tablespoon fresh
    chopped basil
Dash of black pepper

This light glaze enhances, rather than disguises, the flavor of carrots.

1. Steam carrots or cook in boiling salted water until crisp-tender. Drain and set aside.
2. Over low heat, melt the butter in a saucepan.
3. Add the lemon juice, garlic salt, basil, and pepper. Mix well.
4. Add the carrots and stir gently to coat with the lemon basil sauce.
5. Serve hot.

4-6 servings

SPICED CARROTS

6-8 carrots, peeled and cut
    into 3-inch sticks
2   tablespoons vinegar

2   tablespoons sugar
¼   cup butter
5   whole cloves

A tangy dish with a hint of cloves, these carrots would be a nice accompaniment to ham or pork dishes.

1. Steam carrots or cook in boiling salted water until crisp-tender. Drain and set aside.
2. In a separate saucepan mix the remaining ingredients and cook over low heat until butter melts and sugar dissolves.
3. Add carrots to the sauce and simmer about 10 minutes.
4. Serve immediately.

4-6 servings

BROCCOLI-STUFFED TOMATOES

Broccoli is a legacy inherited from the Romans, who referred to it as the Five Fingers of Jupiter. Be sure to include this visually appealing dish on a holiday buffet table.

6 medium tomatoes
Salt and pepper
1 bunch fresh broccoli
1 cup grated Swiss
   cheese
1 cup fresh breadcrumbs
½ cup mayonnaise

2 tablespoons minced
   onion
2 tablespoons freshly
   grated Parmesan
   cheese
Green onion fans, garnish,
   optional

1. Wash tomatoes, cut off tops and scoop out pulp, leaving shells intact.
2. Sprinkle cavities of tomatoes with salt and pepper, and invert on wire rack to drain 30 minutes.
3. Preheat oven to 350°.
4. Remove tough stems from broccoli. Blanch florets in boiling water until crisp-tender (3-4 minutes). Drain and chop coarsely.
5. Combine broccoli, Swiss cheese, breadcrumbs, mayonnaise, and minced onion; mix well.
6. Stuff tomato shells with broccoli mixture; sprinkle with Parmesan cheese. (May be prepared ahead to this point and refrigerated.)
7. Place tomatoes in ovenproof dish and bake 30 minutes.
8. Serve with green onion fans, if desired.

6 servings

Hint: Substitute Monterey Jack or Dilled Havarti for Swiss cheese.

BROCCOLI WITH PECAN SAUCE

Broccoli need never come to the table unadorned again! Try this light and unusual combination.

1 bunch broccoli
½ cup unsalted butter
¼ cup chopped pecans

1 teaspoon tarragon
   vinegar

1. Cut off and discard the leaves and tough stems of the fresh broccoli. Peel the stems and slice the broccoli into florets with short stems. Slice the remaining stems diagonally.

2. Place the broccoli stems and florets in a steamer basket over boiling water and steam covered, about 10-15 minutes or until just tender.
3. In a saucepan over medium heat, melt the butter. Add pecans and stir until lightly toasted.
4. Add vinegar and stir to blend.
5. Place the steamed broccoli in a serving dish, pour the sauce over and serve immediately.

4-6 servings

Hints: One pound of broccoli serves 3 people.
If you prefer, boil the broccoli in lieu of steaming - boiling assures a bright green color.

CHEESE AND ALMOND CAULIFLOWER

1 **small head cauliflower, cut into florets**	½ **cup blanched almonds, lightly toasted**
2 **tablespoons butter**	**Salt and freshly ground pepper to taste**
2 **tablespoons flour**	**Butter**
1 **cup milk**	
¾ **cup grated sharp Cheddar cheese**	

1. Steam or boil cauliflower florets until crisp-tender.
2. While cauliflower is cooking, melt butter in a small saucepan over low heat.
3. Add flour, stirring constantly until smooth. Blend in milk and continue stirring until sauce thickens.
4. Add cheese, stirring until melted. Remove sauce from heat.
5. Preheat oven to 200°.
6. Drain cooked cauliflower and place in a deep casserole dish. Pour cheese sauce over it and top with almonds.
7. Sprinkle salt and freshly ground pepper over all. Dot with butter. Stir several times.
8. Bake for 30 minutes.

4 servings

Even children will enjoy this creamed cauliflower au gratin style. The almonds add a special touch.

MARINATED FRESH VEGETABLES

A bonus for the busy cook, these vegetables must be prepared ahead. Many vegetables work well in this marinade, so use a variety of the season's freshest.

4 stalks fresh broccoli
10 large fresh mushrooms, sliced
1 medium green pepper, chopped
1 small head cauliflower, broken into florets
1 medium red onion, sliced thinly into rings
2 medium carrots, peeled and sliced diagonally
1 medium yellow squash, sliced

Marinade:
¾ cup sugar
2 teaspoons dry mustard
1 teaspoon salt
½ cup vinegar
1½ cups vegetable oil
2 tablespoons Italian seasoning

1. Remove florets from broccoli and cut into bite-size pieces. (Reserve the stalks for another use.)
2. Combine all vegetables in a large bowl.
3. Combine the marinade ingredients in a covered jar or salad cruet. Shake well.
4. Pour the marinade over the vegetables and toss lightly to coat.
5. Chill in the refrigerator at least 3 hours.
6. Serve in a glass bowl.

10-12 servings

VEGETABLE MEDLEY POLONAISE

¼ bunch broccoli
¼ head cauliflower
1 carrot
Seasoned salt
½ teaspoon dried basil
Buttered, toasted
  breadcrumbs

1 hard-cooked egg yolk,
  sieved, optional
Paprika
1 tablespoon lemon juice
1 tablespoon butter or
  margarine, melted

1. Cut the broccoli into bite-size florets. Peel the stems and slice thinly.
2. Break the cauliflower into bite-size florets.
3. Peel and thinly slice the carrot on the diagonal.
4. Place vegetable pieces in a glass pie plate. Arrange them so that parts which take longer to cook, such as stems, are toward the outside of the plate.
5. Cover with plastic wrap (no water is needed) and microwave on high for 5-6 minutes. (The vegetables should remain crunchy.)
6. Before serving, sprinkle the vegetables with the seasoned salt, basil, breadcrumbs, egg yolk (optional), and paprika.
7. Combine the lemon juice and melted butter, pour over the vegetables and serve.

2 servings

Hints: These vegetables may also be steamed or blanched rather than microwaved.
To prepare fresh breadcrumbs: Process 3-4 slices of bread in food processor fitted with steel blade. Melt ⅓ cup butter in small skillet over medium low heat. Add breadcrumbs and stir, continuing to cook until lightly browned.

A vegetable dish that can be prepared with fresh ingredients—even in winter. The seasonings will complement any vegetable so feel free to experiment with personal favorites.

MICROWAVED RATATOUILLE

Vegetables are particularly suited to microwave cookery, and this recipe is no exception. Try this contemporary version of a classic dish.

1 medium eggplant, cut in ½-inch cubes
1 large green pepper, cut into strips
1 large onion, sliced
3 tablespoons olive oil
1 clove garlic, finely chopped
2 medium zucchini, sliced ¼ inch thick

2-3 large fresh tomatoes, cut in wedges, or 1 16-ounce can tomato wedges, drained
2 teaspoons minced fresh parsley
1 teaspoon dried basil, or 1 tablespoon chopped fresh basil
1 teaspoon salt
⅛ teaspoon pepper
1 bay leaf

1. In a 3-quart casserole, combine the eggplant, green pepper, onion, olive oil, and garlic.
2. Cover and microwave on high for 5-6 minutes.
3. Stir in zucchini and microwave on high for 5-6 minutes.
4. Stir in tomatoes, parsley, basil, salt, pepper, and bay leaf. Microwave on medium (50% power) 8-10 minutes or until vegetables are barely tender.

6-8 servings

Hint: If using fresh herbs, adjustment may be needed for amount. Generally, you will need to use at least twice the quantity of fresh herbs as dried.

DILLED ZUCCHINI

The flavor of dill has a natural affinity for many vegetables. These crisp zucchini slices, bathed in a light sauce at the last minute, are superb with grilled fish.

4 medium zucchini
3 tablespoons unsalted butter
Sauce:
3 tablespoons sour cream
1 tablespoon dried dill weed (or 3 tablespoons chopped fresh dill)

3 tablespoons freshly grated Parmesan cheese
½ teaspoon salt
Freshly ground pepper to taste

1. Slice unpeeled zucchini ¼ inch thick.
2. Combine sauce ingredients in small bowl.
3. Melt butter in large skillet over medium-high heat.
4. Sauté zucchini slices in butter until bright green and crisp-tender, 3-5 minutes, stirring frequently. Do not overcook.

5. Pour sauce over zucchini and stir gently until heated through.
6. Serve immediately.

6 servings

GARDEN ZUCCHINI

3-4 medium zucchini,
    quartered lengthwise
Garlic salt to taste
Freshly ground pepper
Oregano to taste (fresh
    preferred)
Basil to taste (fresh
    preferred)

2-3 large fresh tomatoes,
    sliced ¼ inch thick
4-5 ounces sliced cheese
    (Provolone, mozzarella,
    American, Muenster, or
    any combination)
2 medium, sweet onions,
    thinly sliced
4-5 bacon slices

This dish is best made in summer when zucchini and tomatoes are fresh and plentiful. Reminiscent of pizza, this dish combines flavors that bring non-zucchini-lovers back for seconds!

1. Preheat oven to 350°.
2. Generously butter a medium sized shallow baking dish.
3. Place zucchini in dish and season to taste with garlic salt, pepper, and herbs.
4. Place tomato slices in a layer atop zucchini. Season again.
5. Layer cheese slices on top of tomato. Spread onion slices on top of cheese and finish with bacon strips.
6. Bake 45 minutes or until bubbly and zucchini is crisp-tender.

6-8 servings

SAUTÉED ZUCCHINI

6 medium zucchini,
    washed and patted dry
2 tablespoons unsalted
    butter
¼ teaspoon salt

3 twists freshly ground
    black pepper
Freshly grated Parmesan
    cheese

Zucchini prepared the simplest way—a salute to summer's finest.

1. Grate unpeeled zucchini.
2. Drain in colander and press out as much liquid as possible.
3. In large skillet, melt butter.

4. Add the drained, grated zucchini and sauté, stirring with a large wooden spoon for about 3 minutes. (Zucchini will turn bright green and wilt.)

5. Season with salt and pepper, top with grated Parmesan, and serve immediately.

4-6 servings

Hint: Variation: Sauté 1 clove minced garlic and/or shallots in melted butter before adding zucchini.

ZUCCHINI QUICHE CASSEROLE

Wonderful as a meatless main course—summer or winter.

1 tablespoon butter
1½-2 pounds medium zucchini, thinly sliced
1 4-ounce can sliced mushrooms, undrained
2 eggs, separated
8 ounces sour cream

2 tablespoons flour
½ teaspoon salt
1½ cups (6 ounces) grated Cheddar cheese
1 tablespoon butter
¼ cup bread crumbs or wheat germ

1. Preheat oven to 350°.

2. Over medium heat, melt 1 tablespoon butter in skillet; add zucchini and mushrooms and sauté until just tender.

3. Beat egg yolks. Add sour cream, flour, and salt; blend well.

4. In a separate bowl, beat egg whites until stiff and fold into sour cream mixture.

5. In a 12x8x2 inch casserole dish, layer one half each: zucchini, sour cream mixture, and cheese. Repeat layers.

6. Melt 1 tablespoon butter and combine with bread crumbs or wheat germ. Sprinkle on top.

7. Bake uncovered for 35-45 minutes.

6-8 servings

CRANBERRY ORANGE ACORN SQUASH

2 acorn squash, halved lengthwise and seeded
3 tablespoons unsalted butter
3 tablespoons dark brown sugar

3 tablespoons orange marmalade
¾ cup fresh cranberries, coarsely chopped

1. Preheat oven to 350°.
2. Sprinkle cut sides of the squash with salt and place cut side down in a buttered baking dish.
3. Bake 35 minutes.
4. Meanwhile, in a small saucepan over moderate heat, melt the butter.
5. Stir in the sugar and continue stirring until dissolved. Add the marmalade and cranberries. Stir to combine and remove from heat.
6. Turn the cooked squash cut side up, and place ¼ of the cranberry-orange mixture in each cavity.
7. Return to oven and continue baking for 25 minutes (or until tender).

4 servings

Hints: Squash and filling may be prepared ahead. Assemble just before baking.
Frozen cranberries may be substituted if they are thawed first.

A mouth-watering combination of some of winter's best vegetables and fruits. A must for Thanksgiving dinner but don't wait until that late in the season to try this remarkable dish.

Holiday Feast

Crab Mornay in Croustade Shells

Leek & Stilton Creamed Soup

Sausage-Stuffed Cornish Game Hens

Fresh Mushroom Soufflé   Layered Salad

Cranberry Orange Acorn Squash

Buttermilk Rolls

Almond Apricot Bavarian   Chocolate Mousse Pie

GRILLED SQUASH KEBABS

This impromptu vegetable dish was born on a summer evening when the lure of cooking outdoors was irresistible. These kebabs are wonderful companions to any grilled meat or fish and have the added bonus of being very low in calories.

1 **pound small yellow squash**	8 **small skewers (wooden or metal)**
1 **small sweet onion (Vidalia or Walla Walla)**	**Nature's Seasoning (seasoning blend)**
2-3 **large banana peppers**	**Freshly ground black pepper**
⅓ **cup olive oil**	

1. Preheat charcoal or gas grill to medium-high heat.
2. Trim squash and cut into 1-inch lengths.
3. Peel onion and cut into 1-inch squares.
4. Halve banana peppers, remove seeds and membrane, and cut into 1-inch squares.
5. Thread squash, onion, and peppers alternately on skewers. (May be prepared ahead to this point and refrigerated.)
6. Place skewers on a cookie sheet and drizzle with olive oil. Sprinkle generously with Nature's Seasoning and black pepper.
7. Grill approximately 6-8 minutes per side or until vegetables are tender. After turning once, baste with olive oil and season again.
8. Serve immediately.

4 servings

Hints: If using wooden skewers, soak them in water for one hour before threading vegetables. This will help prevent skewers from burning.
Substitute small zucchini for yellow squash, or use a combination of both.

LEMON TARRAGON GREEN BEANS

The simple taste of fresh young beans is enhanced by the addition of tarragon, lemon, and fresh Parmesan. What could be better?

1 **pound fresh green beans**	**Fresh lemon juice to taste**
2 **tablespoons unsalted butter**	**Salt and pepper to taste**
1 **tablespoon tarragon vinegar**	**Freshly grated Parmesan cheese**
	Lemon wedges, optional garnish

1. Snap off tips of beans and remove any strings.

2. Cook beans in boiling salted water until crisp-tender, 5-8 minutes. Green beans should remain crunchy. Do not overcook!
3. Drain and rinse with cold water to stop the cooking process. Pat dry. (May be prepared ahead to this point and refrigerated.)
4. Melt the butter in a frying pan and rewarm the beans in the butter. Add the vinegar, salt, and pepper.
5. Transfer to a serving dish. Sprinkle with lemon juice and Parmesan cheese. Garnish with lemon wedges.
6. Serve immediately.

4 servings

SAUTÉED FRENCH-STYLE GREEN BEANS

1 **pound fresh green beans, cut French-style**	½ **teaspoon salt**
3 **tablespoons pine nuts**	½ **teaspoon freshly ground pepper**
3-4 **tablespoons unsalted butter**	**Lemon pepper, optional**

1. Wash beans and cut, using bean slicer.
2. In small skillet over low heat, toast pine nuts until golden. Reserve.
3. Melt butter in large skillet over medium-high heat. Add beans and stir-fry until crisp-tender, approximately 5-8 minutes.
4. Add salt, pepper(s), and pine nuts. Stir; taste and adjust seasonings, if necessary. Serve immediately.

4-6 servings

Hints: Beans can be sliced ahead of time and refrigerated.
If bean slicer is not available, blanch young whole beans in boiling salted water until crisp. Drain; proceed with recipe.

An inexpensive gadget is available at cookware stores which will simultaneously string and julienne fresh green beans. With a little practice, a pound of beans can be cut "French-style" in less than ten minutes.

BEAN POT

The perfect beans for a barbecue. One tester commented: "I feel I have struck gold—my husband is such a picky eater and he loved these beans!"

4 tablespoons shortening	1 teaspoon salt
2 cloves garlic, minced	1 teaspoon pepper
3 medium onions, thinly sliced	1 16-ounce can pork and beans
½ cup brown sugar	1 16-ounce can lima beans, drained
¼ cup vinegar	1 16-ounce can kidney beans, drained
½ cup catsup	
1 teaspoon dry mustard	

1. Preheat oven to 350°.
2. In a skillet, melt the shortening and sauté the garlic and onion until soft (not brown).
3. In a mixing bowl, combine the garlic and onion with the brown sugar, vinegar, catsup, mustard, salt, and pepper.
4. Add remaining ingredients, mix well, and pour into a 2-quart casserole dish.
5. Bake 45 minutes to 1 hour, covered.

12 servings

LEMON BAKED BEANS

Lemons add a nice tang to traditional baked beans. Tart and unusual, these will be a family favorite for barbecues.

2 1-pound cans baked beans in tomato sauce, undrained	6 slices bacon, cooked and crumbled
½ cup light brown sugar	Several lemons, thinly sliced
1 tablespoon molasses	Several onions, thinly sliced
¼ teaspoon salt	2 slices bacon, partially cooked
⅛ teaspoon pepper	
¼ cup catsup	
¼ teaspoon prepared mustard	

1. Preheat oven to 300°.
2. Season baked beans with the brown sugar, molasses, salt, pepper, catsup, and mustard. Mix well. Add the crumbled bacon and stir.
3. In a buttered 2-quart casserole, layer ⅓ of the lemon and onion slices. Top with ½ of the bean mixture. Repeat once more and end with a layer of lemon and onion slices.
4. Layer top of the casserole with the partially cooked bacon.
5. Cover and bake for approximately 3 hours.

6-8 servings

MAUDE'S RED BEANS AND RICE

1	pound red beans, soaked overnight	1½	pounds pickled pork, smoked ham, smoked sausage, or any combination of the three
1	large onion, chopped		
2	large cloves garlic, pressed		Salt to taste
8	drops Tabasco sauce	8	servings cooked rice
4	bay leaves		

1. Rinse the presoaked beans; drain.
2. Place the beans, onions, garlic, bay leaves, and Tabasco in 4 quarts of water and bring to a boil over medium high heat.
3. Reduce to simmer and cook 4 hours uncovered.
4. Add meat(s).
5. Continue cooking an additional 2-4 hours or until beans are tender and sauce is thick.
6. When finished cooking, remove meat (if desired), salt to taste, and serve over rice.

8 servings

Hint: Sour cream, chopped onions, grated cheese, or a splash of vinegar and wine make delightful toppings.

Once you've sampled this dish, you will understand the current popularity of Cajun cuisine. This early recipe has been handed down through generations—eaten by rich and poor alike— and was traditionally prepared on wash day.

MEXICAN RICE

1	cup rice, uncooked		Salt, pepper, and garlic powder to taste
1	pint sour cream		
1	4-ounce can diced green chilies	10-12	ounces sharp Cheddar cheese, ½ thinly sliced, ½ grated

1. Prepare rice according to package directions.
2. Preheat oven to 350°.
3. In a large bowl, combine the sour cream, chilies, salt, pepper, garlic powder, and rice.
4. Grease a 2-quart casserole.
5. Layer ½ the rice mixture, then the sliced cheese, then the remaining rice mixture, and top with the grated cheese.
6. Bake uncovered 30-35 minutes.

6 servings

Hint: For a milder flavor, substitute banana peppers for the green chilies.

This dish incorporates mild chilies, Cheddar cheese, and sour cream, traditional Mexican condiments that lend a subtle character to rice.

FRESH MUSHROOM SALAD

California cuisine has had a tremendous impact on cooking throughout the country. This is our version of a salad that is clearly California. Make it whenever gorgeous mushrooms are available. A food processor will shorten preparation time, but slice the mushrooms by hand for the prettiest effect.

Dressing:
1 tablespoon fresh lemon juice
1 tablespoon wine vinegar
½ teaspoon dry mustard
¼ teaspoon salt (or more to taste)
¼ teaspoon freshly ground pepper
4 tablespoons vegetable oil
4 tablespoons olive oil
1 green onion or shallot, minced

1 teaspoon chopped fresh basil or tarragon (or ½ teaspoon dried basil or tarragon)
1 tablespoon heavy cream or sour cream
Salad:
1 pound fresh mushrooms, must be best quality, white with tightly closed caps
Bibb or Boston lettuce, for garnish
Cherry tomatoes, garnish

1. Combine all dressing ingredients in a glass jar with top. Shake well.
2. Rinse mushrooms, trim stem ends, and pat dry.
3. Slice very thin. If done ahead, sprinkle with lemon juice, cover with damp paper towel and plastic wrap, then refrigerate.
4. Place lettuce leaves on individual serving plates or large platter.
5. Toss mushrooms with dressing just before serving and place on lettuce.
6. Garnish with tomatoes.

6 servings

Hint: Makes a wonderful first course.

PIONEER LETTUCE SALAD

The dressing is the star in this simple salad. It is very different and quick to prepare.

1 cup heavy cream
2 tablespoons sugar
¼ teaspoon salt

¼ cup wine vinegar
2-3 heads bibb lettuce, washed

1. Tear lettuce into bite-size pieces and place in a large bowl.
2. To prepare dressing, whip cream with sugar and salt until mixture begins to thicken. Stir in vinegar.
3. Pour dressing over lettuce immediately. Toss and serve.

4 servings

19TH HOLE SALAD

Iceberg lettuce (enough for 2 servings), torn into bite-size pieces
Salt and pepper to taste
1 tablespoon freshly grated Parmesan cheese
1 cup cooked, chopped chicken or turkey breast
4 slices bacon, cooked crisp and crumbled
1 ounce blue cheese, crumbled
Cherry tomatoes, halved
Creamy French dressing or French Roquefort Dressing

1. Arrange torn lettuce on 2 serving plates. Sprinkle with salt and pepper.
2. Sprinkle each plate with Parmesan cheese.
3. Add chicken.
4. Top with bacon, then blue cheese.
5. Drizzle with dressing. Garnish with cherry tomatoes. (Do not toss.)

2 servings

Hint: Serve with bran muffins or carrot bread.

Before or after a round of golf, this salad is par for the course. It is a lovely, composed salad and provides a terrific way to use leftover chicken or turkey. Serve with an oaky California Chardonnay or perhaps a white Côtes du Rhône.

CRUNCHY MANDARIN ORANGE SALAD

Dressing:
¼ cup vegetable oil
2 tablespoons vinegar
1 tablespoon minced fresh parsley
½ teaspoon salt
Dash pepper
Dash Tabasco sauce
Salad:
¼ cup sliced almonds
1 tablespoon plus 1 teaspoon sugar
½ head iceberg lettuce
¼ head romaine lettuce
1 cup chopped celery
3 green onions, thinly sliced
1 11-ounce can mandarin orange sections, drained

1. Shake all dressing ingredients in a tightly covered jar. Refrigerate at least one hour.
2. Cook and stir almonds and sugar in skillet over low heat until sugar is melted and almonds are coated. Set aside to cool. Break apart and reserve.
3. Tear lettuce into bite-size pieces.

A solution to wintertime salad doldrums. When the produce department is less than exciting, turn to mandarin oranges and almonds to give pizazz to your salad. Sugar-coating the almonds gives the salad an unexpected crunch!

4. Place lettuce in plastic bag; add celery and onions. Fasten bag securely and refrigerate.

5. Pour dressing in bag 5 minutes before serving. Shake until greens are coated.

6. Add almonds and orange sections, shake, and pour into serving bowl.

4-6 servings

ANTIPASTO SALAD WITH GARLIC WINE DRESSING

An unusual salad that would be good at a luncheon or a late supper after a concert. The combination of ingredients makes it a feast for the eyes as well as the palate.

Dressing:
½ cup wine vinegar
1 clove garlic, halved
¾ cup vegetable oil
1 teaspoon salt
1 teaspoon Italian herbs
½ teaspoon seasoned pepper

Salad:
1 large head of romaine lettuce, torn into bite-size pieces
1 hard-cooked egg, sliced

1 small zucchini, sliced
1 small red onion, sliced
1 3¼-ounce can black olives, halved
½ pound sliced salami, quartered
½ pound Provolone cheese, diced
2-3 tomato peppers, sliced
½ pound fresh mushrooms, sliced
Freshly grated Romano cheese

1. Pour vinegar into a 2-cup jar with a screw top, add halved garlic clove, and cover. Let stand overnight.

2. The next day, remove garlic from vinegar; add oil, salt, herbs, and pepper.

3. Shake well to blend dressing.

4. Combine all salad ingredients in a large bowl.

5. Toss with dressing.

6 servings

Hint: Might include cold pasta with this salad.

FRESH BROCCOLI SALAD

Salad:
1   bunch fresh broccoli
5   hard-cooked eggs, chopped
½   pound fresh mushrooms, sliced
1   small red onion, chopped
½   cup chopped walnuts, optional
½   cup green olives, chopped, optional
½   pound bacon, cooked and crumbled, optional
¼   cup raisins, optional
Mayonnaise Dressing:
¾   cup mayonnaise
Salt and pepper to taste

2   tablespoons tarragon vinegar
2   tablespoons sugar
Vinaigrette Dressing:
1   cup salad oil
⅓   cup vinegar
½   teaspoon sugar
½   teaspoon salt
¼   teaspoon dry mustard
2   teaspoons Italian seasoning
1   clove garlic, minced
No Oil Dressing:
½   cup wine vinegar
¼   cup water
⅛   teaspoon garlic powder
¼   teaspoon crumbled dried basil
1   tablespoon honey
4   scallions, chopped

A broccoli "salad bar"—this may look confusing but give it a try. Start with broccoli, eggs, mushrooms, and onion; then choose the optional ingredients and the dressing. The bacon and raisins are especially good.

1.   For salad: Chop raw broccoli using florets and the tender part of the stem.
2.   Mix broccoli, eggs, mushrooms, onions, and any optional ingredients together in a large bowl.
3.   Pour your choice of dressing over salad, toss gently, and marinate, covered, at least 4 hours - preferably overnight.
4.   For Mayonnaise Dressing: Whisk ingredients together in a small bowl.
5.   For Vinaigrette Dressing: Mix all ingredients together in a jar; cover and shake well.
6.   For No Oil Dressing: In a small saucepan, mix ingredients; bring to a boil.

6-8 servings

SEAWELL'S SPINACH SALAD

The versatility of this salad is limitless. Try it "straight up" or put completed salad in whole wheat pocket bread for lunch. For a light supper, add poached slivered chicken to the salad and accompany with a cup of soup.

Dressing:
½ cup mayonnaise
¼ cup fresh lemon juice
½ cup olive oil
1 tablespoon tarragon vinegar
⅛ teaspoon sugar
Freshly ground black pepper

Salad:
2 quarts spinach, washed and well-drained
½ pound lean bacon, cooked crisp and crumbled
2-3 hard-cooked eggs, sliced
5 green onions, chopped
¾ cup garlic croutons

1. Combine dressing ingredients in a medium bowl and whisk to blend. Cover and refrigerate until ready to serve.
2. Tear spinach into bite-size pieces, removing any tough stems. Place in large serving bowl. Sprinkle with bacon, eggs, green onion. (May be assembled ahead to this point and refrigerated, covered.)
3. When ready to serve, whisk dressing again, if necessary; pour over salad and toss. Sprinkle with croutons.

6-8 servings

Hints: Substitute slivered ham for bacon; add sliced fresh mushrooms.
Top with lightly toasted pine nuts instead of croutons.
Dressing can be used on vegetable fillings for pocket sandwiches.

WILTED SPINACH SALAD

A nice complement to beef and a pleasant change from tossed salad.

Salad:
1 pound spinach leaves, torn into bite-size pieces
1 head iceberg lettuce, torn into bite-size pieces, optional
4 hard-cooked eggs, chopped
⅓ pound fresh mushrooms, sliced
6 green onions, thinly sliced
½ teaspoon freshly ground black pepper
½ pound bacon
Bacon drippings
Dressing:
½ cup wine vinegar
½ cup water
3 tablespoons sugar

1. Place spinach leaves, lettuce, eggs, mushrooms, and onions into a large salad bowl. Season with freshly ground black pepper.

2. In a medium skillet, fry bacon until crisp. Drain well, reserving drippings. Crumble bacon. Set aside.
3. Leave about ⅓-½ cup bacon drippings in pan. To this add vinegar, water, and sugar. Bring mixture to a boil.
4. Pour over greens. Sprinkle on bacon pieces. Serve immediately.

6-8 servings

Hint: Salad will yield more servings if optional lettuce is used.

SPINACH STRAWBERRY SALAD

Dressing:
½ cup sugar
1 tablespoon poppy seeds
2 tablespoons sesame seeds
1½ teaspoons minced onion
¼ teaspoon paprika
¼ cup cider vinegar

¼ cup wine vinegar
½ cup oil
Salad:
¾ cup sliced or slivered almonds
2 tablespoons butter
1 pound spinach, torn into bite-size pieces
1 pint strawberries, sliced

What a wonderful way to welcome spring! If you are fortunate enough to find fresh strawberries in December, this is also a beautiful holiday salad.

1. Mix dressing ingredients together in a bowl. Whisk to combine thoroughly.
2. In a small skillet, melt butter and sauté almonds in it until lightly toasted. Remove from skillet and set aside to cool.
3. Combine spinach, strawberries, and almonds in serving bowl.
4. When ready to serve, pour dressing over salad and toss lightly.

6-8 servings

Spring Brunch

Creamy Cucumber Dip   Avocado Whooper
Chicken Salad in a Cream Puff
Spinach & Strawberry Salad
Lemon Cloud Muffins
Raspberry Cream

BREAD SALAD

Serve this unusual salad pool-side when hot weather demands a cool and refreshing respite.

1   1-pound loaf white bread
½   cup diced red onion
5   hard-cooked eggs, diced
1   cup diced celery
1   7½-ounce can shrimp, drained
1   7½-ounce can crabmeat, drained
2   cups Miracle Whip Salad Dressing (or 2 cups mayonnaise)
6   tomato shells, optional

1.   Trim crusts from bread and cut the bread into small pieces.
2.   Combine bread, onion, and eggs. Cover and refrigerate overnight.
3.   Next day add celery, shrimp, crabmeat, and salad dressing. Mix well. Chill.
4.   If desired, spoon salad into tomato shells before serving.

6-8 servings

Hints: Try adding pickles, relish, and/or pimentos.
Salad may be used as a filling for sweet green or red pepper halves.

BBQ SLAW

North Carolina is famous for its pork barbecue, and true barbecue calls for a tasty slaw on the side. This is a secret recipe from one of the state's best barbecue restaurants. Catsup is the key ingredient.

½   head cabbage, grated
½   cup sugar
½-1 teaspoon ground red pepper
½   teaspoon salt
¼   cup cider vinegar
¼   cup catsup

1.   Sprinkle sugar onto cabbage and let sit until cabbage is watery.
2.   Add pepper, salt, and vinegar.
3.   Add enough catsup to make the slaw red and bind together (as if using mayonnaise).
4.   Taste and adjust seasonings if necessary—adding more sugar if too tart, more vinegar if too sweet, more pepper if not hot enough.
5.   Chill until ready to serve.

6-8 servings

Hints: Great on a barbecue sandwich or as an accompaniment for barbecue or ribs.
Try this on hot dogs.

KIDNEY BEAN SLAW

5 slices bacon
1 cup chopped onion
1 cup mayonnaise
¼ cup vinegar
2 tablespoons sugar
2 tablespoons dried parsley
1 teaspoon salt

½ teaspoon dried oregano
Pepper to taste
4 cups shredded cabbage
2 16-ounce cans kidney beans, drained
1 cup diced celery
1 teaspoon Accent, optional

1. Cook bacon, crumble, and set aside. Reserve pan drippings.
2. Sauté onion in bacon drippings until tender. Remove from heat.
3. Add mayonnaise, vinegar, sugar, parsley, salt, oregano, pepper, and optional Accent to onions. Mix well.
4. In a large bowl, combine bacon, cabbage, beans, and celery.
5. Stir in mayonnaise mixture and chill.

8-10 servings

A pleasant change from the usual slaw.

FRUIT SALAD WITH HONEY DRESSING

Dressing:
¼ cup orange juice
¼ cup vegetable oil
⅓ cup honey
½ teaspoon fresh lemon juice
½ tablespoon poppy seeds
¼ teaspoon salt
¼ teaspoon prepared mustard

Salad:
1 apple, cored and chopped
1 banana, sliced
1 11-ounce can mandarin oranges, drained
1 avocado, peeled and chopped
¼ cup raisins
¼ cup chopped walnuts or pecans

1. Combine all dressing ingredients in a jar; cover and shake well.
2. Place salad ingredients in a glass bowl and stir gently to combine.

Fruit salads are a favorite with children, but this one follows a more sophisticated plan. Try pairing it with bran muffins or ham biscuits for a light lunch.

3. Pour dressing over fruit and toss gently to coat.
4. Chill 1-2 hours before serving.

4-6 servings

Hints: Serve on Boston lettuce leaves.
Good accompaniment to baked ham.

FRESH VEGETABLE MARINADE

Very attractive looking—wonderful on a buffet table. If assembling salad more than 12 hours ahead, blanching vegetables is not necessary.

Dressing:
⅔ cup olive oil
6 tablespoons red wine vinegar
2-3 shallots, minced (may substitute green onion)
2 cloves garlic, pressed
2 teaspoons dried basil
2 teaspoons dried oregano
Salt and freshly ground black pepper to taste

Vegetables:
1 head cauliflower
2 heads broccoli
6-8 thin carrots, peeled and cut in 1-inch strips
8 large fresh mushrooms, quartered
4-6 celery stalks, diced
1 red pepper, cut in strips
½ cup sliced black olives
1 14-ounce can artichoke hearts, drained

1. Combine dressing ingredients thoroughly in a large serving bowl.
2. Divide cauliflower and broccoli into florets.
3. Blanch cauliflower, broccoli, and carrots separately for 15-20 seconds in boiling salted water. Do not overcook. Drain.
4. Toss all vegetables together with dressing in large bowl.
5. Chill at least 2 hours before serving.

8-10 servings

Hint: Substitute other fresh vegetables when they are in season.

COMPANY SALAD

Dressing:
1   cup cider vinegar
1   cup vegetable oil
1   onion, diced
1½ teaspoons seasoned salt
¾   teaspoon seasoned
    pepper
1   teaspoon Accent
1   teaspoon garlic salt
1   teaspoon dried oregano
2   tablespoons sugar
Salad:
2   9-ounce packages
    frozen French-cut
    green beans

1   14-ounce can artichoke
    hearts, drained and
    halved
1   7-ounce can pitted
    black olives, drained
    and sliced
1   4-ounce jar sliced
    pimento, drained
3   small white onions,
    thinly sliced and
    separated into rings
1½ cups sliced fresh
    mushrooms

A favorite every time it is served—an inviting combination of colors, textures, and flavors. Have this in the refrigerator when expecting house guests or take it with you to surprise your weekend hostess.

1. Combine dressing ingredients in a medium saucepan. Bring to a boil, stirring occasionally. Cool.
2. Cook green beans until almost done. Drain.
3. In a large bowl, combine beans with the artichoke halves, sliced olives, pimento, onion, and mushrooms.
4. Pour cooled dressing over vegetable mixture.
5. Refrigerate overnight or longer, stirring gently 2 or 3 times.

8-10 servings

Hint: This will keep for a long time if covered tightly and refrigerated.

SUPER SALAD

Dressing:
¾   cup salad oil
¼   cup wine vinegar
½   teaspoon salt
¼   teaspoon sugar
¼   teaspoon pepper
Salad:
1   14-ounce can artichoke
    hearts, drained and
    quartered
2   cups fresh or frozen
    peas, cooked crisp-
    tender

1   large red onion, thinly
    sliced
½   pound spinach leaves
1   head bibb lettuce
1½ heads iceberg lettuce
2   ripe avocados, sliced
1   11-ounce can mandarin
    oranges, drained
½   cup crumbled blue
    cheese

Artichoke hearts, avocados, blue cheese, bibb lettuce, and fresh spinach—it's easy to see why this is called "Super Salad".

1. Combine dressing ingredients in a jar; shake well.
2. Place artichokes, peas, and onions in a medium bowl. Pour dressing over, cover, and marinate overnight.
3. Just before serving, tear spinach and lettuce into bite-size pieces and place in a large serving bowl. Add avocado and oranges.
4. Pour marinated vegetables over lettuce. Toss.
5. Crumble blue cheese over salad and serve.

10-12 servings

Hint: 1 17-ounce can tiny peas may be used intead of fresh peas.

LAYERED SALAD

Layered salads are plentiful, but don't let that cause you to overlook this one. It combines the best ingredients from several different salad recipes, and the result is wonderful.

1 **pound spinach, cleaned and torn into bite-size pieces**
1 **head iceberg lettuce, cleaned and torn into bite-size pieces**
2 **cups fresh mushrooms, sliced**
1 **cup thinly sliced red onion rings**
½ **cup chopped celery**
½ **cup chopped green pepper**
1 **cup coarsely chopped radishes**
1 **10-ounce package frozen green peas, cooked 1 minute and drained**

1 **cup freshly grated Romano or Parmesan cheese, divided**
2 **teaspoons "Jane's Crazy Mixed Up Salt"**
½ **pound bacon, fried crisp, crumbled, and divided**
Topping:
1 **cup mayonnaise**
1 **cup sour cream**
1 **teaspoon sugar**
8 **ounces Swiss cheese, grated**

1. In a 3-quart glass bowl, layer spinach and lettuce mixed together.
2. Next, layer mushrooms, onion, celery, green pepper, radishes, and peas in that order. Sprinkle with salt.
3. Combine ½ the bacon and ½ cup Parmesan cheese and sprinkle on top.
4. Combine mayonnaise, sour cream, and sugar.
5. Spread over salad, being sure to seal the edge of the bowl.
6. Sprinkle on the remaining ½ cup Parmesan cheese and bacon.
7. Top with Swiss cheese.
8. Cover and refrigerate overnight.

8-10 servings

LAYERED POTATO SALAD

Salad:
1½ pounds medium
     potatoes
½ teaspoon salt
1 medium green pepper,
   cored, halved
   lengthwise, and sliced
1 cucumber, peeled and
   thinly sliced
1 small red onion, thinly
   sliced
1 medium tomato, peeled
   and thinly sliced

2 tablespoons minced
   fresh parsley
Dressing:
¼ cup white vinegar
1 teaspoon salt
¼ teaspoon freshly
   ground pepper
2 tablespoons sugar
1 teaspoon dry mustard
1 small clove garlic,
   crushed
⅔ cup olive oil

1. Cook potatoes in boiling salted water until tender. Cool, peel, and slice thin.
2. Layer potato slices in a bowl, preferably glass, and sprinkle with salt.
3. Layer on top of potatoes: green pepper slices, cucumber, onion, tomato slices.
4. Sprinkle with parsley.
5. Combine all dressing ingredients in a jar; shake until well mixed.
6. Pour dressing over salad, cover and refrigerate several hours or overnight. Baste several times.

6-8 servings

Hints: Potatoes may be cooked in a microwave.
To shorten cooking time, use new potatoes and do not peel.

Potato salads have been around as long as there have been picnics. This contemporary version of an old favorite combines potatoes with summer's bounty and dresses them with olive oil. Especially pretty when served in a glass bowl to let the layers show and shine.

ARTICHOKE GRAPEFRUIT SALAD

¼ cup salad oil
2 tablespoons vinegar
1 teaspoon
   Worcestershire sauce
½ teaspoon salt
⅛ teaspoon pepper
1 tablespoon chopped
   fresh parsley

1 14-ounce can artichoke
   hearts, drained and
   quartered
3 cups lettuce (2 cups
   romaine, 1 cup other
   type lettuce), torn
2 pink grapefruits,
   sectioned
1 ripe avocado, sliced

1. Combine oil, vinegar, Worcestershire, salt, pepper, and parsley. Pour over artichokes.
2. Chill 3 hours.

The inviting appearance and marvelous flavor of this salad make it a favorite of all who try it. Serve with a soup for lunch or as an accompaniment to Veal Marsala. Delicious!

3. Combine lettuce, grapefruit, and avocado.
4. Pour artichokes and marinade over lettuce mixture.
5. Toss and serve.

6-8 servings

MARINATED CARROTS

This salad is very transportable. Take it to the beach for a picnic, to a tailgate party, or to a covered dish dinner.

2 **pounds carrots, peeled and sliced**
Salt and pepper to taste
1 **medium green pepper, sliced**
1 **medium onion, thinly sliced**

1 **10½-ounce can tomato soup**
½ **cup vegetable oil**
1 **cup sugar**
¾ **cup white wine vinegar**
1 **teaspoon Worcestershire sauce**

1. Cook carrots in boiling salted water until crisp-tender; drain and cool.
2. Transfer carrots to large bowl. Add salt and pepper.
3. Combine remaining ingredients and pour over carrots.
4. Cover and marinate overnight. Will keep for 1 week refrigerated.

6-8 servings

Hints: Variations: Substitute zucchini slices for carrots.
Add 2 cups blanched, sliced fresh green beans to carrots or zucchini.

TABBOULEH

½ cup bulgur or cracked wheat
2 cups cold water
3 medium tomatoes, diced
½ cup minced fresh parsley
¼ cup chopped green onions
2 tablespoons chopped fresh mint or 2 teaspoons dried mint

2 tablespoons olive oil or salad oil
2 tablespoons fresh lemon juice
1 teaspoon salt
¼ teaspoon ground allspice
¼ teaspoon freshly ground pepper
Lettuce leaves, garnish
Cherry tomatoes, garnish
Fresh mint leaves
Lemon slices

1. Soak bulgur in 2 cups cold water at least 2 hours.
2. Drain well.
3. Combine bulgur with remaining ingredients and refrigerate for several hours before serving.

6 servings

Hint: This is attractive served on lettuce leaves, garnished with cherry tomatoes, lemon slices, and fresh mint leaves.

Tabbouleh is the star of Lebanese salads. Bulgur, or cracked wheat, is more readily available now than in the past. A simple soaking of this grain will soften it. A chewy texture will remain, affording a flattering background for most any raw or cooked vegetable, as well as leftover meat, poultry, or seafood.

LAYERED MEXICAN SALAD

1 pound ground beef
1-2 tablespoons chili powder
1 16-ounce can red kidney beans, drained
1 cup creamy French dressing, divided
½ teaspoon salt
4 medium, firm tomatoes, chopped
1 cup chopped green pepper, divided
2 medium avocados, peeled and mashed
½ cup chopped mild onion

4 tablespoons crumbled bacon bits
½ teaspoon salt
¼ teaspoon Tabasco sauce
½ cup mayonnaise
4 ounces corn chips, crumbled
3 cups sliced lettuce
4 ounces Monterey Jack cheese, grated
4 ounces sharp Cheddar cheese, grated
Taco sauce
Pitted black olives, garnish

1. In large skillet, brown beef; drain fat.

A deep glass bowl or large platter will show off this beautiful salad. It is a crowd-pleaser and makes other taco salads pale by comparison. Serve it as a light supper or an addition to a salad bar.

2. To beef in skillet, add chili powder, kidney beans, ⅔ cup dressing, and ½ teaspooon salt.
3. Simmer 10 minutes; set aside.
4. Combine tomatoes, ⅔ cup green pepper, and ⅓ cup dressing. Toss lightly. Set aside.
5. Combine avocados, onion, bacon bits, ½ teaspoon salt, Tabasco sauce, and mayonnaise. Mix well; set aside.
6. To assemble salad, layer corn chips, lettuce, tomato mixture, beef mixture, grated cheeses, and avocado mixture.
7. Chill 2-3 hours.
8. Garnish with remaining green pepper and olives.
9. Serve with taco sauce.

8-10 servings

ASPARAGUS MOLD

When your menu includes crabmeat, the occasion becomes a special one—a meal that deserves this asparagus salad. The pimentos lend color, the celery and water chestnuts give it crunch, and asparagus is the queen of vegetables.

⅔ cup sugar
½ teaspoon salt
½ cup vinegar
1 cup water
2 packages unflavored gelatin, softened in ½ cup cold water
Juice of one lemon

1 teaspoon finely grated onion
1 16-ounce can cut asparagus
1 5-ounce can water chestnuts
1 2-ounce jar sliced pimentos
1 cup finely chopped celery

1. Grease a 1½-quart mold.
2. Boil sugar, salt, vinegar, and 1 cup water.
3. Add dissolved gelatin and lemon juice.
4. Add onion.
5. Set aside to cool and congeal slightly.
6. Drain asparagus, water chestnuts, and pimentos.
7. Chop water chestnuts.
8. Place vegetables in mold and add liquid mixture.
9. Chill until firm.

6-8 servings

Hint: For a luncheon, try this salad in individual molds.

CUCUMBER AVOCADO SOUR CREAM MOLD

1   3-ounce package lemon
    gelatin
½   cup boiling water
1   cup sour cream
¾   teaspoon salt
½   cup cucumber, minced
    (remove seeds, do not
    peel)

1   cup diced avocados (2
    medium)
2   teaspoons minced
    onion
Fresh lemon juice

1. Dissolve gelatin in boiling water.
2. Add sour cream and mix thoroughly with an egg beater.
3. If desired, toss avocado with a few drops of lemon juice to prevent discoloration.
4. Combine remaining ingredients with avocado and add to the gelatin-sour cream mixture.
5. Pour into 1-quart mold and chill.

6 servings

Serve this delicious, fresh-tasting salad on a bed of lettuce garnished with sliced avocados, cucumbers, and quartered tomatoes. Be sure to sprinkle the sliced avocados with lemon juice to prevent discoloration.

GRAPEFRUIT CREAM CHEESE SALAD

4   large fresh grapefruit
3   3-ounce packages
    lemon gelatin

1   12-ounce package
    cream cheese
1½ cups mayonnaise

1. Cut grapefruit into halves. Clean out grapefruit shells completely, reserving fruit slices and juices.
2. Allow shells to dry at least 24 hours.
3. Bring 4½ cups grapefruit slices and juice to a boil in a medium saucepan. Remove from heat.
4. Pour gelatin over fruit, stirring until gelatin is dissolved.
5. Divide 2 cups grapefruit-gelatin mixture evenly among shells. Refrigerate briefly to congeal.
6. With electric mixer, combine 1½ cups grapefruit-gelatin mixture, softened cream cheese, and mayonnaise.

The success of a salad depends as much on the eye as on the palate. This stunning salad is wonderful in the winter when fresh grapefruit is at its peak. Be sure to include it on a holiday buffet table.

7. Pour over grapefruit layer in shells and refrigerate to congeal.

8. Cut grapefruit shells in half and serve (one quarter grapefruit per serving.)

16 servings

Hints: Salad can be made in a large glass bowl or ring mold instead of grapefruit shells. Garnish with lemon slices and maraschino cherries.

DILL PARSLEY VINAIGRETTE DRESSING

The tie that binds the various components of a salad into a coherent whole is the dressing—in many cases nothing more than a simple vinaigrette. Here is a classic.

1 small clove garlic, peeled
¾ cup fresh parsley leaves
2 tablespoons red wine vinegar
1 tablespoon fresh lemon juice
¾ cup vegetable oil
¼ teaspoon sugar
1 teaspoon granulated bouillon

1 teaspoon salt
2 teaspoons fresh dill weed, or ¾ teaspoon dried dill
1½ teaspoons fresh oregano, or ½ teaspoon dried oregano
Dash of Tabasco sauce
Freshly ground black pepper

1. Place parsley in bowl of food processor fitted with metal blade. With machine running, drop garlic clove through feed tube and process until parsley is minced.

2. Add remaining ingredients and process until blended, about 2 minutes.

1 pint

*Hints: A wonderful marinade for vegetables.
Good in potato salad.*

ORIENTAL GINGER
SALAD DRESSING

4 ounces peeled fresh ginger root	¼ cup soy sauce or 2 tablespoons water and 2 tablespoons Tamari sauce
½ small onion	
1 stalk celery	
1½ cups vegetable oil	1 tablespoon tomato paste
¼ cup vinegar	

1. Cut ginger, onion, and celery into small pieces.
2. Blend all ingredients in blender or food processor at medium speed for 2 minutes. Texture will not be smooth.
3. Refrigerate. Will keep at least one week.

3 cups

This salad dressing is often served in Japanese restaurants. It is unique and extremely versatile. Try it on shredded iceberg lettuce topped with grated radish or fresh spinach and sliced cucumber. One tester loved it as a topping for hamburgers.

DAD'S DRESSING
FOR TOMATO SALAD

½ cup sugar	½ cup chili sauce
½ cup vegetable oil	1 tablespoon chopped chives
1 clove garlic, crushed	
¼ teaspoon celery salt	Dash salt and pepper
½ cup vinegar	

1. Combine all ingredients in glass jar.
2. Shake well.

1 pint

In summer when garden tomatoes are wonderfully abundant, drizzle this dressing over thick slices of one of summer's greatest gifts. Also try it on a salad of fresh greens.

RUSSIAN DRESSING

This is particularly good on spinach. Don't worry that it makes a lot—this dressing will keep three to four weeks in the refrigerator.

1   10½-ounce can tomato soup
¾   cup cider vinegar
½   cup vegetable oil
1   cup sugar
1   teaspoon salt
1   teaspoon paprika

1   tablespoon prepared mustard
1   tablespoon Worcestershire sauce
1   tablespoon minced onion

Combine all ingredients in a quart jar and shake until completely mixed. (Make certain sugar is completely dissolved.)

1 quart

MOM'S THOUSAND ISLAND DRESSING

This is wonderful to have in the refrigerator. It is much better than "store bought" and is quicker than a trip to the grocery! Try it over a wedge of lettuce or on any green salad.

1   cup mayonnaise
1   cup chili sauce
2   hard-cooked eggs, grated
4   tablespoons sweet pickle relish

1   diced pimento
¼   teaspoon salt
1   tablespoon Worcestershire sauce
Fresh lemon juice to taste

1.   Combine all ingredients in a medium bowl. Stir thoroughly.
2.   Store, refrigerated, in a glass jar.

2 cups

FRENCH DRESSING

1 cup sugar
½ cup catsup
⅔ cup vinegar
1 teaspoon salt
2 teaspoons Worcestershire sauce

2 teaspoons prepared horseradish
1 medium onion, grated
1 dash Tabasco sauce
2 cups vegetable oil

1. Combine all ingredients except oil in a blender and blend well.
2. Add oil slowly, beating continuously.

1 quart

Forget the commercial variety and make your own. This will keep at least two weeks in your refrigerator.

FRENCH ROQUEFORT DRESSING

1 cup vegetable oil
¾ cup catsup
½ cup sugar
½ cup vinegar (cider or wine)
1 teaspoon celery seed
½ teaspoon garlic powder

1 tablespoon minced onion
1 teaspoon fresh lemon juice
3 ounces blue cheese, crumbled
½ teaspoon salt

1. Combine all ingredients in a quart jar.
2. Shake well.

1½ pints

When it comes to salad dressings, everyone has a favorite—but how about combining two favorites? This takes the best of French and the best of blue and makes it even better! Be sure to try this on the 19th Hole Salad.

THE BEST BLUE CHEESE DRESSING

Blue cheese dressing has always been a favorite. This recipe won more accolades from our testers than any other.

2   cups mayonnaise
1   cup buttermilk
½   pound blue cheese, crumbled
1   tablespoon Worcestershire sauce

½   teaspoon salt
¼   teaspoon pepper
¼   teaspoon garlic salt

1.   Combine mayonnaise and buttermilk. Whisk until blended.
2.   Stir in remaining ingredients. (If you prefer chunky dressing, break the blue cheese into small pieces and fold in after all other ingredients have been thoroughly mixed.)

1½ pints

Hints: Try it on baked potatoes.
Substitute Gorgonzola cheese for blue.
Will keep for at least one week in refrigerator.

LEMON HONEY DRESSING

Try this dressing on a fruit salad instead of the traditional poppy seed. For a light summer dessert, serve this dressing as a dip for skewered fresh fruits.

1   cup sour cream
3   tablespoons honey
3   tablespoons fresh lemon juice

½   teaspoon grated lemon zest
½   teaspoon salt

1.   Combine all ingredients, blending well.
2.   Chill thoroughly.

1¼ cups

MOCK SOUR CREAM

2   cups low-fat cottage
    cheese
¼   cup plain low-fat
    yogurt
1   egg
1   tablespoon lemon juice
1   tablespoon water
½   teaspoon dry mustard
¼   teaspoon white pepper
⅛   teaspoon Tabasco sauce

1.   Combine all ingredients in electric blender and process until smooth.
2.   Pour mixture into storage container and chill. Keep mixture refrigerated until ready to use.

2 cups

Hints: Food processor may be used instead of blender.
Great as a base for dips and spreads.

Containing only 14 calories per tablespoon, this sauce is a boon for the weight-conscious.

HOMEMADE MAYONNAISE

1   egg
2   teaspoons onion
    powder
¾   teaspoon dry mustard
1   teaspoon salt
2   tablespoons cider
    vinegar
1   cup corn oil

1.   Blend all ingredients except oil in a food processor or blender.
2.   Very, very slowly add the oil in a thin, continuous stream with processor running.
3.   Place mixture in a storage container and refrigerate. It will thicken.

1 cup

Hints: Very nice for a buffet.
The vinegar may be varied for different flavors.

Make a sandwich or salad special by using homemade mayonnaise. This one is very light and will not overpower the flavor of other ingredients.

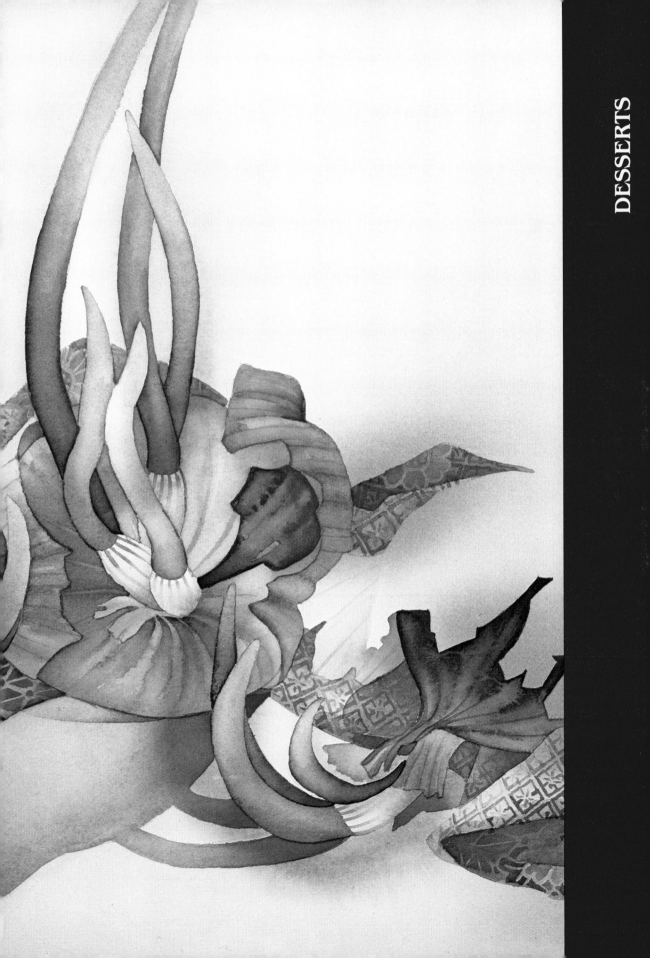

DESSERTS

DESSERTS

ALMOND APRICOT BAVARIAN

A good Bavarian cream requires some effort but the reward is certainly worthwhile, especially since it can be prepared well in advance.

Bavarian Cream:
1 **envelope unflavored gelatin**
½ **cup sugar, divided**
⅛ **teaspoon salt**
2 **eggs, separated**
1¼ **cups milk**
½ **teaspoon almond extract**
1 **cup heavy cream, whipped**

Apricot Sauce:
1 **12-ounce can apricot nectar**
⅓ **cup sugar**
1 **teaspoon lemon juice**
½ **cup quartered dried apricots**
Toasted slivered almonds

1. In a heavy saucepan, combine gelatin, ¼ cup sugar, and salt.
2. Beat together egg yolks and milk and stir into gelatin mixture. Heat gently, stirring, until gelatin completely dissolves. Remove from heat; stir in almond extract. Chill in refrigerator until it begins to gel and mounds slightly.
3. Beat egg whites until soft peaks form. Gradually add remaining sugar (¼ cup); beat until stiff. Fold egg white mixture into gelatin mixture along with whipped cream. Pour into shallow 2-quart serving dish or 8 parfait glasses. Chill until set.
4. In a medium saucepan, combine apricot nectar, sugar, and lemon juice. Add apricots. Bring to a boil, cover, reduce heat, and simmer 20 minutes or until apricots are tender. Chill.
5. To serve, pour apricot sauce over Bavarian pudding and sprinkle toasted almonds on top.

6-8 servings

MOCHA POT DE CRÈME

Everyone has a favorite chocolate mousse recipe, and this is ours. The combination of chocolate and fresh strawberries is a winner.

½ **cup water**
½ **cup sugar**
1½ **teaspoons instant coffee**
1 **6-ounce package semi-sweet chocolate bits**

2 **eggs**
1½ **cups heavy cream (no substitute)**
1-2 **pints fresh strawberries, garnish**

1. Combine water, sugar, and instant coffee in a saucepan and bring to a boil. Boil 3 minutes, stirring constantly.

2. Place chocolate chips in blender or food processor fitted with steel blade. Add hot sugar syrup and blend for 6 seconds. Add eggs and blend for 1 minute.
3. Whip cream until soft peaks form. Fold into chocolate mixture. Pour into 1½-quart soufflé dish or, if desired, a 9-inch square glass pan. Cover and refrigerate at least 8 hours.
4. To serve, scoop into small balls from soufflé dish or cut into squares from pan. Garnish with fresh strawberries.

10 servings

STRAWBERRY CHARLOTTE

1½ packages unflavored gelatin	6 eggs, separated
¼ cup hot water	1 9-ounce package lady fingers
1 3⅝-ounce package vanilla pudding	Light rum
1 8-ounce package cream cheese	1 quart fresh sliced strawberries or 2 10-ounce packages frozen sliced strawberries
1 cup unsalted butter, melted	1 cup heavy cream, whipped
1 cup sugar	

1. Soften gelatin in ¼ cup hot water. Cool slightly.
2. Combine pudding mix, cream cheese, melted butter, sugar, and egg yolks, beating with electric mixer until creamy. Mix in softened gelatin.
3. Beat egg whites until stiff, then carefully blend into creamed mixture.
4. Put a circle of waxed paper on the bottom of a 9-inch springform pan. Split lady fingers in half and stand around edge (curved side out) of form. Fill in bottom with remaining fingers.
5. Lightly sprinkle rum on the lady fingers. If moistened too much they will disintegrate.
6. Spoon half the batter onto fingers, arrange half the strawberries over this, and top with remaining batter. Refrigerate approximately 12 hours until firm. Refrigerate remaining strawberries in covered container.
7. Before serving, spread whipped cream on top and arrange strawberries decoratively. Remove from pan and serve at once on cake stand or plate.

10-12 servings

A charlotte is always an impressive dessert. This one is no exception.

TONKONISE

Calling all chocolate lovers! This rich, lavish dessert is irresistible.

3 eggs, separated
1 cup confectioners' sugar
3 ounces unsweetened chocolate, melted
1 teaspoon vanilla extract
1 dozen lady fingers, split
1 cup heavy cream, whipped
1 10-ounce jar maraschino cherries
½ cup broken walnuts or pecans

1. Beat egg yolks; add sugar and beat 1 minute with mixer. Quickly blend in melted chocolate and vanilla. Work fast; mixture gets firm quickly.
2. Beat egg whites until stiff but not dry. Fold into chocolate mixture.
3. On a cake platter or in 9-inch springform pan, layer ⅓ of split lady fingers. Spread with ⅓ of chocolate filling. Continue for three layers. Turn lady fingers in alternating directions with each layer. (Can be made ahead to this point. Cover and refrigerate.)
4. Prior to serving, remove band from springform pan, if used. Frost entire tonkonise with whipped cream. Garnish with cherries and nuts.

6-8 servings

Hints: This dessert is even better if refrigerated overnight. Use red and green cherries for Christmas.

Rites of Spring

Herbed Boursin with Crackers

Spring Soup

Grilled Lamb Chops   Layered Vegetable Salad

Lemon Asparagus   Braided Dill Bread

Strawberry Charlotte

PRUNE BAVARIAN

½ cup granulated sugar	¼ teaspoon salt
1 envelope unflavored gelatin	¼ teaspoon cream of tartar
1¼ cups orange juice, preferably fresh	¼ cup sugar
	1 cup heavy cream
1½ teaspoons grated orange zest	1 cup finely chopped, cooked prunes
3 large eggs, separated	Whipped cream, garnish

1. Combine ½ cup sugar with gelatin in a double boiler. Stir in orange juice and zest.
2. Beat egg yolks lightly and add to orange gelatin mixture. Cook over hot water for 8-10 minutes, stirring constantly until mixture thickens slightly. Do not boil.
3. Remove top of double boiler and refrigerate to chill, stirring occasionally until mixture begins to set.
4. With electric mixer beat egg whites, salt, and cream of tartar until soft peaks form. Beat in ¼ cup sugar one tablespoon at a time until a stiff meringue is formed.
5. Whip cream to soft peaks.
6. Fold prunes into orange mixture. Fold in meringue and whipped cream.
7. Rinse a 1-quart melon shaped mold with cold water. (Do not oil mold.) Pour Bavarian cream into mold and chill 12 hours before unmolding onto platter. (If served in sherbet glasses the Bavarian needs to be chilled only 4 hours.)
8. Garnish with dollop of whipped cream.

6-8 servings

Hint: You can put pudding in a lady finger-lined 9-inch springform pan: Split lady fingers, put curved sides against the form. To cover bottom, trim end of lady fingers to a point and fit them around like spokes of a wheel. A circle of lady fingers can be placed in the center. Refrigerate 12 hours before unmolding.

Forget any ideas you have about prunes— this Bavarian is scrumptious.

CARAMEL FLAN

This is an exceptionally smooth, creamy flan with a great deal of character. For a seasonal touch, try serving with fresh fruit.

⅓ cup sugar
4 eggs
½ cup sugar
¼ teaspoon salt
⅛ teaspoon ground cinnamon

⅔ cup water
1 13-ounce can evaporated milk, undiluted
1 teaspoon vanilla extract

1. Preheat oven to 350°.
2. In a small heavy saucepan over medium heat, stir the ⅓ cup sugar constantly until it has melted to a golden-brown syrup. Quickly spoon equal amounts of the syrup into each of six 6-ounce custard cups to coat the bottom. Set aside.
3. Slightly beat eggs with ½ cup sugar, salt, and cinnamon. Stir in water, milk, and vanilla.
4. Pour equal amounts of egg mixture into each of the prepared custard cups. Place cups in a large baking pan. Place in oven and fill pan with hot water to within ¾ inch of tops of cups.
5. Bake 35-40 minutes or until a knife inserted in the center comes out clean. Remove custard cups from the water immediately. Cool slightly, then chill thoroughly in refrigerator.
6. To serve, run knife around edge of each custard cup. Turn onto individual dessert plates.

6 servings

PECAN CREAM ROLL

6   eggs, separated
⅔   cup sugar
1½ cups finely chopped
    pecans
1   teaspoon baking
    powder

1½ cups heavy cream
1   cup confectioners'
    sugar
1   teaspoon vanilla

1.   Preheat oven to 350°.
2.   Beat egg whites until stiff.
3.   In separate bowl, cream yolks with sugar. Add nuts and baking powder; mix well.
4.   Fold in egg whites.
5.   Grease a sheet of aluminum foil the same size as a jelly roll pan. Take care not to tear the foil or crinkle it too much. Place foil in pan; spread mixture onto foil. Bake in preheated oven for 20 minutes.
6.   Cool on rack. Gently loosen edges of foil. Cover with a damp cloth and refrigerate until ready to use.
7.   Prior to serving, beat 1½ cups heavy cream and add confectioners' sugar. Continue beating until mixture is stiff and of spreading consistency. Stir in vanilla.
8.   Remove foil from cake. Trim off any hard edges. Spread with whipped cream, then roll. Dust with confectioners' sugar and serve.

10 servings

Hint: During the summer, put finely sliced strawberries into the whipped cream before spreading it on the roll. Then garnish with whole fresh strawberries.

This easy, light dessert has a gourmet flair. Great summertime fare served with seasonal fresh fruit.

RASPBERRY CREAM

1   envelope unflavored
    gelatin
1   cup cold water
1   pint heavy cream
¾-1 cup sugar to taste
1   pint commercial sour
    cream

2   teaspoons vanilla
    extract
2   6-ounce packages
    frozen raspberries,
    thawed

1.   Sprinkle gelatin onto one cup of water and let sit until it dissolves.

This is truly a luscious dessert that is simple, yet sophisticated. Only the unique flavor of raspberries will work with this cream. No other fruit will do.

2. Combine heavy cream and sugar in top of double boiler and warm until sugar is dissolved.
3. Add gelatin to heavy cream mixture in double boiler. Stir to dissolve gelatin; do not allow mixture to get hot.
4. Refrigerate mixture in double boiler top for 2-3 hours to thicken slightly. If it gets lumpy, whisk it.
5. Mix sour cream and vanilla. Combine with heavy cream mixture using wooden spoon. Mix well.
6. Pour into 8 serving glasses. Refrigerate. (Do ahead to this point.)
7. When ready to serve, spoon defrosted raspberries and a little juice over top.

8 servings

SHERRY GELATIN

This 150-year-old recipe is unusual, light, and refreshing—the perfect ending to a heavy meal.

Gelatin:
2 packages unflavored gelatin
½ cup cold water
1⅔ cups boiling water
1 cup sugar
⅓ cup strained fresh orange juice
3 tablespoons strained fresh lemon juice

1 cup sherry, Port, or Madeira
Topping:
1 cup heavy cream
½ teaspoon vanilla extract
1 tablespoon sugar
Sprig of mint

1. Soften gelatin in cold water. Dissolve gelatin mixture in boiling water.
2. Add sugar and strained juices. When cool, add sherry. Pour into molds or bowl and refrigerate several hours or overnight to congeal.
3. Beat cream flavored with vanilla and sugar until peaks form.
4. To serve, unmold gelatin onto plate decorated with mint leaves. For individual servings, cut gelatin into cubes and serve in dessert glasses. Top with whipped cream and mint sprigs.

6-8 servings

Hint: If using cream sherry, use slightly less sugar.

PLAIN PASTRY

1½ cups sifted all-purpose flour	½ cup shortening
½ teaspoon salt	4 tablespoons cold water

1. Preheat oven to 425° if pie shell is to be baked.
2. Sift together flour and salt into medium bowl. Cut shortening into mixture with pastry blender or two knives until it resembles coarse crumbs. Sprinkle cold water over dough one tablespoon at a time and work in with fork; do not allow dough to get sticky. Gather dough into ball. Dust lightly with flour; cover with waxed paper. Chill 30 minutes.
3. Roll out dough between two sheets of waxed paper. Use short strokes moving from center of dough to outside perimeters. Carefully lift dough and reflour paper as you roll it out.
4. Remove top sheet of paper. Turn into 9-inch pan and peel off second waxed sheet. Flute edge, if desired. Prick dough for baked shell and bake 10 minutes. Leave unpricked for filled pies and bake as directed in recipes.

One 9-inch crust

Hint: This recipe may be doubled if a lattice top or double crust is needed.

FOOD PROCESSOR PIE SHELLS

2 cups all-purpose flour	7 tablespoons cold water
¼ teaspoon salt	2 tablespoons sugar, optional for sweet pastry
6 tablespoons frozen butter, cut into 6 slices	

1. Preheat oven to 425° if pie shells are to be baked.
2. In food processor fitted with steel blade, mix flour, salt, and butter for 8-10 seconds or until consistency of coarse meal.

With the advent of the food processor, pastry novices have become pastry experts. However, the original "hands-on" method is still preferred by many cooks. Here is a sampling of recipes which includes both methods.

3. While processor is running, pour cold water steadily into feed tube until ball of dough forms on blades. If dough feels too soft, 2 tablespoons additional flour may be added and processed 5 seconds.

4. Turn onto waxed paper. Divide and shape into 2 flat disks. Wrap in plastic wrap or waxed paper and chill in refrigerator 30 minutes or more. (May freeze at this point for later use.)

5. To roll out dough, allow to soften at room temperature. Roll out on floured surface ⅛ inch thick. Fit into 8 or 9-inch pie pans. Fill and bake as directed. For baked shells, prick bottom with fork and bake for 10 minutes until lightly browned.

Two 8 or 9-inch pie shells

BROWN SUGAR PECAN CRUST

1 cup sifted all-purpose flour	1 cup chopped pecans
½ cup butter or margarine, softened	¼ cup brown sugar

1. Preheat oven to 350°.

2. Mix flour, sugar, and pecans. Add butter and stir to combine. Mixture will be crumbly.

3. Press into bottom and sides of a greased 9-inch deep dish pie pan.

4. Bake for 10 minutes. Let cool to room temperature.

One 9-inch deep dish pie crust

Hint: Try this pie shell with your favorite chocolate filling.

VINEGAR PIE CRUST

4 cups all-purpose flour	½ cup water
1 tablespoon sugar	2 tablespoons cider
2 teaspoons salt	vinegar
1¾ cups shortening	1 egg

1. Preheat oven to 425° if pie shells are to be baked.
2. In large bowl mix flour, salt, and sugar together. Cut in shortening until mixture resembles coarse crumbs.
3. Combine water, vinegar, and egg. Beat mixture with a fork. Gradually pour egg mixture into dry ingredients. Mix until pastry holds together; dough will be slightly sticky.
4. Divide into four flat disks and dust lightly with flour. Cover with waxed paper. Chill one hour.
5. Roll out on floured surface to fit four 9-inch pie pans.
6. Place dough in pans. For baked shell, prick crust and bake for 10 minutes. Leave unpricked for filled pies and bake as directed in recipes.

Four 9-inch pie crusts

TART PASTRY

1⅓ cups sifted all-purpose flour	¾ cup butter or margarine
⅓ cup sugar	1 slightly beaten egg
¼ teaspoon salt	

1. Sift flour, sugar, and salt into medium bowl. Cut in butter with pastry blender until coarse crumbs form. Stir in egg with fork. Knead slightly with hands until mixture holds together. Wrap in waxed paper; chill 2-3 hours.
2. Preheat oven to 375°.
3. Roll out dough on lightly floured surface. Using sharp edged tart shells, cut with shells and fit into shell pan bottoms. Press a similarly shaped empty mold on top of pastry. Place both on cookie sheet and bake for 5 minutes. Remove empty mold and prick shell with fork. Return to oven and bake 5 minutes longer. Remove to cool on racks.

2 dozen 1½-inch tarts or one 9-inch tart shell

Hint: Can use unbaked shells in filled tart recipes.

WHISKEY PIE CRUST

This pie crust is good with mincemeat, raisin, or apple filling. It is very easy to roll out.

1 **cup all-purpose flour**
½ **teaspoon salt**

⅓ **cup shortening**
2 **tablespoons whiskey**

1. Preheat oven to 425° if pie shell is to be baked.
2. Mix flour and salt together with fork.
3. Cut in shortening with a pastry blender until dough forms balls the size of peas.
4. Sprinkle with whiskey. Form ball of dough. Wrap dough in waxed paper and chill in refrigerator for 1 hour.
5. Roll out ⅛ inch thick on lightly floured surface. Fit into 8 or 9-inch pie pan. Flute edges.
6. Prick dough for baked shell and bake 10 minutes. Leave unpricked for filled pies and bake as directed in recipe.

One 8 or 9-inch pie shell

CRUMB CRUST PIE SHELLS

Chocolate Crumb Crust:
18 2¾-inch chocolate wafers, finely rolled
3 tablespoons butter or margarine, melted

Graham Cracker Crust:
1⅓ cups graham cracker crumbs
⅓ cup brown sugar, firmly packed
½ teaspoon cinnamon
⅓ cup butter, melted

Cereal Crust:
6 cups unsweetened cornflakes, crushed
¼ cup granulated sugar
½ cup butter, melted

Gingersnap Crust:
1½ cups crushed gingersnaps
¼ cup sifted confectioners' sugar
6 tablespoons butter, melted

Zwieback Crust:
1½ cups crushed Zwieback toast
¼ cup sifted confectioners' sugar
6 tablespoons butter, melted

Vanilla Wafer Crust:
24 2-inch vanilla wafers, finely crushed
¼ cup butter, melted

1. Preheat oven to 300°.
2. Combine crumbs and any other dry ingredients in a medium bowl.
3. Add butter and stir with a fork until thoroughly combined.
4. Using the back of a spoon, press crumb mixture into pie pan, spreading evenly. Press a second pie pan of the same size firmly into crust, then remove. Trim off any excess crumb mixture at top edge.
5. If used unbaked, crust must be thoroughly chilled for at least 1 hour before filling, otherwise it will disintegrate.
6. For a baked crust, bake for 10-15 minutes. Cool before filling.

One 9-inch pie shell

NO ROLL PIE CRUST

1½ cups all-purpose flour
1 teaspoon salt
1½ teaspoons sugar
2 tablespoons milk
½ cup cooking oil

1. In a 9-inch pie pan, mix flour, salt, and sugar.
2. Slowly add milk and oil. Mix carefully.

Mix this one in the pie pan for an easy, delicious pie shell!

3. Using hands, pat dough outward from center along bottom and sides of pan. Crimp edges with tines of fork.
4. If recipe calls for an unbaked pie crust, cover with foil and bake at 350° for 5 minutes. If recipe calls for baked pie shell, bake at 425° for 10 minutes.

One 9-inch pie shell

Hints: Do not attempt to roll out this dough. It won't work. Good for dessert pies. Excellent for meat pies such as shepherd's pie or open-faced chicken pies.

CHOCOLATE MOUSSE PIE

Rich mousse in a crumb crust! A very sophisticated dessert.

Crust:
18 **chocolate wafers, finely rolled**
3 **tablespoons butter or margarine, melted**
Pie Filling:
1 **6-ounce package semi-sweet chocolate chips**
1 **whole egg**

2 **eggs, separated**
1 **teaspoon dark rum**
1 **teaspoon vanilla extract**
1 **cup heavy cream, whipped**
Topping:
½ **cup heavy cream, whipped**
3 **tablespoons shaved or grated semi-sweet chocolate**

1. Preheat oven to 375°.
2. Mix butter and cookie crumbs and press into 9-inch pie plate. Bake for 8 minutes. Set aside to cool.
3. Melt chocolate chips in top of double boiler. Remove from heat. Add whole egg and egg yolks one at at time, beating well. Add rum and vanilla extract.
4. Beat egg whites until stiff and combine with whipped cream. Fold into chocolate mixture.
5. Pour filling into prepared pie shell and freeze for 6 hours or overnight.
6. Transfer pie to refrigerator one hour before serving.
7. When ready to serve, top pie with dollops of whipped cream and sprinkle with shaved chocolate.

8 servings

Hint: May use graham cracker crumb shell or vanilla cookie crumb shell.

LEMON FLUFF PIE

Pastry for two single crust pies
½ cup butter
2 cups granulated sugar
Juice of 2 lemons
Grated zest of 1 lemon

6 eggs, separated
1 cup whole milk or cream
1 tablespoon corn meal
⅛ teaspoon salt

The refreshing flavor of lemon is a logical choice for desserts which follow a heavy meal.

1. Prepare and roll out pastry. Line two 9-inch pie plates. Set aside.
2. Preheat oven to 350°.
3. Cream butter and sugar with electric mixer until fluffy and lemon colored. Add lemon juice and zest. Add egg yolks, beating well. Stir in milk, then corn meal.
4. Using electric mixer, beat egg whites and salt until stiff peaks form.
5. Fold egg whites into lemon mixture.
6. Pour into prepared pastry crusts. Bake for 40 minutes until top is golden and custard is set.

Two pies - 8 servings each

GRANDMOTHER'S BUTTERMILK COCONUT PIE

Pastry for two single crust pies
2 cups sugar
½ cup butter or margarine, softened
5 eggs

1½ cups shredded coconut
¾ cup buttermilk
1 teaspoon vanilla extract

This is a lovely, rich pie guaranteed to please coconut lovers. With frozen pastry on hand, this pie can be assembled in minutes.

1. Prepare and roll out pastry. Line two 9-inch pie plates. Set aside.
2. Preheat oven to 350°.
3. Cream butter and sugar together with mixer at medium speed.
4. Add eggs, coconut, buttermilk, and vanilla extract. Mix well.
5. Pour half of batter into each prepared pie shell.

6. Bake in center of oven for 45 minutes. Great served warm or cold.

Two pies - 8 servings each

Hint: Before cooking, sprinkle top of pies with cinnamon sugar (1 tablespoon cinnamon mixed with 1 cup of sugar).

MOCHA PIE WITH PECANS

A rich pecan pie with the added bonus of chocolate and coffee. Top with lightly whipped cream or homemade vanilla ice cream.

Pastry for single crust pie
2 **tablespoons instant coffee**
¼ **cup boiling water**
2 **ounces unsweetened chocolate**
2 **tablespoons butter**

4 **large eggs**
½ **cup sugar**
1 **cup dark corn syrup**
Dash of salt
1½ **cups coarsely chopped pecans**

1. Prepare and roll out pastry. Line a 9-inch pie plate. Set aside.
2. Preheat oven to 375°.
3. In medium saucepan dissolve coffee in boiling water. Add chocolate and butter stirring constantly. Continue stirring mixture over low heat until ingredients are melted and smooth. Remove from heat and cool slightly.
4. In large bowl, beat eggs with wire whisk until lemon colored. Beat in sugar and corn syrup. Add dash of salt.
5. Gradually stir chocolate mixture into egg mixture until well blended. Stir in pecans.
6. Pour into unbaked pie shell and bake 40-45 minutes. Pie is done when knife inserted halfway between outside and center comes out clean.
7. Cool on wire rack.

8 servings

OLD FASHIONED SWEET POTATO PIE

Pastry for single crust pie
Filling:
2   **cups cooked, peeled, mashed sweet potatoes**
¼   **cup butter, melted**
2   **eggs**
1   **cup granulated sugar**
¼   **teaspoon salt**
¼   **teaspoon cinnamon**
¼   **teaspoon ground ginger**
1   **teaspoon vanilla extract**
1   **cup milk**
Meringue Topping:
3   **egg whites**
¼   **cup granulated sugar**

This pie brings to mind the country cooking of the deep South. Its delicate spiciness makes it a marvelous dessert to serve in the fall.

1.   Prepare and roll out pastry. Line a 10-inch pie plate. Set aside.
2.   Preheat oven to 350°.
3.   In a large mixing bowl combine potatoes, butter, eggs, sugar, salt, spices, and vanilla. Mix thoroughly. Add milk, stirring well.
4.   Pour mixture into prepared pastry shell. Bake for 45-50 minutes or until knife inserted in center comes out clean. Cool on rack to room temperature before covering with meringue topping.
5.   Using mixer beat egg whites until soft peaks form, then beat in sugar, one tablespoon at a time. Continue beating until sugar dissolves and mixture is glossy and stiff, but not dry.
6.   With rubber spatula spoon meringue onto pie, forming peaks. Make sure meringue touches crust edge all around pie shell. Sprinkle with a pinch of granulated sugar.
7.   Bake at 350° for 5-10 minutes until delicately browned. Cool and serve.

8-10 servings

Hints: You may substitute 1-2 tablespoons bourbon for vanilla extract.
Mash sweet potatoes in a blender or food processor fitted with steel blade. This will produce a smooth, creamy pie with no lumps.

FRENCH SILK CHOCOLATE PIE

Judith Stern, Sc.D.,Vogue magazine's nutrition columnist, once said: "Emotionally, I think chocolate should be declared an honorary vitamin." The dosage in this pie will satisfy even the most avid chocoholic.

Pie Shell:
4 egg whites
¼ teaspoon cream of tartar
1 cup sifted sugar
½ cup chopped pecans
Filling:
2 ounces unsweetened chocolate
½ cup butter, softened
¾ cup sugar

3 eggs
1 teaspoon vanilla extract
Topping:
1 cup heavy cream, whipped
2 tablespoons confectioners' sugar
½ ounce shaved unsweetened chocolate

1. Preheat oven to 275°.
2. Beat egg whites until foamy, add cream of tartar, and add sugar slowly one tablespoon at at time. Beat until stiff peaks are formed. Do not over beat.
3. Add chopped pecans. Spread in a greased 10-inch glass pie plate and bake for 1 hour. Cool before adding filling.
4. For filling, melt chocolate over low heat; set aside to cool. Cream butter and sugar for 5 minutes using medium speed on mixer. Add eggs and beat for full 5 minutes after each. Add cooled melted chocolate and beat for 5 minutes. Add vanilla and beat 5 minutes. Strict adherence to instructions is mandatory.
5. Pour filling into pie shell and chill for minimum of 3 hours or overnight.
6. Two hours prior to serving, cover chocolate mixture with whipped cream sweetened with sugar. Decorate with shaved chocolate.

8-10 servings

Hints: Variation for coconut pie crust: Mix 2 cups shredded coconut and ⅓ cup melted butter and press into 9-inch pie pan. Press second pan against crust to smooth out; remove second pan. Chill in freezer while making filling.

PAPER BAG APPLE PIE

Pastry for single crust pie
6-7 cups peeled sliced
    apples
1 cup sugar
½ cup plus 2 tablespoons
    all-purpose flour

½ teaspoon nutmeg
2 tablespoons lemon
    juice
½ cup butter or
    margarine, softened

1.   Prepare and roll out pastry. Line a 9-inch pie plate. Set aside.
2.   Preheat oven to 425°.
3.   Combine apple slices, ½ cup sugar, and 2 tablespoons flour; add nutmeg and toss to mix well. Turn into unbaked pie shell and sprinkle with lemon juice.
4.   Combine remaining ½ cup sugar with remaining ½ cup flour; mix with softened butter. Sprinkle topping evenly over apples.
5.   Place pie in large brown paper bag, folding the end over twice and clipping with paper clips. Place bag on a cookie sheet. Bake for 1 hour.

8 servings

Hints: This is wonderful served with ice cream or a slice of Cheddar cheese.
Try this "Apple Pie en Papillote." Bring it straight from the oven to the table; split the bag open for a dramatic burst of aroma.

SOUR CREAM APPLE PIE

Pastry for single crust pie
Filling:
1 cup sour cream
¾ cup sugar
1 egg
2 tablespoons flour
1 teaspoon vanilla
    extract
¼ teaspoon nutmeg
⅛ teaspoon salt

2 cups peeled, shredded,
    tart apples
Topping:
⅓ cup brown sugar,
    firmly packed
⅓ cup flour
1 teaspoon cinnamon
2 tablespoons butter,
    melted
½ cup chopped pecans

The lastest culinary trend sweeping the country is American food, and what could be more American than apple pie? Here is a sampling of the best apple pies we have tasted anywhere.

1.	Prepare and roll out pastry. Line a 9-inch pie plate. Set aside.
2.	Preheat oven to 400°.
3.	In bowl, combine sour cream, sugar, egg, flour, vanilla, nutmeg, and salt. Blend well. Stir in apples. Pour into unbaked pie crust.
4.	Bake 15 minutes at 400° in lower third of oven. Reduce heat to 350° and bake until apples are tender, about 25-30 minutes longer. Remove pie from oven.
5.	Combine topping ingredients and mix well. Sprinkle over pie. Return to oven and bake 10 minutes longer. Serve hot.

8 servings

APPLE CHEDDAR CRUMB PIE

Pastry:
1	cup sifted all-purpose flour
½	teaspoon salt
⅓	cup shortening
3	tablespoons cold water
Filling:
8	cored, peeled, thinly sliced cooking apples
1	tablespoon cornstarch
⅔	cup granulated sugar
1½	teaspoons cinnamon

½	teaspoon nutmeg
⅛	teaspoon salt
1	tablespoon lemon juice
1	tablespoon butter
¼	cup shredded sharp Cheddar cheese
Crumb Topping:
½	cup butter, softened
¼	cup shredded sharp Cheddar cheese
⅓	cup light brown sugar, firmly packed
1	cup all-purpose flour
Confectioners' sugar

1.	For crust, sift flour and salt into medium mixing bowl. Cut in shortening until mixture resembles corn meal. Sprinkle with cold water one tablespoon at a time. Mix with fork until dough forms ball. Form flattened disk; wrap in waxed paper. Chill one hour. Roll out pastry on floured surface. Fit into 10-inch deep dish pie pan. Flute edges.
2.	Preheat oven to 400°.
3.	Prepare apples. In separate bowl mix cornstarch, sugar, cinnamon, nutmeg, salt. Toss mixture over apples. Sprinkle with lemon juice and set aside.
4.	Prepare crumb topping by blending softened butter, ¼ cup cheese, sugar, and flour with fingers until crumbs are formed.

5. To assemble pie, carefully spoon apple mixture into crust. Press down gently. Dot with butter. Sprinkle with ¼ cup shredded Cheddar. Place cheese crumbs on top. Bake for 30-40 minutes. Watch pie, and if crust and topping brown too quickly, cover loosely with foil. Dust with confectioners' sugar before serving.

8-10 servings

Hints: If plain crumb pie is desired: Omit ¼ cup shredded cheese and cheese topping. Use the following: ½ cup light brown sugar, firmly packed, ½ cup sifted all-purpose flour, ½ teaspoon cinnamon, ¼ cup butter, softened. Combine all ingredients and make crumbs. Sprinkle over pie. Bake as above.

APPLE MACAROON PIE

Pastry for single crust pie
Filling:
4 cups peeled, cored, sliced apples
½ cup sugar
1 tablespoon flour
½ teaspoon salt
1 tablespoon butter

Topping:
½ cup sugar
1 tablespoon butter, melted
1 cup shredded coconut
1 egg, beaten
¼ cup milk

1. Prepare and roll out pastry. Line a 9-inch pie plate. Set aside.
2. Preheat oven to 400°.
3. Place apple slices in unbaked pastry shell. Combine flour, sugar, and salt and sprinkle over apples. Dot with butter. Bake for 20 minutes.
4. While pie is baking, prepare topping. Combine sugar, melted butter, coconut, egg, and milk.
5. Remove pie from oven. Reduce temperature to 350°. Spread topping on hot pie, return to oven, and bake 30 minutes longer.

8 servings

Sunday Night Supper

Oyster Cracker Tidbits   Texas 12-Bean Soup
Green Salad with Dill Parsley Vinaigrette
Processor French Bread
Paper Bag Apple Pie

BAVARIAN APPLE TORTE

An unusual combination of cheesecake and apple pie.

Crust:
½ cup butter, softened
⅓ cup sugar
¼ teaspoon vanilla
    extract
1 cup all-purpose flour
Filling:
1 8-ounce package cream
    cheese, softened

¼ cup sugar
1 egg
½ teaspoon vanilla
    extract
Topping:
4 cups peeled, cored,
    sliced apples
⅓ cup sugar
½ teaspoon cinnamon

1. Preheat oven to 450°.
2. To make crust, cream butter and sugar. Stir in vanilla. Add flour and mix well. Spread in bottom and 2 inches up sides of a greased 9-inch springform pan.
3. For filling, combine softened cream cheese and sugar. Add egg and vanilla, mixing well. Spread evenly over pastry.
4. In large mixing bowl sprinkle sugar and cinnamon over apples. Toss well. Spoon apples over filling.
5. Bake at 450° for 10 minutes. Reduce temperature to 400° and bake torte 25 minutes longer. Cool before removing from pan.

8-10 servings

MUD SUNDAE

The ultimate ice cream pie—dieters should be forewarned to leave the room during dessert!

Crust:
18 chocolate cream
    sandwich cookies
¼ cup melted butter
Filling:
1 quart coffee ice cream,
    softened

Fudge Sauce:
2 ounces unsweetened
    chocolate

1 tablespoon butter
½ cup sugar
4 ounces evaporated
    milk
Topping:
1 cup heavy cream
½ ounce Kahlua liqueur,
    optional
½ cup chopped pecans or
    almonds

1. With a rolling pin, crush cookies between layers of waxed paper until they are coarse crumbs. Stir melted butter into crumbs and press into bottom of an 8 or 9-inch square pan. Chill 30 minutes.
2. To prepare sauce, melt chocolate in top of double boiler. Add sugar and butter, stirring well. Slowly add milk and stir until thickened. Chill 30 minutes or more.

3. Spread softened ice cream evenly on crust. Refreeze until hard.
4. Cover ice cream with cold fudge sauce (sauce spreads easier if placed in freezer 5 minutes before spreading).
5. Whip the cream and add Kahlua if desired. Spread in swirls over fudge sauce. Garnish with nuts. Cover and refreeze for 10 hours or overnight.
6. Remove from freezer 30 minutes before serving. Cut into squares.

8-10 servings

Hints: A finishing accompaniment to this dessert is mocha java coffee.

PUMPKIN ICE CREAM PIE

Crust:
1½ cups finely crushed
    gingersnaps
1 tablespoon sugar
¼ cup melted butter or
    margarine
Filling:
1 pint softened vanilla
    ice cream
1 cup cooked pumpkin

¾ cup sugar
½ teaspoon ground ginger
½ teaspoon cinnamon
½ teaspoon salt
¼ teaspoon nutmeg
1 cup heavy cream
½ teaspoon vanilla
    extract
**Pecan halves, optional
    garnish**

An unusual dessert that provides that great "fall pumpkin taste" in hot summer months.

1. Preheat oven to 300°.
2. To prepare crust, combine cookie crumbs with sugar, then add butter.
3. Press crust firmly onto sides and bottom of 9-inch pie pan. Bake 12-15 minutes. Cool crust, then chill 30 minutes.
4. To assemble pie, spread softened ice cream over chilled crust. Freeze 15 minutes.
5. In a large bowl combine pumpkin, sugar, spices, and salt. In a separate bowl whip cream and vanilla until soft peaks form. Fold into pumpkin mixture. Pour over ice cream layer, swirl top with spatula and garnish with pecan halves.
6. Freeze pie at least 2 hours.
7. To serve: Let stand at room temperature 10-15 minutes before slicing.

6-8 large servings

Hints: Butter pecan ice cream can be substituted for vanilla. Will keep in freezer 3-4 weeks if tightly wrapped.

FROZEN MOCHA TOFFEE DESSERT

This rich, cool dessert is sure to be a hit. Crème de cacao combined with whipped cream makes an elegant topping.

5 lady fingers, split, or graham cracker crust
3 tablespoons dry instant coffee
1-3 tablespoons boiling water, enough to dissolve coffee
1 half-gallon carton vanilla ice cream, softened

8 Heath bars, frozen and crushed (1 cup)
½ cup heavy cream
2 tablespoons white crème de cacao
Graham cracker crust:
2½ cups crushed graham crackers
½ cup sugar
¾ cup melted butter

1. Line bottom of buttered 8-inch springform pan with lady fingers. If using graham cracker crust, combine crushed graham crackers, sugar, and melted butter. Press into bottom of buttered 8-inch springform pan.
2. Dissolve coffee in water and cool. Stir coffee, softened ice cream, and Heath bars together.
3. Spoon into pan and freeze at least 2 hours.
4. Combine cream and crème de cacao. Whip to soft peaks. Add to top of dessert when serving.

8-10 servings

Hints: Can substitute coffee ice cream for vanilla ice cream and instant coffee.
Can substitute 8 Skor bars for Heath bars.

PEACHES 'N' CREAM ICE CREAM

3 cups mashed fresh peaches (sweeten to taste, if desired)	1½ cups sugar
	1 teaspoon vanilla extract
1 tablespoon fresh lemon juice	1 teaspoon almond extract
4 cups milk	¼ teaspoon salt, optional
3 cups heavy cream	

1. Combine peaches and lemon juice.
2. In a separate large bowl, combine milk, heavy cream, sugar, vanilla, almond extract, and salt (if used). Add peaches. Chill.
3. Churn in ice cream maker according to manufacturer's directions.

One gallon

Peaches and cream have always captured the essence of summer. Try serving this with a slice of Classic Pound Cake.

EXPRESSO ICE CREAM

1¼ cups double strength coffee	2 tablespoons dark rum
¾ cup sugar	½ teaspoon cinnamon
½ cup dark corn syrup	2 cups heavy cream

1. Combine coffee, sugar, corn syrup, rum, and cinnamon. Stir until sugar dissolves.
2. Stir in heavy cream.
3. Freeze in ice cream maker according to manufacturer's directions.

8 servings

Hint: Top with shaved semi-sweet chocolate or warmed chocolate sauce.

A delightful conclusion to a heavy meal.

RICH VANILLA ICE CREAM

Ice cream the old fashioned way—creamy, rich, and smooth. Combine this with any of the toppings on the following pages for an unforgettable dessert.

3 cups heavy cream	4 egg yolks, lightly beaten
1 cup whole milk	1 tablespoon vanilla extract
¾ cup sugar	

1. In medium saucepan, combine cream, milk, and sugar. Cook, stirring, over medium heat until mixture is very hot.
2. Add about 1 cup of hot cream mixture to egg yolks and stir to blend.
3. Return yolk mixture to saucepan. Stir in vanilla. Lower heat and cook, stirring constantly, until custard is slightly thickened and will coat the back of a spoon.
4. Remove from heat. Strain custard and chill.
5. When custard is chilled, freeze in ice cream maker according to manufacturer's directions.

8-10 servings

Hint: When ice cream is almost frozen, stir in crumbled Oreo cookies, chocolate chips, fresh fruit, or toasted nuts.

FRESH BLUEBERRY SAUCE

Serve this sauce atop vanilla ice cream or, for breakfast, with waffles or pancakes.

1 pint fresh blueberries	1 tablespoon fresh lemon juice
Zest of 1 lemon	½-¾ cup sugar, to taste

1. In medium saucepan, combine all ingredients.
2. Cook over medium-low heat until sugar is dissolved and sauce has thickened slightly. (No more than 10 minutes.)

6-8 servings

Hint: Sauce may be prepared ahead and reheated.

BUTTERSCOTCH SAUCE

1 cup brown sugar, firmly packed	¼ cup light corn syrup
1 cup sugar	¼ teaspoon salt
1 cup evaporated milk	1½ teaspoons vanilla extract
½ cup unsalted butter	

1. Combine all ingredients except vanilla in heavy bottomed saucepan.
2. Cook over medium heat until sauce reaches 230° on candy thermometer. Immediately remove from heat.
3. Stir in vanilla and cool until warm.
4. When cooled, beat vigorously for 1 minute. Serve warm over ice cream.

Hint: May be prepared ahead and refrigerated. Reheat before serving.

Try this classic sauce over Rich Vanilla Ice Cream.

HOT PLUM AND CURRANT SAUCE

2 tablespoons butter	¼ teaspoon almond extract
3 fresh ripe plums (red or purple)	Vanilla ice cream
⅓ cup red currant jelly	½ cup almond slivers, toasted

1. Melt butter in a saucepan over low heat.
2. Peel and slice plums into bite-size pieces. Sauté in butter for 2-3 minutes until softened.
3. Add jelly. Heat until melted.
4. Stir in almond extract.
5. Spoon immediately over ice cream. Sprinkle with toasted almonds.

4 servings

This unusual sauce is wonderful spooned over ice cream.

CHOCOLATE FUDGE SAUCE

This is an incredible chocolate experience your friends will not forget.

4 squares unsweetened chocolate
1 cup heavy cream or half and half
1½ cups sugar
3 tablespoons butter
1 teaspoon vanilla
¼ cup sherry or favorite liqueur

1. Melt chocolate in double boiler over low heat.
2. Add cream, sugar, and butter. Stir until well blended.
3. Remove top of double boiler and place over low flame. Boil without stirring for 5-7 minutes.
4. Stir in sherry and vanilla. Serve warm over ice cream.

6 servings

PRALINE SAUCE

A sophisticated cousin of butterscotch sauce.

3 tablespoons unsalted butter
1 cup brown sugar, firmly packed
½ cup half and half
1 cup chopped pecans
1 teaspoon vanilla

1. In small saucepan, melt butter.
2. Add brown sugar and cook over medium low heat, stirring constantly, for 5-8 minutes. Remove from heat.
3. Gradually stir in half and half. Return to heat and cook 1 minute.
4. Stir in pecans and vanilla. Serve warm atop ice cream.

6-8 servings

GOLDEN FRUIT ICE

1½ cups sugar
2 cups water
3 well-mashed bananas
Juice of 3 lemons

Juice of 3 oranges
3 tablespoons crushed pineapple

1. Combine sugar and water in saucepan and boil for 5 minutes while stirring. Remove from heat and chill.
2. Put fruit and juices in blender or food processor fitted with steel blade. Mix quickly to attain a uniform consistency.
3. Add fruit and juices to sugar-water mixture, stirring until well blended.
4. Process in ice cream maker according to manufacturer's directions, or, place "ice" in a covered mold or refrigerator tray. Cover with foil and place in freezer. While still slushy, stir or beat ice from front to back of tray to reduce size of crystals. Repeat stirring at half-hour intervals until desired consistency is achieved.

6-8 servings

Hints: Serve in a fruit shell. Prepare fancy cut and hollowed out navel oranges or thick-skinned lemons: cut a scalloped opening near top (this later can serve as a lid). Hollow out pulp and fill with ice. Garnish the cases with fresh green leaves.
A dab of orange marmalade can be placed on top of the fruit ice. Accompany with sugar cookie.
Fresh strawberries dipped in sugar, kiwi fruit slices, or lemon and orange slices with fresh mint leaves can serve as garnish.

Sorbets, or ices, are French sherbets which are first cousins of ice cream, sans the cream. They are most commonly served as desserts in this country, though the French often prefer them as a palate refresher before the main course. With the recent emphasis on lighter food, popularized by nouvelle cuisine, the sorbet's qualities of refreshing versatility, taste, and color make it a great choice for dessert. Here is a selection of sorbets for you to try.

Beach Picnic

Patricia's Pâté with Crackers

Chilled Melon Soup

Dilled Havarti Pocket Sandwiches

Orange Ice   McIntosh's Shortbread

ORANGE ICE

1 cup water
1½ cups granulated sugar
Grated zest of 1 orange

2 cups fresh orange juice
½ cup fresh lemon juice

1. Combine sugar and water in saucepan and boil for 5 minutes, stirring occasionally. Remove from heat and stir in orange zest.
2. When mixture is cool, strain it through a sieve.
3. Add the orange juice and lemon juice to the strained mixture and stir until well blended.
4. Freeze in ice tray according to instructions for Golden Fruit Ice.

8-10 servings

Hints: May be served in orange rind cup.
May be served in green apples which have been cored and pulp scooped out. Sprinkle inside of apple with lemon juice to prevent remaining flesh from browning.

CRANBERRY ICE

1 egg white
2 tablespoons sugar
¼ cup powdered skim milk
¼ cup ice water

1 tablespoon fresh lemon juice
1 cup water
½ cup sugar
4 cups fresh cranberries, sorted and rinsed

1. In a large saucepan, combine ½ cup sugar, 1 cup water, and fresh cranberries. Heat to boiling, continuing to cook and stir until cranberries no longer pop (about 7 minutes).
2. Purée cranberries in food processor fitted with steel blade. Cover surface of cranberry purée with plastic wrap and chill.
3. In a small bowl, beat egg white until frothy; add 2 tablespoons sugar and continue beating to a meringue consistency. (May use electric mixer.)
4. In a medium bowl, beat powdered skim milk, ice water, and lemon juice until thick. Add to meringue.
5. Fold chilled cranberry mixture into skim milk-meringue combination. Pour into desired container and freeze until firm.

1 quart

CHAMPAGNE SORBET

| 3 cups chilled Champagne | 1½ cups simple syrup (recipe follows) |

1. Combine champagne and simple syrup.
2. Freeze in ice cream maker according to manufacturer's directions.

5 cups

Hint: Serve as a palate cleanser between courses or as a dessert with fresh strawberries.

FRESH PINEAPPLE SORBET

| 1 small ripe Hawaiian pineapple | 2 tablespoons fresh lemon juice |
| 1 cup simple syrup (recipe follows) | |

1. Peel, core, and cube the pineapple.
2. Place cubes in food processor fitted with steel blade and process until very smooth. (Puréed pineapple should measure 2½ cups.)
3. Stir in simple syrup and lemon juice. Taste and add more syrup or lemon juice if necessary.
4. Process in ice cream maker according to manufacturer's directions.

1 quart

Hint: Garnish with kiwi slices and sprigs of mint.

STRAWBERRY SORBET

| 2 10-ounce packages frozen strawberries, packed in syrup | 3 tablespoons fresh lemon juice |
| 1 cup simple syrup (recipe follows) | |

1. In a food processor fitted with steel blade, purée the strawberries with their syrup.
2. Stir in the simple syrup and lemon juice.
3. Process in ice cream maker according to manufacturer's directions.

1 quart

Hint: Garnish with sliced fresh strawberries.

SIMPLE SYRUP

4 cups water	4 cups sugar

1. In a medium saucepan, combine sugar and water.
2. Simmer until sugar is dissolved.
3. Cool to room temperature and refrigerate in a covered jar.

1 quart

Hint: Will keep indefinitely in refrigerator.

FRANGO MINTS

An irresistible chocolate and mint after-dinner confection. Include it in a dessert buffet or by itself with coffee.

4	ounces unsweetened chocolate	2	teaspoons vanilla extract
1	cup butter, no substitute	2	teaspoons pure peppermint or rum flavoring
2	cups confectioners' sugar	4	eggs

1. Melt chocolate in double boiler.
2. Combine chocolate, butter, sugar, and flavorings in blender or food processor fitted with steel blade. Process 5 seconds, scraping bowl.
3. Add and blend eggs one at a time.
4. Pour into 1 or 1½-inch paper muffin cups.
5. Freeze.
6. Serve frozen.

2 dozen 1½-inch cups or 3 dozen 1-inch miniatures

CHOCOLATE COCONUT CANDY

2   14-ounce bags coconut
1   cup unsalted butter, softened
1   14-ounce can sweetened condensed milk
1   box confectioners' sugar
2   12-ounce bags semi-sweet chocolate chips
1½ bars paraffin

1.   Combine first four ingredients. Pour into a jelly roll pan and freeze.
2.   Melt chocolate and paraffin in a double boiler. Keep warm over low heat.
3.   Cut frozen coconut mixture into 1-inch squares. Using a toothpick, dip squares into chocolate-paraffin mixture.
4.   Let squares harden on waxed paper. Store in a cool place.

Approximately 48 pieces

Hints: Almonds are a wonderful addition to this candy. Candy will keep indefinitely in refrigerator.

The ultimate chocolate coconut experience!

ENGLISH TEA CAKES

1½ cups all-purpose flour
½   teaspoon salt
1½ teaspoons baking powder
½   cup sugar
½   cup solid vegetable shortening
1   egg
2   tablespoons milk
1   tablespoon vanilla
½   cup currants or raisins
Frosting:
¼   cup margarine
1   cup confectioners' sugar
1   teaspoon milk
1   teaspoon vanilla

1.   Preheat oven to 350°. Grease two cookie sheets.
2.   Sift dry ingredients into a medium bowl.
3.   Cut in shortening.
4.   In a separate bowl, beat egg until light colored, then add milk and vanilla.
5.   Add egg mixture to dry ingredients and shortening.
6.   Stir in currants or raisins. Dough will be stiff.
7.   Spoon dough onto cookie sheet in small chunks or roll into 1-1½ inch diameter balls.

Decorate these festive cookies for different holidays by tinting the frosting. Children love to help.

8. Bake about 15 minutes or until faintly brown on the bottom.

9. When cookies are cool, combine frosting ingredients and beat into a stiff frosting.

10. Frost each cookie and dip in colored sugar or decorating candies.

2-3 dozen

Hints: Do not substitute margarine for shortening.
The currants or raisins may be omitted and chopped nuts may be substituted. Frosting may be flavored with brandy, etc. and colored pink for Valentine's Day or green for St. Patrick's Day.

McINTOSH'S SHORTBREAD

Shortbread has been a popular cookie for decades thanks to its melt-in-your-mouth texture and buttery flavor. Serve with fresh fruit or sorbet.

2 cups all-purpose flour	**½ cup confectioners'**
1 cup butter	**sugar**

1. Preheat oven to 350°.

2. Measure flour first, then sift three times.

3. Using mixer or processor, cream butter and sugar. Add flour cup by cup. Mix until dough leaves sides of bowl.

4. Roll out on lightly floured surface and cut into small rounds ½ to ¾ inches thick.

5. Prick rounds with fork and place on ungreased cookie sheet.

6. Bake for 5 minutes at 350°. Turn oven back to 300° and continue baking for 20-30 minutes or until bottoms of cookies are light tan. Cool on rack.

7. If desired, roll in powdered sugar. Store in air-tight container.

2 dozen

Hints: These will keep for weeks in an air-tight container.
Shortbread acquires its flavor from real butter, so no substitutions, please.

TRUDIE'S COOKIES

2 cups all-purpose flour	1 cup brown sugar,
½ teaspoon baking soda	firmly packed
½ teaspoon cream of	1 teaspoon vanilla
tartar	extract
¼ teaspoon salt	1 large egg
¾ cup butter	¾ cup chopped pecans

1. Sift together flour, baking soda, cream of tartar, and salt.
2. In a large bowl, cream butter, adding a little of the flour mixture.
3. Beat in sugar.
4. Add vanilla, egg, chopped nuts, and remaining flour.
5. Divide dough in half. Form into two long rolls wrapped in waxed paper. Chill.
6. When ready to bake, preheat oven to 400° and grease several cookie sheets.
7. Slice dough thinly, place on cookie sheets, and bake about 12 minutes, or until golden.
8. Remove from pan and cool on wire racks.

5 dozen

Hint: The rolls of raw cookie dough may be frozen until needed.

We finally convinced one grandmother to write down the recipe while she made these thin, crisp, butter-nut delicacies.

MOLASSES COOKIES

4 cups all-purpose flour	1 teaspoon ground ginger
1 teaspoon ground cloves	½ cup dark molasses
2 teaspoons cinnamon	1 teaspoon salt
1½ cups shortening	2 eggs
2 cups sugar	Granulated sugar
4 teaspoons baking soda	

1. Preheat oven to 350°. Grease several cookie sheets.
2. Mix ingredients in order listed; you may want to use your hands.
3. Roll dough into 1-inch balls, roll in sugar, and bake on prepared cookie sheets about 7-8 minutes. DO NOT OVER COOK!

Greet the kids after school with these chewy, old-fashioned cookies. Be sure to have enough on hand for seconds!

4. Remove to wire rack to cool.

5-6 dozen

Hints: This recipe can be halved.
For a crisper cookie, use ¾ cup butter and ¾ cup shortening.

WHOLE WHEAT BRAN COOKIES

Here is an afternoon snack you'll want your children to eat. They will never guess that these tasty cookies are good for them.

½ cup unsalted butter	¼ teaspoon salt
½ cup brown sugar, firmly packed	½ cup bran cereal
½ cup granulated sugar	¾ cup chopped pecans or walnuts
1 egg	½ cup flaked coconut
1 teaspoon vanilla	
1 teaspoon water	
1 cup whole wheat flour	
½ teaspoon baking soda	

1. Cream butter and sugars, then beat in egg, vanilla, and water.
2. Stir in flour, baking soda, and salt.
3. Stir in bran cereal, nuts, and coconut.
4. Refrigerate dough for 30 minutes.
5. Preheat oven to 350° and grease a large cookie sheet.
6. Drop 1 teaspoonful of dough at a time onto greased cookie sheet.
7. Bake for 12-14 minutes.
8. Remove from cookie sheet immediately and cool on wire racks.

2-3 dozen

Hint: Store in well-sealed container.

RASPBERRY JAM COOKIES

This pretty cookie is flexible, too. Use your favorite jam in place of raspberry for a change of color and taste.

1½ cups butter	3 cups all-purpose flour
1 cup sugar	Raspberry jam
2 egg yolks	
1 teaspoon vanilla	

1. Preheat oven to 400°.

2. Cream butter and sugar.
3. Add egg yolks, flavoring, and flour.
4. With your hands, roll dough into 1-inch balls and place on an ungreased cookie sheet.
5. With a small spoon, make a small indentation on top of each ball.
6. Place a touch of raspberry jam in each indentation.
7. Bake for 8-10 minutes. Cookies should turn light brown on the bottom and outer edges.

7 dozen

Hints: This dough can be rolled out to make cut cookies.
You may substitute ½ teaspoon vanilla and ½ teaspoon almond extract for the flavorings.

OATMEAL PEAR SQUARES

2 cups all-purpose flour	4 medium pears, peeled,
1 cup quick cooking oats	cored, and chopped
1 cup flaked coconut	(approximately 2 cups)
1 cup brown sugar,	½ cup chopped nuts
firmly packed	¼ cup granulated sugar
1 teaspoon baking soda	¼ teaspoon cinnamon
¼ teaspoon salt	¼ teaspoon ground ginger
1 cup butter	3 tablespoons butter

1. Preheat oven to 375°. Grease a 9x13 inch pan.
2. In a large bowl, stir together flour, oats, coconut, brown sugar, baking soda, and salt.
3. Cut in 1 cup butter until mixture is crumbly.
4. Pat half of mixture into pan. Cover with pears.
5. Combine nuts, sugar, and spices and sprinkle over fruit.
6. Dot with 3 tablespoons butter.
7. Pat remaining oat mixture over all.
8. Bake for 45-50 minutes. Cool and cut into squares.

2½ dozen

Try these tasty squares for a change of pace. Their spicy goodness will win over all who taste them.

STRAWBERRY CHEESECAKE BARS

Trying to find that special dessert for a bridge game or luncheon? These colorful bars freeze well so make them ahead.

25 graham cracker squares
½ cup butter, softened
½ cup chopped pecans
3 eggs
1 cup sugar
1 8-ounce package cream cheese

1 pint sour cream
1 package unflavored gelatin
1 cup boiling water
1 16-ounce package frozen strawberries

1. Preheat oven to 325°.
2. Crush graham crackers to make crumbs and mix with soft butter and chopped pecans.
3. Press crumb mixture into 8x8 inch glass dish.
4. Beat together eggs, sugar, and cream cheese.
5. Pour this mixture over crust and bake for 30-40 minutes.
6. Immediately remove cheese cake from oven and spread sour cream over it. Return to oven and bake 10-15 minutes. Remove from oven.
7. Dissolve gelatin in boiling water. Add frozen strawberries and stir.
8. When cake is completely cooled, pour strawberry mixture over it and refrigerate for 24 hours.
9. Cut in squares and serve. Keep any remaining bars in the refrigerator.

12 bars

Hint: Could use 2 cups of graham cracker crumbs instead of crackers.

CAPE COD OATMEAL COOKIES

Oatmeal cookies are great, but these are extra special because of their unique molasses flavor.

1 egg
1 cup sugar
½ cup butter, melted
½ cup margarine, melted
2 tablespoons molasses
¼ cup milk
1¾ cups oatmeal

1½ cups all-purpose flour
½ teaspooon baking soda
½ teaspoon salt
1 teaspoon cinnamon
½ cup raisins
½ cup finely chopped pecans

1. Preheat oven to 325°. Grease several cookie sheets.

2. Sift together flour, soda, salt, and cinnamon and set aside.
3. Beat egg well and add all ingredients in order listed. Mix well.
4. Drop batter by teaspoonfuls onto greased cookie sheets.
5. Bake 10-15 minutes. Cool on wire racks.

5-6 dozen

Hint: For a thicker cookie, increase oats to 2 cups and flour to 1¾ cups.

FRUIT CAKE COOKIES

6 slices candied pineapple	1 cup brown sugar, firmly packed
8 ounces candied cherries	2 eggs
8 ounces dates	2¼ cups self-rising flour
All-purpose flour for dredging	1½ tablespoons milk
6 cups pecans	½ teaspoon baking soda
1 cup butter	½ teaspoon vanilla
	1 cup pineapple preserves

1. Preheat oven to 325°. Grease several cookie sheets.
2. Chop pineapple, cherries, and dates; dredge with flour.
3. Chop pecans.
4. Cream butter and sugar together.
5. Add eggs, flour, milk, soda, vanilla, and preserves. Mix well.
6. Stir in floured, chopped fruit and pecans.
7. Drop batter by the teaspoonful onto cookie sheets and bake for 15 minutes.
8. Remove to wire racks to cool.

6 dozen

Hints: This recipe can be doubled. Use 3 eggs when doubling. Chop fruit ahead of time - this makes the process shorter.

Move over fruit cake! Here's a worthy competitor in a different form to tempt those for whom Christmas would be incomplete without fruit cake.

DATE FILLED CHEDDAR TURNOVERS

The contrast between savory cheese pastry and rich date filling in these turnovers makes a very appealing combination.

Pastry:
½ cup margarine, softened
1   cup grated New York sharp Cheddar cheese, at room temperature
1⅓ cups all-purpose flour
½ teaspoon salt

Filling:
½ cup dark brown sugar, firmly packed
8   ounces chopped dates
2-3 tablespoons water

1.   Cream together softened margarine and cheese. Combine flour with salt and gradually add to cheese mixture. Blend well. Wrap in waxed paper and chill in refrigerator 1 hour.
2.   Prepare filling by cooking brown sugar, dates, and water in small saucepan, stirring constantly 5 minutes until well-blended and slightly thickened. Do not overcook. Cool before using to fill pastries.
3.   Preheat oven to 350°.
4.   Roll out dough ⅛ inch thick on lightly floured surface. Cut into 2-inch circles.
5.   Place teaspoonful of date filling in each circle. Fold dough in half. Moisten inside edges with cold water; crimp together with tines of fork. Place on ungreased cookie sheet and bake for 10 minutes or until golden brown.

4 dozen 2-inch turnovers

Hints: Substitute mincemeat for date filling.
Use cheese pastry for tart shells with apple filling.

E. T. COOKIES

Don't be surprised when mothers of your children's friends "phone home" to ask you for this original recipe.

1   16-ounce package Reese's pieces
1   cup margarine, softened
¾   cup granulated sugar
¾   cup brown sugar, firmly packed
2   eggs

1   teaspoon vanilla extract
2½ cups all-purpose flour
½   teaspoon baking soda
½   teaspoon salt
1   cup chopped nuts, optional

1.   Preheat oven to 350°. Grease several cookie sheets.

2. Coarsely chop 1½ cups of candy by hand or in food processor. Reserve remaining candy for decoration.
3. Beat together margarine and sugars until light and fluffy. Blend in eggs and vanilla.
4. Combine flour, soda, and salt and add to margarine-sugar mixture. Beat well. Stir in chopped candies and nuts.
5. Drop by rounded tablespoons onto greased cookie sheet. Bake for 9-11 minutes.
6. Remove from oven and immediately press 3 reserved candies on the top of each cookie. Cool on wire rack.

5 dozen

PEANUT SQUARES

1 cup unsalted butter	2 cups sifted all-purpose
½ cup granulated sugar	flour
1½ cups brown sugar,	1 teaspoon baking soda
firmly packed	¼ teaspoon salt
2 eggs, separated	1 6-ounce package
1 tablespoon water	chocolate chips
1 teaspoon vanilla	1 cup chopped, salted
	peanuts or cashews

Peanuts have never tasted so good. After sampling these, you'll be adding another cookie to your Christmas baking.

1. Preheat oven to 375°. Grease a 15½x10½x1 inch jelly roll pan.
2. Cream butter with electric mixer, gradually adding ½ cup of each type of sugar. Beat well.
3. Beat in egg yolks, water, and vanilla.
4. Sift together flour, soda, and salt and add to butter mixture. Blend thoroughly for 2 minutes.
5. Spread mixture into jelly roll pan and sprinkle with chocolate chips. Press chips into batter.
6. Beat egg whites until stiff, about 3 minutes. Add remaining 1 cup brown sugar and beat until frothy peaks form.
7. Spread egg white mixture over batter and sprinkle with chopped nuts.
8. Bake for 20 minutes. Cool and cut into squares.

2 dozen

CHOCOLATE FUDGE COOKIES

The dough for these cookies is so good that it may disappear before you start baking. But if you can resist, you'll be rewarded with a moist, chewy, chocolate cookie that was worth the wait!

3 tablespoons margarine
1½ cups semi-sweet chocolate chips
1 15-ounce can sweetened condensed milk

1 cup all-purpose flour
1 cup chopped pecans
1 teaspoon vanilla

1. In a double boiler, melt margarine and chocolate together.
2. Remove from heat and stir in condensed milk.
3. Add flour and mix well.
4. Stir in nuts and vanilla.
5. Cover and chill for at least 4 hours or overnight.
6. Preheat oven to 325°. Grease two cookie sheets.
7. Use a spoon to dip chunks (1-1¼ inch diameter) of the stiff dough onto cookie sheets.
8. Bake about 10 minutes. Be careful not to overcook.
9. Cool on wire racks.

4 dozen

Hint: Dough must be refrigerated or cookies will go flat when you bake them.

DOUBLE FUDGE BROWNIES

Chocoholics beware! These rich brownies are impossible to resist.

2 eggs
1 cup sugar
½ cup butter
2 ounces unsweetened chocolate
½ cup all-purpose flour
¼ teaspoon salt
¼ teaspoon baking powder

1 teaspoon vanilla
1 cup chopped pecans
Icing:
1 cup sugar
¼ cup cocoa
¼ cup milk
¼ cup butter
½ teaspoon vanilla

1. Preheat oven to 325°. Grease and flour an 8-inch square pan.
2. With electric mixer, beat eggs and sugar.
3. Melt butter and chocolate together and add to egg mixture.

4. Sift flour, salt, and baking powder together and stir lightly into chocolate mixture until blended.
5. Add vanilla and nuts.
6. Pour mixture into prepared pan.
7. Bake for 25-30 minutes.
8. To make icing, combine all ingredients in a saucepan, bring to a boil, and boil briskly for 1 minute.
9. Remove from heat and beat until creamy. Spread on brownies.
10. Cool brownies completely, then cut into squares.

2 dozen

CLASSIC POUND CAKE

2	cups butter, at room temperature	¼	teaspoon baking soda
3	cups sugar	2	teaspoons vanilla extract
6	eggs, at room temperature	1	8-ounce carton sour cream, at room temperature
3	cups all-purpose flour		
½	teaspoon salt		

1. Grease and flour a 10-inch tube pan and set aside.
2. In a large bowl, cream butter and sugar well. Add 2 eggs, beating well.
3. Combine flour, salt, and baking soda in a separate bowl.
4. Add the flour mixture to the butter alternately with the 4 eggs until all is added.
5. Stir in vanilla extract and sour cream. Spoon batter into prepared pan.
6. Place pan in the middle of a cold oven. Set temperature at 325° and bake for 1½ hours. Do not open oven door for the first hour of cooking time.
7. Cool cake in pan on a wire rack for 10-15 minutes before removing from pan.

16 servings

Hints: This cake freezes well or may be kept for a month in an airtight container.
You may substitute almond or lemon extract for vanilla.

This is an old family recipe that will soon become a tradition in your home, too. Serve it plain year round, or for a special summer treat, top with fresh peaches or peach ice cream.

CHOCOLATE CINNAMON CAKE

This dark, rich chocolate cake has a hint of cinnamon flavor.

1 cup water	2 eggs
1 cup butter or margarine	½ cup buttermilk
4 tablespoons cocoa	1 teaspoon baking soda
2 cups all-purpose flour	1 teaspoon cinnamon
2 cups sugar	1 teaspoon vanilla extract

1. Preheat oven to 350°. Grease and flour a tube pan.
2. Bring water, butter or margarine, and cocoa to a boil. Remove from heat and set aside.
3. In a bowl, combine flour and sugar.
4. Pour cocoa mixture over flour and sugar. Beat well.
5. Add eggs, buttermilk, baking soda, cinnamon, and vanilla. Beat well.
6. Pour batter into prepared pan and bake for 50-60 minutes.

12-16 servings

Hints: Frosting variation: 1 6-ounce package semi-sweet chocolate chips, ½ cup half and half, 1 cup butter, 2½ cups confectioners' sugar. Combine chocolate chips, half and half, and butter in a saucepan. Cook over medium heat until chocolate is melted. Remove from heat. With mixer, blend in confectioners' sugar until smooth. Set saucepan in a pan of ice in the sink, and beat until frosting holds its shape.
Cake could be garnished with sifted confectioners' sugar or drizzled with melted chocolate.

SWEDISH GINGER CAKE

Imported from a Swedish friend via Germany, this gingerbread recipe is exceptional.

1-2 tablespoons butter	1 teaspoon ground cloves
¼ cup fine dry bread crumbs	1¾ cups all-purpose flour
½ cup butter, softened	1 teaspoon baking soda
1 cup sugar	⅔ cup sour cream
3 eggs	Glaze:
1 teaspoon cinnamon	⅔ cup confectioners' sugar
1 teaspoon ground ginger	4 tablespoons brandy

1. Preheat oven to 325°. Butter and lightly sprinkle sides and bottom of bundt or tube pan with bread crumbs.
2. In mixing bowl, cream ½ cup butter and sugar until light and fluffy. Add eggs and spices.

3. Sift together flour and baking soda. Add this alternately with sour cream to butter mixture. Stir well.
4. Pour mixture into prepared pan and bake at 325° for 15 minutes. Reduce heat to 250° and continue baking for 30-45 minutes longer.
5. Cool cake in pan for 10 minutes, then remove to wire rack.
6. If glaze is desired, mix brandy and confectioners' sugar to form a syrup-like sauce. Pour over warm cake.
7. Serve warm.

10-12 servings

Hint: Be careful not to overcook.

CHOCOLATE BAVARIAN CREAM CAKE

Chocolate Angel Food Cake:
¾ cup sifted all-purpose flour
¼ cup cocoa
¼ cup sugar
12 egg whites
1 teaspoon cream of tartar
1 cup sifted sugar
1½ teaspoons vanilla extract
Bavarian Cream:
¼ cup cold water

1 envelope unflavored gelatin
4 eggs, separated
⅛ teaspoon salt
½ cup sugar
1 cup milk
2 ounces unsweetened chocolate, melted
1 cup heavy cream
1 teaspoon vanilla
Assembling the cake:
2 cups heavy cream
¼ cup Kahlua

Special occasions will be memorable when you serve this spectacular dessert. Your efforts will be rewarded with raves from satisfied guests.

Cake:
1. Preheat oven to 350°.
2. Sift flour, cocoa, and sugar together 5 times and set aside.
3. Beat egg whites and cream of tartar in an extra large bowl until they form peaks.
4. Beat sifted sugar into whites 1 tablespoon at a time, until whites are stiff and all sugar is used.
5. Add vanilla.
6. Sprinkle flour mixture over batter and fold in until all of the mixture is used up.
7. Pour batter in an ungreased 9-inch tube pan and bake 40-45 minutes.
8. Invert the pan and let the cake cool for 1½ hours upside down. Then remove from pan by turning over and running a knife around all edges.

The chocolate angel cake may be made several days ahead and refrigerated or frozen.

Bavarian Cream:
1. Soften gelatin in ¼ cup cold water and set aside.
2. Mix egg yolks, salt, and sugar together in the top of a double boiler.
3. Gradually blend in milk and cook over hot water, stirring constantly until thickened.
4. Add softened gelatin and stir until dissolved. Remove from heat, add melted chocolate, and cool.
5. Beat egg whites and fold into cooled custard.
6. Whip cream, add vanilla, and fold into chocolate custard.

After making Bavarian Cream proceed to assemble cake.

Assembling the cake:
1. Line the bottom and sides of a 9-inch tube pan with waxed paper.
2. Tear angel cake into bite-size pieces.
3. Starting with cake, alternate cake and Bavarian cream until the pan is full.
4. Chill for 12 hours before unmolding.
5. Unmold on serving plate.
6. Whip heavy cream and add Kahlua.
7. Frost cake with flavored cream. Refrigerate until ready to serve.

16 servings

Hints: Wet tube pan and waxed paper will adhere to sides.
Could layer slivered almonds in body of cake.
For a lighter flavor, omit Kahlua and sweeten whipped cream to taste with confectioners' sugar.

SNOWBALL

Children are fascinated by the appearance of this dessert glowing with candles on a tall cake plate. Make it for your next birthday celebration.

2	tablespoons unflavored gelatin	⅛	teaspoon salt
4	tablespoons cold water	1	pint heavy cream
1	cup boiling water	1	small angel food cake, torn into small pieces
1	cup orange juice, fresh if possible		**Frosting:**
	Juice of 1 lemon	1	cup heavy cream, whipped
1	cup granulated sugar	2	cups flaked coconut

1. Dissolve gelatin in cold water.
2. Add boiling water, orange and lemon juice, sugar, and salt. Mix well.

3. Chill until partially set.
4. Whip 1 pint heavy cream and fold into partially jelled mixture.
5. Line large mixing bowl with waxed paper.
6. Put handful of small cake pieces into bowl alternately with gelatin mixture until ingredients are completely used.
7. Chill until firm.
8. Turn onto plate with rounded side up. Frost with remaining whipped cream. Cover with coconut.

10-12 servings

Hints: This is beautiful unmolded on glass or silver cake plate. Can be prepared a day ahead and refrigerated.

PHILADELPHIA CHRISTMAS CAKE

2¼ cups all-purpose flour, divided	1½ cups sugar
1 cup candied fruit	1½ teaspoons vanilla extract
½ cup chopped pecans	4 eggs
1 8-ounce package cream cheese	1½ teaspoons baking powder
1 cup margarine	1 teaspoon mace

1. Preheat oven to 325°. Grease and flour a 10-inch tube pan or 2 loaf pans.
2. Combine ¼ cup flour with candied fruit and chopped pecans; set aside.
3. Blend cream cheese, margarine, sugar, and vanilla, mixing well.
4. Add eggs one at a time, mixing well after each.
5. Sift together 2 cups flour, baking powder, and mace. While mixing at low speed, gradually add dry ingredients to cream cheese batter.
6. Fold in candied fruit and nuts.
7. Place batter in prepared pan. Bake for 1 hour 20 minutes for tube pan or approximately 45 minutes for 2 loaf pans.
8. Cool for 10 minutes in pan before removing to rack to completely cool.

12-16 servings

Christmas gifts can be easy and fun, especially when you make this delicious fruit cake early and put it in your freezer. Dress this cake up with an Orange Glaze. Add orange juice to confectioners' sugar until it is a thin consistency. Apply to warm cake.

FRESH APPLE CAKE

Let your children help with this cake. Simply dump everything into a bowl and mix. What could be easier?

3 cups chopped apples
2 cups all-purpose flour
2 cups sugar
1 cup oil
3 eggs

1 teaspoon baking soda
1 teaspoon salt
1 teaspoon cinnamon
1½ cups chopped pecans or walnuts, optional

1. Preheat oven to 325°. Grease and flour a bundt pan.
2. Place all ingredients in a large bowl. Stir well.
3. Pour batter in bundt pan and bake for 1½ hours.
4. Leave in pan to cool for at least 10 minutes.
5. Remove cake from pan and cool on wire rack.

12-16 servings

Fall Brunch

Hot Bacon & Mushroom Dip

Cream of Onion Soup

Broccoli & Feta Cheese Tart

Microwaved Ratatouille   Dill Rolls

Fresh Apple Cake

FROSTED BROWN SUGAR POUND CAKE

This cake is perfect for a picnic or pot luck dinner. Serve with homemade vanilla ice cream, and you will receive many requests for a return engagement.

1 16-ounce box brown sugar
¾ cup granulated sugar
1½ cups butter, at room temperature
5 eggs, at room temperature
1 cup evaporated milk
3 cups all-purpose flour
½ teaspoon baking powder
1 teaspoon salt

1 teaspoon vanilla extract
Frosting:
1 16-ounce box brown sugar
½ cup evaporated milk
½ cup butter
1 teaspoon vanilla extract
½ teaspoon baking powder

1.   Preheat oven to 325°. Grease and flour a 10-inch tube pan or 2 loaf pans.
2.   Cream sugars and butter. Add eggs, mixing well.
3.   Sift together dry ingredients and add to sugar mixture alternately with milk.
4.   Stir in vanilla.
5.   Pour into prepared pan.
6.   Bake for 1 hour 15 minutes for tube pan or approximately 45 minutes to 1 hour for loaf pans.
7.   Cool cake 10 minutes in pan, then remove to wire rack to complete cooling.
8.   When cool, spread with frosting.
9.   To make frosting, bring brown sugar, evaporated milk, and butter to a boil in a saucepan. Cook for 3 minutes.
10.   Remove from heat; add vanilla and baking powder.
3.   Place in a pan of ice water and beat until frosting attains spreading consistency.

16 servings

Hint: This cake freezes beautifully.

CHOCOLATE ZUCCHINI CAKE

3 ounces unsweetened chocolate	3 cups unpeeled, grated zucchini
3 cups all-purpose flour	Frosting:
1½ teaspoons baking powder	1 3-ounce package cream cheese
1 teaspoon baking soda	1 tablespoon butter
1 teaspoon salt	1 ounce unsweetened chocolate, melted and cooled
4 eggs	
3 cups sugar	2 cups sifted confectioners' sugar
1½ cups salad oil	
1 cup chopped pecans or walnuts	Milk as needed

This rich, dark cake has a texture similar to carrot cake.

1.   Preheat oven to 350°. Grease and flour a tube pan.
2.   Melt chocolate and cool.
3.   Sift together flour, baking powder, soda, and salt.
4.   With mixer at high speed, beat eggs until light. Add sugar ¼ cup at a time, beating well after each addition.
5.   Add salad oil and chocolate.
6.   Beating at low speed, add sifted dry ingredients. Beat until well mixed.
7.   Stir in nuts and zucchini.
8.   Pour into prepared pan and bake for 1 hour 15 minutes. Cool 10 minutes in pan, then remove to wire rack.
9.   For frosting, beat cream cheese and butter with mixer until fluffy.
10.   Add chocolate and sugar and beat again.

11. Stir in a little milk. Beat in more milk until frosting reaches spreading consistency.
12. Frost cooled tube cake.

12-16 servings

Hints: This is a versatile batter that may also be baked in three cake pans for 30-35 minutes. Or try three small loaf pans for 25-30 minutes. Whatever size pan you use, fill no more than ⅔ full. Double frosting recipe for layer cake.

HOT MILK CAKE

Start with this basic but delicious recipe the next time you make a birthday cake. Frost with your family's favorite icing to create an original.

4 **eggs**	½ **cup butter**
2 **cups sugar**	1 **cup milk**
2 **cups all-purpose flour**	1 **teaspoon vanilla**
2 **teaspoons baking powder**	**extract**
¼ **teaspoon salt**	

1. Preheat oven to 350°. Grease and flour three 9-inch round cake pans, a tube pan, or a 9x13 inch pan.
2. Beat eggs with mixer until very light, about 5 minutes. Gradually add sugar and continue to beat.
3. Sift together flour, baking powder, and salt; add to egg mixture.
4. Heat butter and milk until butter is melted; do not boil. Add to batter all at once, stirring well. Add flavoring.
5. Pour into prepared pan(s).
6. Bake round cake layers for 25 minutes, tube cake for about 1 hour, and 9x13 inch cake for about 45 minutes.
7. Turn cake out immediately and cool on wire racks.

12-16 servings

Hints: After baking, the cake may be frozen. Add your favorite frosting, glaze, or fresh fruit to finish this easy recipe.
Batter may be halved to make an 8-inch square pan.

COCONUT CREAM FROSTING

1 fresh coconut	6 tablespoons sugar
1 pint heavy cream	½ teaspoon vanilla extract

1. Break coconut, reserving milk.
2. Peel pieces of coconut and grate finely.
3. Pour cold cream into a chilled bowl and beat with mixer until it starts to thicken.
4. Gradually add sugar and beat until stiff.
5. Add vanilla.
6. Pour the coconut milk over the layers of any yellow or white cake.
7. Ice by putting a layer of cream then coconut between cake layers. Frost outside of cake with remaining cream and sprinkle with coconut.

Ices one 2-layer cake

Hints: This frosting is best if the cake and frosting are served the day after being made.
Grating the coconut by hand seems to yield the best texture.

Bring the flavor of the tropics to your table by gracing one of your favorite cakes with this luscious icing.

CARROT CAKE

Cake:
2 cups all-purpose flour
2 cups sugar
2 teaspoons baking soda
1 teaspoon salt
2 teaspoons cinnamon
4 large eggs
1 cup vegetable oil
4 cups (1 pound) grated carrots
Coconut Frosting:
4 tablespoons butter, divided
2 cups flaked coconut
1 8-ounce package cream cheese, softened

2 teaspoons milk
3½ cups sifted confectioners' sugar
½ teaspoon vanilla extract
Lemon Cream Cheese Frosting:
1 8-ounce package cream cheese, softened
¼ cup butter, softened
2 cups confectioners' sugar
1½ teaspoons vanilla extract
1 tablespoon grated lemon zest

A rich, moist cake with two delicious icing variations.

Cake:
1. Preheat oven to 350°. Grease and flour three 9-inch round cake pans.
2. Mix together dry ingredients and set aside.

3. In large bowl, beat eggs until foamy. Slowly add oil. Add dry ingredients slowly and mix well.
4. Add grated carrots and mix well.
5. Pour batter into prepared pans and bake for 25 minutes.
6. Cool 10 minutes in pans and remove to rack.
7. When completely cool, frost between layers and on top and sides with Coconut Frosting or Lemon Cream Cheese Frosting.
8. Store cake in an air-tight container in refrigerator until ready to serve.

12 servings

Hints: For a bundt pan, cook 45 minutes to 1 hour.
Variation: Use 3 cups grated carrots and 1 8½-ounce can of crushed pineapple, drained. It's also good to add ½ cup chopped walnuts and/or ½ cup raisins.
Use food processor for grating carrots and making frosting.

Coconut Frosting:
1. In a medium skillet, melt 2 tablespoons of butter; add coconut and brown. Set aside.
2. Cream last 2 tablespoons of butter with cream cheese in food processor or mixer.
3. Alternate milk and confectioners' sugar until all is added to the butter mixture. Add vanilla.
4. Stir in toasted coconut.

Lemon Cream Cheese Frosting:
1. In a large mixing bowl or food processor, beat cream cheese. Add butter and cream until fluffy.
2. Add sugar, processing until smooth. Blend in vanilla and lemon zest.

FAN'S PRUNE CAKE

1   cup prunes
1   cup oil
1½ cups sugar
3   eggs
2   cups all-purpose flour
1   teaspoon baking soda
1   teaspoon cinnamon
1   teaspoon ground
    nutmeg
1   teaspoon allspice
1   cup buttermilk

1   teaspoon vanilla
    extract
1   cup chopped pecans
Glaze:
1   cup sugar
1   cup buttermilk
½   teaspoon baking soda
2   tablespoons white corn
    syrup
¼   cup butter
½   teaspoon vanilla
    extract

Bring this winning dessert to a tailgate picnic or, on a fall day, score inside by serving it warm with a dab of whipping cream.

1. Preheat oven to 350°. Grease an 11x13 inch baking dish.
2. Boil 1 cup of prunes in enough water to cover until they have plumped up and are soft. Reserve liquid. Remove seeds and chop prunes.
3. Mix oil and sugar. While mixing, add eggs one at a time.
4. Sift dry ingredients together. Add to batter alternately with buttermilk.
5. Stir in vanilla, chopped pecans, and prunes including liquid.
6. Pour batter into prepared pan and bake for 40 minutes.
7. In a medium saucepan, combine glaze ingredients - except vanilla. Cook to a soft ball stage, 240° on candy thermometer.
8. Stir in vanilla and pour on warm cake. Cool in pan.

12-16 servings

Hint: For glaze: If you don't have a candy thermometer, try drizzling some of mixture into a cup of cold water. Test it by trying to make a soft ball of it with your fingers.

FRESH BLUEBERRY CAKE

A wonderful, quick recipe for fresh blueberries. Serve it warm, topped with vanilla ice cream.

¼ cup margarine, softened
½ cup sugar
1 egg
1 cup all-purpose flour
1½ teaspoons baking powder
Pinch of salt
⅓ cup milk

Topping:
2 cups fresh blueberries
½ cup sugar
¼ cup butter, softened
⅓ cup all-purpose flour
1 teaspoon cinnamon

1. Preheat oven to 375°. Grease a 9-inch square pan.
2. Cream ¼ cup margarine and sugar. Add egg, flour, baking powder, salt, and milk; mix until smooth.
3. Pour into prepared pan.
4. Mix ingredients for topping and pour over batter in pan.
5. Bake for 35-45 minutes. Cool in pan or serve warm.

6-8 servings

NO-CRUST CHEESECAKE

This deli-style cheesecake is irresistibly rich and creamy. With no crust to prepare, it takes only minutes to assemble.

4 8-ounce packages cream cheese, at room temperature
2 cups sugar
5 eggs, at room temperature
3 tablespoons melted butter
2 tablespoons lemon juice

2 teaspoons vanilla extract
3½ tablespoons cornstarch
1 pint sour cream, at room temperature

1. Preheat oven to 325°. Grease and flour a 9 or 10-inch springform pan.
2. Cream sugar and cream cheese. Add eggs one at a time, beating thoroughly.
3. Add remaining ingredients and beat for 15 minutes with mixer.
4. Pour batter into prepared pan.
5. Bake 1 hour. Do not open oven door.

6. Turn oven off and leave cake in oven for an additional hour.
7. Refrigerate cake in pan for at least 10 hours before serving.

12 servings

Hint: This is an easy cheesecake that does not sacrifice flavor.

I LOVE NEW YORK CHEESECAKE

1½ tablespoons butter, at room temperature
1 cup fine crumbs from pound cake
1¼ pounds cream cheese, at room temperature
¾ cup heavy cream
3 tablespoons fresh lemon juice
2 teaspoons vanilla extract
4 large eggs, at room temperature
¾ cup sour cream
1¼ cups sugar

1. Place rack in center of oven and preheat to 325°.
2. Coat butter evenly on 8-inch springform pan. Place cake crumbs in pan; tilt and rotate to coat sides and bottom evenly.
3. Beat cream cheese at medium speed until completely smooth.
4. Slowly add cream, lemon juice, and vanilla, beating until smooth.
5. Add eggs one at a time, beating after each addition.
6. Add sour cream and sugar, beating at medium speed until blended.
7. Pour batter into springform pan, gently rotating pan to settle batter.
8. Bake for 1 hour 15 minutes - for firm center bake 10 minutes longer.
9. Turn off oven and let cake stand in oven for 1 hour. DO NOT OPEN THE DOOR.
10. Remove from oven and let cool to room temperature.
11. Remove sides of pan and refrigerate cake uncovered, until serving time, overnight or at least 8 hours.

10 servings

You'll savor every delectable bite of this creamy cheesecake whether it is served plain or topped with sour cream or fresh berries.

MACK'S TUMBLEWEED
HOPE VALLEY COUNTRY CLUB

Hope Valley Country Club is Durham's oldest country club, and the Tumbleweed is a long-time favorite.

Ice
1 pint vanilla ice cream
1 ounce Drambuie
1 ounce Kahlua

1 ounce dark crème de cacao
2 ounces Cognac or brandy

1. In a 5 cup blender, put a few small pieces of ice.
2. Add vanilla ice cream.
3. Add all the remaining ingredients.
4. Blend to a smooth consistency at medium speed.
5. Serve in chilled wine or champagne glass.

4-6 servings

LEMON TAMARI DRESSING
PYEWACKET

Pyewacket is located at The Courtyard, Franklin Street, in Chapel Hill. It features vegetarian and seafood cuisine.

½ medium yellow onion
1 small green pepper
2 stalks celery
1 teaspoon white pepper
1 teaspoon garlic powder
1 cup tahini (sesame paste)
¾ cup fresh lemon juice

½ cup soy oil
1 cup sesame oil (be sure to use the light-colored type of sesame oil rather than the dark oriental variety)
¾ cup tamari
1 tablespoon honey

1. Combine all ingredients in blender or food processor.
2. Blend until mixture is smooth.

Approximately 1 quart

SPINACH LASAGNE PYEWACKET

1 10-ounce package frozen chopped spinach, thawed and drained
4 cups cottage cheese, drained
1 egg yolk
½ teaspoon black pepper
½ teaspoon salt
3¾ cups meatless Italian tomato sauce, divided
2 cups grated mozzarella cheese
12 lasagne noodles
1½ cups freshly grated Parmesan cheese
16 slices mozzarella cheese

1.   Cook and drain lasagne noodles.
2.   Grease a 9x13 inch pan.
3.   Combine spinach, cottage cheese, egg yolk, black pepper, salt, ¼ cup tomato sauce, and grated mozzarella cheese.
4.   Layer in the pan in the following manner: 1 cup Italian sauce, 6 noodles, 3½ cups spinach/cottage cheese mixture, 1¼ cups Italian sauce, 8 slices mozzarella cheese, 6 noodles, 3½ cups spinach/cottage cheese mixture, 1½ cups Parmesan cheese, 1¼ cups Italian sauce, 8 slices mozzarella cheese.
5.   Cover pan and bake at 450° for 35 minutes.
6.   Uncover pan and continue to bake 5-10 minutes until top starts to brown.

10-12 servings

SOUPE LYONNAISE RESTAURANT LA RÉSIDENCE

12 large white or yellow onions, thinly sliced
½ pound unsalted butter
¼ cup sugar
1 cup brandy
1 gallon duck stock*
4 bay leaves, whole

1.   Sauté onions in butter (very slowly until translucent).
2.   Add sugar, stirring constantly over high heat to caramelize.
3.   Add brandy and allow to burn until flame dies out.
4.   Add stock and bay leaves.
5.   Simmer up to 3 hours.

Restaurant La Résidence, specializing in French cuisine, is located at 220 W. Rosemary Street in Chapel Hill.

6. Season to taste with Madeira, Tabasco, Worcestershire, salt, and pepper.
7. To serve: Sauté 1-inch slices of French bread in olive oil until golden. Float one in each bowl, sprinkle with grated Jarlsberg cheese, and give a dash of brandy (optional: 8-10 julienne strips of cooked duck in each bowl).

12-16 servings

*Hint: This can be made with beef stock or any combination of beef, chicken, or duck. *Duck stock is made with roasted carcasses and standard stock ingredients plus red wine.*

RASPBERRY VINAIGRETTE
RESTAURANT LA RÉSIDENCE

This vinaigrette can be used with any salad greens, especially bitter ones such as endive and arugula.

¼ cup raspberry vinegar
¼ teaspoon dry mustard
¼ teaspoon sugar
1 cup olive oil

¼ cup minced shallots
1 teaspoon fresh thyme
(or ½ teaspoon dried)

1. In food processor fitted with steel blade, combine raspberry vinegar, mustard, and sugar. Process 30 seconds.
2. With machine running, slowly drizzle in olive oil.
3. Stir in shallots and thyme.

1½ cups

PEAR SORBET
RESTAURANT LA RÉSIDENCE

The sorbet is best when eaten no more than two days after being made. Bon Appétit!

2 cups sugar
2 cups water
4 cups Bartlett pear purée (approximately 16 medium size, ripe pears)
3 tablespoons fresh lemon juice

⅓ cup white rum
Garnish:
4 Bartlett pears
White rum
1 teaspoon fresh lemon juice
Mint sprigs

1. Make a simple syrup by combining sugar and water in saucepan and placing over medium heat.

2. Bring to a full boil; remove from heat.

3. Stir to make certain that sugar has completely dissolved.

4. Set aside to cool to room temperature.

5. Place 1 tablespoon lemon juice in a bowl.

6. Stem, peel, quarter, and core pears for purée.

7. Place pear sections in bowl and stir to coat each section with lemon juice to keep pears from turning brown.

8. Purée pears by pressing through a food mill or strainer. (Or use a food processor fitted with steel blade.)

9. Measure out 2 cups of simple syrup. Save remaining for garnish.

10. Combine 2 cups syrup with 4 cups pear purée, 2 tablespoons lemon juice, and ⅓ cup white rum.

11. Churn in ice cream maker according to manufacturer's directions, 25-30 minutes.

12. Remove the semi-frozen sorbet from the ice cream maker and place sorbet in separate container.

13. Put in freezer and allow to harden for at least 8 hours.

14. To serve: Stem, peel, quarter, core, and slice 4 pears. Place in bowl with remaining simple syrup; add a splash of white rum to taste and 1 teaspoon lemon juice. Allow to macerate for 2 hours. Place small scoops of sorbet in a serving bowl. Top with macerated pear slices and a sprig of mint.

10-12 servings

GUACAMOLE PAPAGAYO

12 pounds peeled and pitted avocados	**1½ tablespoons jalapeño purée**
1½ cups lemon juice	**¾ tablespoon black pepper**
2 cups diced onions	
¼ cup minced garlic	**1½ tablespoons salt**
2 pounds diced green chilies	**Diced fresh tomatoes**
	¼ cup olive oil

1. Sauté the onions and garlic in olive oil.

2. Mash the avocados; add the onion mixture and all of the remaining ingredients.

3. At the time of serving, fold in 4 cups of drained, diced tomatoes per gallon of guacamole.

25-30 servings

Mexican food is the specialty at Papagayo, located at 501 Douglas Street in Durham and at NCNB Plaza, Franklin Street, in Chapel Hill.

GAZPACHO PAPAGAYO

5 green peppers, diced	8 cups diced tomatoes
1 carrot, diced	1 quart tomato juice
5 stalks celery, diced	1 tablespoon sugar
2 cups diced onions	1 tablespoon salt
5 scallions, minced	1¼ teaspoons pepper
1 bunch parsley, chopped	2 teaspoons basil
	½ cup lemon juice
1 teaspoon minced garlic	2 cups chicken stock
½ cup good quality olive oil	2 tablespoons vinaigrette
	¼ teaspoon Tabasco
6 peeled, seeded, and chopped cucumbers	

1. Cook the onions, scallions, and garlic in ½ cup olive oil. (Note, this is more oil than is necessary for sautéing the vegetables but essential for the soup.)
2. Combine with the remaining ingredients. Chill.
3. Garnish with homemade French bread croutons.

20 servings

MARGARITA PIE PAPAGAYO

1 baked 10-inch pie crust	2 tablespoons Grand Marnier
1 envelope gelatin	
1 cup sugar	2 teaspoons grated lime
1 teaspoon salt	¼ cup heavy cream, whipped and sweetened
4 eggs, separated	
1 cup lime juice	
⅓ cup tequila	8 lime peel twists and slices

1. Combine gelatin, ½ cup sugar, and salt in saucepan.
2. Beat yolks and lime juice until foamy.
3. Stir into gelatin mixture.
4. Cook over low heat to dissolve gelatin.
5. Stir in tequila, Grand Marnier, and lime peel.
6. Cool, refrigerate until thick.
7. Beat whites and ½ cup sugar.
8. Combine ¼ gelatin mixture with egg whites. Fold remaining gelatin mixture into egg whites.
9. Pour into pie shell and top with whipped cream. Garnish with lime twists and slices.

8 servings

ESCARGOTS EN CROÛTE
SLUG'S AT THE PINES

Pastry:
1 **pound all-purpose flour**
¾ **pound shortening**
1 **tablespoon sugar**
1 **teaspoon salt**
1 **cup ice water**
Herb butter:
2 **pounds margarine**

1 **pound butter**
½ **cup buttermilk**
1 **teaspoon dill weed**
1 **teaspoon garlic powder**
1 **small onion**
1 **green onion**
10 **sprigs parsley**
36 **snails**
1 **egg combined with 1 tablespoon milk**

1. Combine dry ingredients for pastry in mixer bowl. Cut in shortening. Add water; mix and let rest a couple of hours. Roll out in circles to fit top of crocks.
2. For herb butter, chop onions and parsley. Combine margarine and butter in mixer; add buttermilk slowly. Add onions, dill, garlic powder, and parsley; whip for 10 minutes. Chill.
3. Place 6 snails in each crock and pack with herb butter, filling all available space.
4. Cover with dough circles and make border designs with a fork.
5. Brush with egg wash and bake at 400° for 8-12 minutes until brown and butter has melted.
6. Serve with parsley sprig in center and cocktail fork with lemon wedge.

6 servings

Hint: Serve in a ceramic crock with 6 holes for snails and herb butter, topped with a light pastry sheet.

Slug's At The Pines, known for its beef and seafood, is located on N.C. 54 East in Chapel Hill.

BLUE CHEESE DRESSING
SLUG'S AT THE PINES

1	pound blue cheese, crumbled	
1	quart buttermilk	
1	quart mayonnaise	
1	quart sour cream	

2 teaspoons Worcestershire sauce
½ cup fresh chives, minced
1 pinch black pepper
½ pinch salt

Mix thoroughly and chill.

1 gallon

CRAB DIP
CROASDAILE COUNTRY CLUB

Seafood buffets are always a highlight at Croasdaile Country Club.

1 pound lump crabmeat
2 pounds cream cheese
¼ cup butter
1½ cups minced onion
½ teaspoon garlic salt

2 teaspoons Tabasco sauce
2 teaspoons Worcestershire sauce
Crackers or patty shells

1. Sauté onions in butter until transparent.
2. Add cream cheese, stirring until consistency is smooth.
3. Add crabmeat and remaining ingredients.
4. Simmer for 5 minutes.
5. Serve in chafing dish accompanied by crackers or patty shells.

15-20 servings

BEEF OSCAR
CROASDAILE COUNTRY CLUB

4 5-ounce fillets of
tenderloin
1 pound crabmeat
¼ cup finely chopped
onion

Cracker meal
16 fresh asparagus spears
Bearnaise sauce (your
favorite recipe)

1. Combine crabmeat, onion, and enough cracker meal to hold crab together. Form into 4 patties.
2. Sauté crabmeat patties until lightly browned, turning once. Keep warm.
3. Cook asparagus until crisp-tender.
4. Cook fillets. As steaks finish, place on warm plate. Top each with a crabmeat patty and 4 asparagus spears. Top with bearnaise sauce.

4 servings

SAUSAGE AND CHICKEN
JAMBALAYA — RHUMBA'S

½ pound unsalted butter
1 pound raw white rice
1 8-ounce can tomato
sauce
1 1-pound can whole
tomatoes
1 cup chopped green
pepper
1 cup chopped onion
1 pound chopped
chicken

1 pound Polish sausage,
sliced
1 cup chopped celery
3 cups chicken stock
1 teaspoon salt
1 teaspoon white pepper
1 teaspoon black pepper
½ teaspoon thyme
½ teaspoon cayenne
pepper
½ teaspoon sage
½ teaspoon oregano

1. Sauté onion, green pepper, celery, and sausage in butter until tender.
2. Add remaining ingredients.
3. Place mixture in large casserole.
4. Bake uncovered at 375° for 1 hour.

6-8 servings

Rhumba's MexiCajun Cafe specializes in two popular cuisines. Rhumba's is located at 800 W. Main Street, Durham.

GUMBO YA YA RHUMBA'S

1 cup corn oil	1 teaspoon dried savory
1 cup flour	½ teaspoon dried oregano
1 cup chopped green onion	½ teaspoon dried thyme
1 cup minced fresh parsley	½ teaspoon cayenne pepper
1½ cups cubed uncooked chicken	½ teaspoon black pepper
1½ cups cubed country ham	½ teaspoon white pepper
1 cup diced green pepper	½ teaspoon Tabasco sauce
3 cups chicken stock	1 tablespoon fresh lemon juice
	Zest of 1 lemon

1. Make roux using corn oil and flour; brown ever so lightly.
2. Add green onion and stir until it turns dark green.
3. Add parsley.
4. Cook 2 minutes.
5. Add chicken and ham; cook until tender.
6. Add green pepper.
7. Add chicken stock; bring to a boil.
8. Add spices and simmer for 20 mintues.
9. Serve over rice.

4-6 servings

DILLED SHRIMP RALEIGH'S

Raleigh's, Ltd., serves continental and American dishes. It is located on 15-501 South, Chapel Hill.

1 cup sliced fresh mushrooms	1 teaspoon dried dill weed or 3 teaspoons finely minced fresh dill
2 tablespoons Chablis	
4 tablespoons crème fraîche	Salt and pepper (white) to taste
1½ cups heavy cream	Cornstarch
	32-48 peeled, uncooked shrimp

1. Simmer mushrooms and Chablis in large enameled skillet or Teflon coated fry pan.

2. Stir in crème fraîche.
3. Add heavy cream.
4. Bring to boil; reduce to simmer for 5 minutes.
5. Add dill.
6. Thicken with cornstarch dissolved in water (to the consistency of slightly diluted mushroom soup).
7. Just prior to serving, add shrimp.
8. Raise heat and cook shrimp until firm (about 2-3 minutes); do not overcook.
9. Serve with hot rice.

4 servings

ELEGANT RASPBERRY SATIN PIE — RALEIGH'S

1 **baked pie crust (ready made or homemade)**	¾ **pound unsalted butter, softened**
½ **cup raspberry purée**	¾ **cup fine granulated sugar**
3 **tablespoons raspberry liqueur**	**Whipped cream**
2 **eggs, well beaten**	

1. In mixer bowl, beat butter until fluffy and light in color.
2. Gradually add sugar, beating until no granules are evident when a dab is pressed between thumb and forefinger.
3. Add well beaten eggs, raspberry purée, and liqueur, incorporating completely.
4. Spoon into pie crust.
5. Cover and chill until firm.
6. Cut in 8 servings; top with whipped cream.

8 servings

Hint: Use a food processor for finest grain in sugar.

OLIVER'S SIGNATURE SHRIMP — OLIVER'S SIGNATURE RESTAURANT

Oliver's is a continental restaurant located at The Sheraton University Center, 2800 Middleton Street, Durham.

6	large Gulf shrimp	¼	seeded tomato
1	ounce backfin crabmeat	2	ounces white wine
¼	ounce shallots, finely chopped	1	pinch saffron
		2	ounces heavy cream

1. After peeling and deveining shrimp, broil for approximately 1½ minutes until done.
2. In saucepan, sauté crabmeat, shallots, and tomato in white wine for 30 seconds; add cream and saffron and cook for 2-3 minutes. (The sauce will thicken as it reduces.)
3. Place shrimp over sauce and serve immediately.

1 serving

VEAL FRANCES PINO'S

Pino's is an Italian restaurant located on Interstate 85 at Hillsborough.

2	eggs	1	cup oil
4	ounces Romano cheese	1	tablespoon butter
1	ounce milk	6	ounces chicken broth
½	teaspoon basil	¼	lemon
Pinch of black pepper		2	ounces dry white wine
8	ounces veal scallops	4	mushrooms, sliced

1. Beat eggs, cheese, milk, basil, and pepper in mixing bowl.
2. Place veal in mixture.
3. In heavy pan, heat oil until very hot; fry veal until brown on both sides.
4. Remove veal from skillet and drain.
5. Pour excess oil from skillet.
6. Return veal to skillet and add butter, chicken broth, lemon, white wine, and mushrooms.
7. Cook 4 minutes.
8. Serve immediately.

2 servings

STUFFED POTATOES
ANGUS BARN

6 large Idaho baking potatoes
1 teaspoon salt
1 tablespoon chopped chives
2 tablespoons finely crumbled, cooked bacon

½ cup butter
3½ tablespoons Parmesan cheese, grated
½ teaspoon black pepper
⅛ teaspoon msg
1 tablespoon sour cream

The Angus Barn, renowned for steaks, is located on U.S. 70 West between Durham and Raleigh.

1. Grease and bake potatoes at 400° for 45 minutes.
2. Cut potatoes in half lengthwise. Spoon out pulp while potatoes are hot. Save shells.
3. Combine pulp with remaining ingredients.
4. Spoon mixture back into skins.
5. Brown in hot oven for 4 minutes.

12 servings

BREAD PUDDING WITH WHISKEY SAUCE
THE CAROLINA INN

⅛ cup butter
1 small loaf French bread (day old)
4 eggs
1 quart milk
1 cup sugar
1 cup raisins

1 tablespoon vanilla
Whiskey Sauce:
1 pound butter
1½ cups sugar
2 eggs
¾ cup bourbon

The Carolina Inn is located on The University of North Carolina campus in Chapel Hill. Fine southern cooking is its trade mark.

1. Soak the bread in water first - not too long.
2. Whisk eggs, milk, sugar, and vanilla together.
3. Add the soaked, drained bread.
4. Add raisins and mix well.
5. Melt butter in a baking dish.
6. Pour in the bread pudding mixture.
7. Place the dish inside roasting pan.
8. Pour small amount of hot water into roasting pan.
9. Cook 1 hour at 350°.

10. To make Whiskey Sauce: Melt butter in double boiler. Whisk sugar and eggs together in a separate bowl.
11. Add to butter; whisk until eggs are cooked. Cool a little and add the bourbon.
12. Serve over the hot bread pudding.

8 servings

SEAFOOD CHOWDER
THE CAROLINA INN

2 carrots	4 tablespoons flour
2 onions	1 cup heavy cream,
1 bunch celery	scalded
2 green peppers	¼ pound shrimp
4 tablespoons butter	¼ pound clams
6 strips bacon, cooked	Thyme
2 potatoes	Salt and pepper
1½ quarts fish stock	Bay leaf
4 tablespoons butter	

1. Dice carrots, onions, celery, and peppers.
2. Sauté in 4 tablespoons butter.
3. Add chopped bacon and broth.
4. Bring to boil and simmer gently for 10 minutes.
5. Add diced potatoes, clams, and shrimp.
6. When potatoes are finished cooking, melt remaining 4 tablespoons butter in a separate saucepan. Add flour and cook, stirring constantly for 1-2 minutes.
7. Slowly stir in some stock from the soup pot to make a thickened sauce. Pour sauce into soup pot and stir well to blend.
8. Season to correct taste.
9. Add scalded heavy cream.

6-8 servings

SALAD VINAIGRETTE
THE CAROLINA INN

1 cup oil
⅓ cup vinegar or lemon juice
1 teaspoon Dijon mustard

1 teaspoon chopped parsley
Salt
Pepper

1. Combine all ingredients and whisk until blended.
2. Add salt and pepper to taste.
3. Store in refrigerator.

1⅓ cups

Hints: Selection of greens: iceberg, romaine, Boston, bibb, chicory, spinach, watercress. Any flavor of vinegar may be used. Adds an extra touch to your salad.

SHRIMP SALAD
ANOTHERTHYME

2½ pounds shrimp (fresh, peeled)
8 cups water
2 tablespoons salt
2 tablespoons granulated garlic
3 bay leaves
1 teaspoon black pepper
½ cup dry white wine
⅓ cup lemon juice

Dressing:
⅓ cup mayonnaise
1 teaspoon dried dill weed
¼ teaspoon white pepper
1 tablespoon Pommery mustard
2 teaspoons fresh lemon juice

1. Combine water, salt, garlic, bay leaves, pepper, wine, and lemon juice.
2. Bring to a boil; simmer uncovered for 10 minutes.
3. Skim off spices.
4. Cook shrimp in 3-4 batches. (To cook shrimp, put in strainer; lower into spice water and poach gently for 2 minutes or until shrimp is pink and tender. Cool shrimp.)
5. Combine mayonnaise, dill weed, white pepper, mustard, and lemon juice.
6. Add shrimp. Toss gently.
7. Serve on a bed of lettuce.

6-8 servings

Seafood and vegetarian dishes are the specialities at Anotherthyme, located at 109 N. Gregson Street in Durham.

CHOCOLATE ROULAGE
APPLES

Apples, a New York style deli, is located at Brightleaf Square, Gregson and Main Streets, Durham.

Cake:
5   eggs, separated
1   cup confectioners' sugar
⅛   teaspoon salt
3   tablespoons cocoa
Filling:
1½ cups heavy cream
½   cup cocoa
¼   cup confectioners' sugar

2   tablespoons Kahlua
Frosting I:
3   ounces semi-sweet chocolate
½   ounce butter
3   tablespoons milk
1   tablespoon corn syrup
Frosting II:
½   cup confectioners' sugar
2   teaspoons water

1.   Preheat oven to 400°. Grease and flour a jelly roll pan.
2.   Beat egg whites until soft peaks form. Add ½ cup sugar; beat until stiff.
3.   Beat egg yolks until thick. Add salt, ½ cup sugar, and cocoa.
4.   Fold whites into yolk mixture.
5.   Spread in jelly roll pan and bake 15 minutes.
6.   Sprinkle a towel with cocoa. Remove cake from pan and roll in towel immediately, starting at narrow end. Cool.
7.   Combine all ingredients for filling and beat until stiff.
8.   Unroll cake and spread with filling. Re-roll.
9.   For Frosting I, melt chocolate and butter. Remove from heat and add milk and corn syrup. Spread over cake roll.
10.   Combine ingredients for Frosting II and drizzle over cake in stripes.

6-8 servings

McCARTHY'S HOUSE DRESSING — McCARTHY'S

2 pints mayonnaise	¾ cup honey
2 cups vegetable oil (preferably cottonseed)	1 8-ounce jar Poupon mustard
¾ cup fresh lemon juice (or Realemon juice)	1 bunch fresh parsley, coarsely chopped

1. In a large bowl, combine mayonnaise, lemon juice, honey, and mustard.
2. Mix with whisk by hand, or use hand mixer on low speed.
3. Slowly add oil while mixing.
4. Fold in parsley.
5. Pour into air-tight container.
6. Store in refrigerator.

Generous 2 quarts

McCarthy's serves soups, salads, sandwiches, and continental cuisine. The restaurant is located at Kroger Plaza Shopping Center, Elliott Road, Chapel Hill.

RUMANIAN CHICKEN ORIENT-EXPRESS

2 tablespoons butter	½ cup chicken stock
3 tablespoons olive oil	1 pint sour cream
1½ pounds boneless chicken breast	2-3 tablespoons poppy seeds
½ cup dry white wine	3-4 cloves garlic, minced

1. Pound the chicken breasts to an even thickness to assure even cooking.
2. Sauté breasts in butter and olive oil.
3. Pour off extra oil mixture and deglaze the pan with white wine.
4. Reduce to 3-4 tablespoons liquid.
5. Add the stock and continue to cook for a few minutes to blend the flavors.
6. Add 1 pint sour cream, garlic, poppy seeds, and salt and pepper to taste.

6 servings

Hint: A Beaujolais goes well with this dish.

The Orient-Express serves Eastern European and Austro-Hungarian cuisine. It is located at 201 E. Main Street in Carrboro.

BUTTERMILK PECAN PIE CLAIRE'S

Claire's Cafe serves new American cuisine. Its home is a Victorian house at 2701 Chapel Hill Road, Durham.

½ cup butter, softened
4 cups sugar
3 tablespoons flour
¼ teaspoon salt
3 eggs
1 cup buttermilk

¾ teaspoon vanilla extract
1 cup pecans
1 9-inch unbaked pie crust

1. Preheat oven to 350°.
2. Cream butter and sugar in mixing bowl.
3. Add flour and salt.
4. Add eggs, one at a time, while still beating.
5. Add buttermilk and vanilla; mix until smooth.
6. Sprinkle pecans in bottom of 9-inch unbaked pie crust.
7. Pour in custard.
8. Bake 1½ hours.

6-8 servings

CHILLED GRAND MARNIER SOUFFLÉ — HOTEL EUROPA

Hotel Europa specializes in continental cuisine. It is located on the Durham-Chapel Hill Boulevard, Chapel Hill.

8 egg yolks
5 eggs
12 ounces sugar

1 quart heavy cream
½ cup Grand Marnier

1. Beat first 3 ingredients in top of double boiler over warm water to dissolve sugar. Remove.
2. Whip in mixer on high speed until "strands" form when beater is removed.
3. Whip heavy cream until peaks form. Fold into egg and sugar mixture. Add Grand Marnier.
4. Spoon mixture into 10-inch mold or 14-inch tube pan and freeze.
5. When frozen, remove from mold or tube by dipping into warm water. Place soufflé on flat surface and return to freezer to firm up.
6. Just before serving, slice and garnish with dollop of whipping cream and shaved chocolate.

8-10 servings

INDEX

The Junior League of Durham and Orange Counties would like to thank its members and their friends who contributed so much to this book.

Kay N. Abbott
Cathryn Filkins Abernathy
Anne Adams
Cynthia Clay Adams
Jean Taylor Adams
Dorea D. Akers
Kathy Moore Aldridge
Susan Fleming Aldridge
Laura Emerson Alexander
Kaye Benfield Amick
Emmy Lou Anderson
Jane Hubbard Anderson
Nancy Walker Anderson
Susan Kimball Anderson
Claudia Lynn Andrews
Vickie Yarbrough Atwater
Dial D. Baker
Joy B. Baldwin
Leigh Shelton Ballou
Betty Lou S. Barnes
Diane Smith Barr
Gayle Sanderson Bergamini
Sally Tart Bethune
Judith Sigmon Bishop
Debbie Blaylock
Virginia Bohannon
Jan Y. Bolick
Ethel Chaffin Bollinger
Susan A. Booth
Marilyn Myers Boulton
Jetta Purcell Boyd
Sharon Puryear Boyd
Michaella Brabec
Marjorie Sealy Bradshaw
Anita Wilkinson Brame
Bob Brame
Caroline M. Brame
Marcie Bynum Brame
Barbara Richie Branch
Valerie Baker Brannon
Katherine Kimbrough
  Brenneman
Barbara Bressler
Dede O'Briant Brockwell
Gin-gin Brogden
Jane Davenport Brown
Kathy LeSac Bruch
Katharine Wilson Bryan
Ruth Smitherman Buchanan
Karen Budin
Sally M. Bugg
Martie Bynum
Marsha Hallman Cadwallader
Anita M. Caldwell
Leesa Heydenreich Campbell
Anne Stahl Carr
Debbie Carver
Susan Smith Cavanagh
Sarah H. Chandler
Brandon Boyd Chapman

Elizabeth Chapman
Leigh O. Cherry
Charlotte Reeves Clark
Rae Schwalbe Clark
Kate Bradshaw Cloninger
Jennifer Ann Cobb
Sheila Sellers Cochrane
Janice Grier Corley
Barbara Bitler Coughlin
Michele S. Council
Kris S. Coupland
Virginia Johnson Crane
Susan Barwick Curlee
Jeanmarie Eaves Curtis
Katherine Powe Dauchert
Margaret S. Davenport
Holly Green Davis
Susan DeLoatche
Betty B. Dewar
Cindy Scott Dickerson
Cynthia Henmon Diehl
Caroline H. Dixon
Lucy Bratton Doak
Nancy Roach Dougherty
Patricia Dougherty
Claudia Rutledge Draffin
Gail M. Drew
Robin B. Drew
Carmen Elizabeth Durack
Meredith Millspaugh Durham
Audrey S. Earle
Judith Farris Easley
Marilyn F. Edmondson
Lyn L. Edwards
Betsy Elkins-Williams
Kathryn Rush Elkins
Stuart Robinson Embree
Annie Thomasina Herrick
  Evans
Scottie L. Evans
Sara Hubbard Fairey
Mary Faulkenberry
Elizabeth Moore Feifs
Martha Buckner Finn
Ann Reesman Fisher
Ele Fisher
Evelyn Wells Fisher
Louise A. Fisher
Margaret S. Fitch
Winston Fitzpatrick
Sims Brockenbrough Foulks
Mishew Smith Fouts
Adele Phillips Freeman
Nancy B. Freeman
Cindy Gardiner
Adrienne Weber Gantt
Lesli A. Garrison
Lorene Gates
Diana Payne Getzelmann
Louise S. Glenn

Marie Wallace Goldenberg
Ruth Harris Goldsmith
Judy Mulholland Grady
Lucy Anne Grant
Nancy M. Grayiel
Alyson Daily Green
Jane Moore Green
Mary S. Griffin
Susan Griffin
Leesie Pettrey Guthridge
Margaret Erickson Haber
Betsy Hardison Hamer
Richard Hamilton
Carroll G. Haney
Bobbie Tomb Hardaker
Chasie Harris
Nancy Rawlinson Harvell
Mary Rawlinson Haywood
Barbara J. Heagren
Marsha Turner Herbert
Susie Werber Hill
Daniel L. Hoffman
Mary Dameron Holderness
Katherine Holeman
Joy Walker Hollar
Frances Holman
Lloydette Humphrey Hoof
Alice Horton
Joanne Hubbard
Reba Golden Huckabee
Rebekah Allen Huckabee
Vicki Powell Hunt
Patricia M. Hutchings
Suzanne Dragge Icaza
Judy Miller Jay
Ellen Phillips Jeffrey
Susan Thurston Jenkins
Vickie Riddle Jernigan
Judy Wily Jervis
Caroline Dern Johnston
Janet Sullivan Johnston
Catherine Monaghan Joyner
Mary-Margaret Justis
Connie P. Kearney
Patricia N. Keicher
Ken Kenyon
Julia DuRant Kimbrell
Sue Lyon Kimbrell
Brenda B. Kincade
Sandra Moody King
Virginia V. King
Chris Skinner Kirkland
Sandy Kopp
Trish Lanier
Mary Downey Lavinder
Peggy Harp Lee
Aggie Leshner
Page Littlewood
Yolanda Old Litton
Isabella Pescud Long

Joy Farthing Long
Virginia Stanley Long
Cindy Elkins Lowe
Sandra Wrenn Lutz
Kathy M. Lyon
Betsy W. Mangum
Catherine Manning
Dorothy W. Manning
Robin Green Marin
Mary Beth Markham
Sally B. Markham
Sarah Wilson Markham
Lee Branch Marks
Anne D. Marshall
Leslie Montfort Marsicano
Elizabeth Holland Maxwell
Deborah Koss McCarthy
Allison Haltom McClay
Doris Cooper McCoy
Gigi McKee
Anne McNamara
Kathryn Davenport
  McPherson
Mary Jane Boren Meeker
Barbara Bush Merten
Peg Midyette
Mary Myers Miller
Virginia Miller
Marelle Yeaman Molbert
Bonnie B. Moore
Kathleen Bryson Moore
Margaret Myers Morris
Glenda Bowers Moser
Nancy H. Myers
Jean Wetzel Nance
Jean Healy Neville
Frances M. Newsom
Elise C. Nunley
Sandy Ogburn
Mary Oliver-Boeckel
Betsy Norman Overton
Kendall Hill Page
Lynda Lambert Painter
Evelyn D. Evans Palmer
Phyllis Foster Parker
Margaret Blair Parks
Elizabeth Bradshaw Patterson
Ruth Dissinger Patterson
Barbara Scott Patton
Katherine Anne Patton
Blanche P. Paul
Gayle and Dave Pierce
Dian H. Poe

Rhonda Pollard
Sandi Prentis
Becky Rhoads Prestwood
Martha Leslie Bennett
  Pritchett
Nancy Hager Rand
Alison Ravin
Jo Ann F. Reeves
Katharine K. Richman
Nancy G. Riefkohl
Dorothy Poole Ritchie
Hanley Testerman Roach
Betty Robinson
Jessie Roche
Ellen Rock
Deborah Eliason Rollins
Donna Cooper Ross
Eda D. Ross
Ruth W. Ross
Susan Cranford Ross
Kristie Rotz
Joyce Nichols Roughton
Margaret Allen Rouse
Stuart Camblos Royall
Jane Roycroft
Margo Crafton Rundles
Nancy Howard Saitta
Janet Sanfilippo
Laurie Gilbert Sanford
Caroline Byerly Sasser
Anita Adamitis Scarborough
Anne Luper Schmitt
Kathryn Byerly Searles
Hollace Selph
Teresa Jansen Senter
Margaret Brinkley Sigmon
Debi Silber
Ruth Simione
Mary Thompson Skinner
Susan A. Sloat
Debbie Nichols Smalley
Emma Kiser Smart
Pamela P. Smith
Frances Sparks
Kathleen Bryan Stallings
June L. Steel
Diane Stephens
Tricia Howell Stewart
Shannon St. John
Sherry McCoy Stubbs
Catherine M. Stull
Gwen Ellingson Swenberg
Mary Wellens Tatum

Cecelia S. Taylor
Lynn Templeton
Lyn Anne Wattley
  Terrebonne
Ashlin Thomas
Virginia Ashlin Thomas
Judy Thompson
Jane Bohannon Thorn
Tricia M. Toher
Edith Sprunt Toms
Marian M. Tyson
Cary Campbell Umhau
Debbie Ungeleider
Muff Shawger Urbaniak
Aggie Ushner
Martha Erwin Uzzle
Perry Grimes Van Dyke
Spot Hawfield Vicars
Diane Stockard Wade
Sandra Weigle Wainio
Kathryn Powers Walker
Charlotte A. Wallace
Kathryn H. Wallace
Heidi Fullerton Warburton
Connie Ward
Beverley Brockenbrough
  Watts
Gail Weinerth
Martha Huffstetler Welborn
Elaine Smith Westbrook
Pam Teer Whilden
Brenda Whisnant
Joan Farabow Whisnant
Deborah Miller White
Judy Atkins White
Mary W. White
Ann Wilder
Sterly L. Wilder
Lee Walker Willard
Suzanne Smith Williams
Valerie Tullai Williams
Patricia Parker Willimon
Frances Horn Wilkinson
Kathryn Y. Wilson
Alice M. Wiprud
Judy Johnson Wooden
Judy Watterson Woody
Susan G. Yancy
Anne Hutchins Young
Nancy Adams Young
Barbara Dimmick Yowell
Anne Rawls Zollicoffer

JUNIOR LEAGUE OF DURHAM AND ORANGE COUNTIES, INC.
900 S. Duke St. • Durham, North Carolina 27707

Please send _____ copies @ $14.95 each $ _____
Postage and handling @ $1.75 each $ _____
North Carolina residents add 4½% @ $0.60 each $ _____

Total enclosed $ _____
Make checks payable to Special Publications.
Please charge to VISA/MASTERCARD card number _____
Expiration date _____ Interbank number (MC only) _____
Signature of card holder _____

Name _____
Address _____
City _____ State _____ Zip _____

All profits from *Even More Special* are returned to the community through projects of the Junior League of Durham and Orange Counties.

JUNIOR LEAGUE OF DURHAM AND ORANGE COUNTIES, INC.
900 S. Duke St. • Durham, North Carolina 27707

Please send _____ copies @ $14.95 each $ _____
Postage and handling @ $1.75 each $ _____
North Carolina residents add 4½% @ $0.60 each $ _____

Total enclosed $ _____
Make checks payable to Special Publications.
Please charge to VISA/MASTERCARD card number _____
Expiration date _____ Interbank number (MC only) _____
Signature of card holder _____

Name _____
Address _____
City _____ State _____ Zip _____

All profits from *Even More Special* are returned to the community through projects of the Junior League of Durham and Orange Counties.

All copies will be sent to same address unless otherwise specified. If you wish one or any number of books sent as gifts, please furnish a list of names and addresses of recipients. If you wish to enclose your own gift card with each book, please write name of recipient on outside of envelope, enclose with order and we will include it with your gift.

Prices subject to change without notice.

All copies will be sent to same address unless otherwise specified. If you wish one or any number of books sent as gifts, please furnish a list of names and addresses of recipients. If you wish to enclose your own gift card with each book, please write name of recipient on outside of envelope, enclose with order and we will include it with your gift.

Prices subject to change without notice.